Contents

Figures

Tables

Authors

David Moseley leads and contributes to a number of research projects in the Centre for Learning and Teaching at the University of Newcastle upon Tyne (UK). As Reader in Applied Psychology, he was responsible for the postgraduate training in educational psychology for 21 years and since 1997 has initiated and managed several large-scale projects in educational and health contexts, working with voluntary bodies and public policy and research organisations. His publications include learning and assessment materials for use by children and adults, Open University course units and papers on: informatics; emotional intelligence; literacy and ICT; and constructs of teaching and learning. In 2002 he and his colleagues were funded by the national Learning and Skills Research Centre to evaluate theories of thinking skills – work which led to an ESRC-funded series of seminars and to the present handbook.

Vivienne Baumfield is a Senior Lecturer in Education at the University of Newcastle upon Tyne. Her research focuses on the role of enquiry in pedagogy and professional learning, with a particular interest in the potential of thinking skills interventions to provide stimulus and support for teacher change. As part of her work in the Centre for Learning and Teaching, she has lectured to networks of teachers and researchers interested in thinking skills and professional development in Hong Kong, Singapore, the Netherlands and Peru as well as across the UK. She is also involved in Initial Teacher Education and remains focused on the daily realities of teaching and learning in classrooms.

Julian Elliott is a Professor of Education at the University of Durham. Formerly a teacher in mainstream and special schools, he subsequently practised as an educational (school) psychologist before entering higher education. His research and publication interests include: achievement motivation, the treatment of children's disorders, cognitive education and dynamic assessment, and teachers' skills of behaviour management. From 2003–2005 he was President of the International Association for Cognitive Education and Psychology, and is an Affiliate of the Centre for the Psychology of Abilities, Competencies, and Expertise at Yale University.

Maggie Gregson is a Senior Lecturer in post-compulsory Education in the School of Education and Lifelong Learning at the University of Sunderland (UK). Through her research, Maggie has explored models of reflection in relation to the social, cultural and psychological realities of helping student teachers to think critically and creatively about their practice. Her research includes an evaluation of 'thinking skills' interventions in schools and colleges across the North East of England. She is also involved in an evaluation of the impact of post-compulsory educational policy upon teaching, learning and assessment, especially in relation to adult literacy and numeracy.

Steve Higgins is a Senior Lecturer at Newcastle University and is Director of the Centre for Learning and Teaching. His research interests are in the area of developing children's thinking, ICT and mathematics in primary education. He has written a number of books on developing thinking and on the effective use of ICT in primary schools.

Jennifer Miller is a Senior Lecturer at Newcastle University with responsibility for initial teacher education. Educated in the USA and the UK her first degree was in librarianship and information science with further postgraduate study in business management. During her career, she has worked for local government in an advisory capacity supporting the use of ICT to improve teaching and learning. She is currently a member of the Centre for Teaching and Learning with research interests in e-learning and teaching for thinking.

Douglas Newton is an Emeritus Professor of Education at Newcastle University and a Professorial Fellow at Durham University. His research interests include the nature of understanding and how its thinking processes can be supported. He has published widely and his work has been translated into other languages.

Foreword

I have two reproductions of great art on my desk. One is an inexpensive copy of Auguste Rodin's imponderable masterpiece, the Thinker, hunched over in his familiar pose that portrays 'every man' who is 'lost in thought'. The other 'objet d'art' is an inflatable replica of Edvard Munch's depiction of mental anguish in his renowned painting 'The Scream'. As I think about the task of integrating and classifying the last 50 years of theory and research in critical thinking, these two images come to mind and merge. In my mind's eye, I can see Rodin's inscrutable Thinker contort his face into that of the one depicted in 'The Scream' when the thoughtful, and presumably silent, Thinker is faced with organising and evaluating the literature on thinking skills. Fortunately, for those of us who care about improving how students think, we can all save our voices from the possible harm caused by a shrill scream because of the excellent work toward creating an organising taxonomy of thinking skills presented in *Frameworks for Thinking: A Handbook for Teaching and Learning*.

David Moseley and his able band of co-authors have boldly sorted through a mountain of literature to create a thinking skills taxonomy, so that we can identify what, when, and how well different methods and theories work to develop students' critical thinking abilities. Although it has always been true that the ability to think critically is necessary for democracies to flourish and for economies to succeed, modern technology now makes it necessary for increasing proportions of the population to develop their critical thinking abilities. In *Frameworks for Thinking: A Handbook for Teaching and Learning*, Moseley et al. provide a categorisation system that allows readers to understand essential elements among different ways of thinking about thinking and theories of teaching for thinking. They review the research designed to enhance thinking and identify the variables that promote better thinking—explicit instruction in thinking skills, emphasis on metacognition, good teaching, attention to dispositional aspects, and opportunities to practise across domains with collaborative group work. The authors took on a difficult task and performed a great service for all of us. Everyone who cares about the next generation of learners and thinkers and those who will teach them will find great food for thought in *Frameworks for Thinking*. It is one handbook that many people will keep handy. *Frameworks* is interesting reading for thinkers of all sorts.

Diane F. Halpern, PhD
Professor of Psychology
Claremont McKenna College
Past-president 2004,
American Psychological Association

Acknowledgments

This handbook could not have been produced without the foresight and support of the Learning and Skills Development Agency (LSDA). They funded a large part of the research on which the handbook is based, seeking to provide a sound theoretical basis for post-16 teaching and learning. They hold the copyright of material taken (with permission) from our 2004 report: *Thinking skill frameworks for post-16 learners: an evaluation.*

Thanks are also due to two members of our original team (Mei Lin and Sue Robson) who have not contributed directly to the present volume. The Centre for Learning and Teaching at Newcastle University and the School of Education and Lifelong Learning at Sunderland University have provided support and encouragement throughout.

We are grateful to Diane Halpern, Robert Marzano, Paul Pintrich and Robert Sternberg for providing feedback on early drafts.

Introduction

This handbook is about thinking. More specifically, it is about theoretical frameworks and classificatory systems developed since the Second World War to help educators understand the processes and products of thinking and learning. By setting out the ideas and beliefs of various system builders it raises questions about human nature and the nature of knowledge. However, it is far from comprehensive in its treatment of philosophical issues, since the starting point for our work was a brief from the Learning and Skills Research Centre (LSRC), based in London, to evaluate thinking skills taxonomies which may be relevant in post-16 education and training. Our main purpose is practical, so we are more interested in how frameworks can be used than in theoretical elegance.

Everyone involved in education and training needs to talk about thinking and learning. Frameworks for thinking can provide shared understandings which can help improve the quality of instructional design, course and lesson planning, teaching, learning and assessment. We therefore believe that this handbook will be useful for practitioners, students and academics as well as for policy-makers and others wanting to find out more about certain frameworks.

Here, as in the published report of our work for the LSRC (Moseley et al., 2004),[1] we include frameworks and models as well as taxonomies, and are just as interested in school education as the post-16 sector. However, by focusing on analyses of thinking and learning which are concerned with structure as well as function, we largely

---

[1] Copies of this report can be downloaded from: http://www.lsda.org.uk/pubs/dbaseout/download.asp?code=1541

exclude holistic and narrative accounts of thinking, many of which are critical of attempts to impose categories on organic and dynamic experiences.

Our interests and the concerns of many of the authors represented here extend well beyond the cognitive domain, since people think and learn in social and cultural contexts and experience an interplay of cognitive, emotional, motivational and social energies. Education is widely seen as being about social and emotional learning as well as the acquisition of academic knowledge and skills. Illeris (2004) located learning theorists in a triangular space defined by three dimensions of learning (cognitive, emotional and social). However, it is noticeable that few of those in the social corner have put forward ways of classifying thinking. Consequently, most of the frameworks outlined and evaluated in this handbook have a cognitive and affective emphasis. One (that of Pintrich, 2000) is solely concerned with motivation, dealing with processes and strategies where thinking, feeling and will (conation) are intertwined.

Selection of frameworks

We began by conducting a comprehensive and systematic literature search of electronic and paper-based sources, initially confining ourselves to the term 'taxonomy', but later extending this to 'framework' and 'model'. Over 400 articles and books were identified as relevant and we read most of these. We also found a large number of useful websites, many of which are gateways to other sources. We included 55 thinking skills frameworks in our LSRC report, with evaluations of 35 of these. In the present handbook, as in our LSRC research, we have excluded unsystematic ways of describing thinking skills, including lists with no organising principles. We have also excluded frameworks which add little to existing formulations. Decisions as to what to include in the handbook in order to extend its age coverage downwards were made after discussion within the writing team. We have ended up with 41 individual frameworks, plus a composite evaluation of theories of executive function.

Description and evaluation of individual frameworks

After describing the main features of each framework, we evaluate it in terms of purpose(s) and actual and potential use(s), applying a consistent set of criteria. We deal with each framework under three main headings: *description and intended use, evaluation,* and *summary* (in tabular form).

The following aspects are taken into account:

Description and intended use
nature and function: taxonomy / framework / model / map / list
the domains and / or sub-domains addressed
the principle or principles used in constructing the framework
structural complexity and level of detail
broad categories covered
thinking skill categories
thinking skill elements
stated purpose

Evaluation
how well the domains and / or sub-domains are covered
extent to which categories overlap
overall coherence
distinctiveness
justification for choice of underlying principles
explanatory power
compatibility with similar systems
consistency with well-supported theories
pedagogical stance (if any)
values: explicit / non-explicit; descriptive / prescriptive
clarity of formulation
accessibility for teachers and learners

Relevance for teachers and learning
actual and potential areas of application
implications for understanding teaching and learning

implications for practice

actual and potential use in research.

As we became familiar with an increasing number of frameworks, we noted many common features regarding scope and structure and asked ourselves whether it might be possible to formulate an integrated 'meta-model' against which we could compare the scope and structure of each framework. We agreed on the following set of broad categories, and use them in our summary tables:

- self-engagement
- reflective thinking
- productive thinking
- building understanding
- information gathering

These broad categories are not meant to be interpreted as a hierarchy of levels, but are seen as interactive systemic processes (Moseley et al., 2004, 2005).

How to use this handbook

Mode of use will depend on purpose. Many readers will be interested in a limited number of theorists and will use the handbook for reference purposes, perhaps in connection with a student assignment. Others will be interested in a tradition of thought or practice, such as critical thinking or instructional design. They can learn about a 'family' of frameworks, presented in chronological order in one of the four main content chapters (Chapters 3–6).

If the reader's purpose is to select one or more frameworks for professional use, they would be well advised to read Chapters 1 and 7 in preparation for the task and to consider the relevance for a particular subject area of theoretical issues about the psychology of thinking and learning (covered in Chapter 5). A quick reading of a selection of summary tables will then help the reader to choose a small number of frameworks for more detailed study, before making a final choice.

The first two chapters are helpful for people who value clarity in the use of terms and wish to make analytic comparisons between frameworks. Chapter 2 contains some illustrations of how this may be done, encouraging the reader to go beyond the present text and work at some depth. With the same end in view, each of the 'family group' chapters ends with a section raising issues for further investigation. These sections may also be used as advance organisers for critical reading.

The handbook is an excellent resource for comparing and contrasting theories and models. We anticipate that at college level teachers will often want to challenge students to identify the strengths and weaknesses of contrasting frameworks in relation to a subject area or field of study. For example, medical students might be asked how far King and Kitchener's model of reflective judgment and Vermunt and Verloop's categorisation of learning activities illuminate their understanding of problem-based learning.

Teachers and other professionals who wish to acquaint themselves with a wider range of disciplinary approaches to the study of teaching and learning will find this a useful introductory text. The first chapter provides an overview of the field and a number of all-embracing frameworks are described in Chapter 6. Chapter 3 has a mainly educational emphasis, while philosophical frameworks predominate in Chapter 4 and psychological frameworks in Chapter 5.

A superficial flicking through the handbook would equate with a 'pre-structural' understanding, in SOLO taxonomy terms (Biggs and Collis, 1982). Reading about one or more frameworks without relating them to each other or to one's own experience would be to gain knowledge at the 'unistructural' level, whereas 'multistructural' understanding would be to notice a number of similarities and differences without fully grasping their significance. The authors hope that readers will seek to develop new understandings of ideas, values and practices within their fields of enquiry and that by critically engaging with the text and consulting original sources a deeper appreciation of trans-disciplinary themes will result.

Overview of what follows

Chapter 1 The nature of thinking and thinking skills

This introductory chapter provides an overview in which theories, models, and concepts underpinning cognitive education are described and discussed. It reflects the current emphasis upon the strategic and self-regulatory nature of learning and provides detailed accounts of theoretical and practitioner use of such terms as metacognition, critical thinking, creative thinking and self-regulation. Other terms describing cognitive processes (e.g. analysis, synthesis, problem-solving, information-processing) are discussed or defined as necessary.

Chapter 2 Lists, inventories, groups, taxonomies and frameworks

This chapter explains the nature and function of ways of organising fields of study, with special attention to taxonomies. It then demonstrates their application in different fields, including three examples of frameworks which deal with aspects of thinking.

Chapter 3 Frameworks dealing with instructional design

This family group includes conceptions by Bloom, Anderson and Krathwohl, Biggs and Collis, Gagné and Feuerstein. All authors seek to create a structured learning environment, whether the emphasis is on content or process, knowledge acquisition or creativity.

Chapter 4 Frameworks dealing with productive thinking

Here we focus upon frameworks used for understanding critical and 'productive' thinking. Conceptions by de Bono, Halpern, Ennis, Lipman and Paul are included, as well as the TRIZ theory of inventive problem-solving.

Chapter 5 Frameworks dealing with cognitive structure and/or development

This group includes models of cognitive structure and/or cognitive development. As a 'family' it is relatively diverse and includes different approaches to analysing the concept of intelligence. It includes well-established theories such as those of Piaget, Guilford and Gardner, as well as a recent synthesis of components of self-regulation by Pintrich.

Chapter 6 Seven 'all-embracing' frameworks

Members of this family group are relatively all-embracing in scope, covering personality, thought and learning. Included here is Wallace and Adams' 'Thinking Actively in a Social Context' framework as well as some recent conceptions such as Vermunt and Verloop's categorisation of learning activities, Marzano's taxonomy of educational objectives and Sternberg's model of abilities as developing expertise.

Chapter 7 Moving from understanding to productive thinking: implications for practice

This chapter examines how various taxonomies can inform differing forms of cognitive education. It will explain the particular emphases of some of those that the authors deem most relevant for different types of thinking programme. Finally, we outline the value to practitioners of a four-category framework (information-gathering, basic understanding, productive thinking, strategic management/reflective thinking) that has arisen from our evaluation.

Without downplaying the importance of unconscious and social processes, we believe that thinking skills approaches focus attention on self-aware goal-directed thinking, in which there is strategic management of attention and working memory, supported by various 'habits of mind', including critical reflection. The goals of thinking and learning may be concerned with information-gathering, with building understanding, with thinking that generates productive outcomes, or with dynamic combinations of all three.

1

The nature of thinking and thinking skills

Perspectives on thinking

To be genuinely thoughtful, we must be willing to sustain and protract that state of doubt which is the stimulus to thorough enquiry, so as not to accept an idea or make a positive assertion of a belief until justifying reasons have been found.

Dewey, 1933, p. 16.

The aim of this book is to summarise and evaluate a number of systematic approaches to describing thinking and its relation to learning and teaching which have been developed over the last 50 years or so. We believe that each of these frameworks and taxonomies have value in attempting to describe aspects of thinking. The purpose of this collection is therefore to provide a resource for teachers, learners and researchers in order to make explicit a vocabulary with which to describe aspects of thinking which are relevant across a range of situations and contexts. Without a vocabulary to describe aspects of thinking that we believe to be teachable it is hard to develop teaching approaches or pedagogies that are effective. As a learner it is difficult to understand and make connections with what we have learned at different times and to plan how to take more control of our learning in the future without the language to describe our thinking and learning. For educational researchers it is impossible to describe aspects of the educational experience without developing concepts and terminology that can be identified with some reliability (or at least agreed regularity) across teaching and learning situations. With some clarity in these descriptions it may be possible to tackle important questions about how to improve education by attempting to measure aspects of these essential components and therefore evaluate the impact of different approaches and techniques.

Thinking skills (or at least those skilled in thinking) are needed, not only in the worlds of work, education and training, but in the contexts of family, friendship and community and in the construction of personal and shared beliefs and values. There is good evidence that organisations are more successful the more they involve their members in the processes of problem-solving and decision-making. In the 'information age' qualities of independence and flexibility are highly valued and 'learning to learn' has become an important goal. A well-functioning democracy is not only one in which people feel that their views can be freely expressed and are adequately represented; but one where those views are informed by reliable information, critical appraisal of ideas, creative thinking and open debate.

A range of academic traditions has considered and examined thinking as an aspect of human experience. In particular, various philosophical, psychological and sociological perspectives provide insight into thinking and learning at both an individual and cultural level. Whereas psychology has always been interested in learning about the development of thinking and hence teaching and learning, the philosophical tradition has usually viewed thinking in terms of the theory of (adult) mind and the theory of knowledge (rather than learning or coming to know). Sociological tools offer valuable perspectives on what occurs in terms of the systems, their structures and functions in schooling and educational practices, and especially about the relation of the individual to the wider society with regard to customs, power and authority. Each of these traditions has influenced the frameworks, taxonomies and descriptions of thinking that we have collected and which we review in this handbook. Other traditions, of course, have relevance. Politics exert powerful influences on the educational practices of different cultures and eras and economic factors are often cited as having a significant impact on the policies that are implemented. Cognitive neuroscience and neurophysiology are beginning to have an impact on aspects of teaching and learning, despite the fact that descriptions of brain functioning are hard to translate into clear messages for classroom practice. In terms of the accounts of thinking described in this book, the various influences have largely been mediated through psychological and philosophical traditions and their conceptualisations about thinking and learning to think.

In this first chapter we provide some background to these perspectives on thinking in education. A number of key terms and issues are outlined and discussed, since the evaluations of the frameworks and taxonomies which follow make some assumptions about the concepts and ideas that they rely upon. We give a brief overview of psychological, sociological and philosophical perspectives on thinking, and especially critical thinking. We then turn to the development of thinking skills approaches in education, including various programmes designed to develop particular aspects of thinking.

What is thinking?

Trying to understand how people think and learn is in some ways an impossible challenge, since we can only try to understand these things by using the very processes that we do not fully understand. In such circumstances choices are available. We can choose to focus on measurable aspects of human behaviour rather than on lived experience; or we can resort to metaphors which have personal or group appeal; or we can do what scientists have often done when entering a new and complex field – look for patterns and regularities between situations. All three approaches are evident in the theoretical frameworks and taxonomic approaches to thinking and learning that are described in this handbook and they all involve classification. Moreover, they all result in simplified accounts, since the human mind can only operate consciously with limited amounts of information.

Dewey's (1933) classic introduction to 'How We Think' offers an overview of some of the different senses in which the term *thinking* is used:

- thinking as a 'stream of consciousness' and the everyday 'uncontrolled coursing of ideas through our heads', including dreaming and daydreams (p. 3)
- thinking as imagination or mindfulness which is 'usually restricted to things not directly perceived' since we tend to say 'I saw a tree'

rather than 'I thought of a tree' if we are actually standing with our eyes open in front of one (p. 5)

- thinking as synonymous with *believing* expressed in statements such as 'I think it is going to rain tomorrow': in this sense it is contrasted with knowledge and the level of confidence with which we express such a belief (p. 6)
- reflective thinking as a chain of thought leading, through enquiry, to a conclusion (p. 9): this, of course is Dewey's aim in defining and recommending reflective thinking as the basis of both rationality and action.

Another sense implicit in the term *thinking* is more often explicit in the related term *thoughtful*: the sense of care and attention. When we are thoughtful we are either being considerate (usually towards another person) or spending time in deliberating about or considering a course of action. The critical thinking movement in the US has often identified this aspect of thinking and Matthew Lipman's framework makes 'caring thinking' explicit. The value that this implies is not always made so obvious. Thinking is, perhaps, generally a good thing, but there may be occasions where some kinds of thinking are more valuable than others. For example in a dangerous situation, such as when someone swimming is in difficulties, it may be more effective to recall what to do (and do it quickly) than thoughtfully identify all of the possible rescue options and evaluate their merits. A further issue here is that thinking usually implies a process or at least a state which continues for some time. However, when used in the past tense it can have the briefer sense of recall or remembering: 'I heard this tune and thought of you.'

The term 'thinking' can therefore be used in many senses: to describe mental activity that we may not be fully aware of (semi-conscious thought): from the everyday things that we perceive and routinely act upon, but which require little direct attention or effort; to the more conscious or deliberate act of reflecting or bringing to attention particular aspects of our experience. A number of the general issues in the frameworks which we have evaluated relate to these different senses and resulting connotations of the term.

It is hard to disentangle each of these various senses and we therefore acknowledge the complexity surrounding the terminology involved in each of the sections of the book. What we can say is that the word 'thinking', particularly in educational contexts, is usually used to mean a consciously goal-directed process, such as remembering, forming concepts, planning what to do and say, imagining situations, reasoning, solving problems, considering opinions, making decisions and judgments, and generating new perspectives. When there is some uncertainty that a satisfactory end is achievable, it is useful to think. This has clear resonances with Dewey's definition of reflective thinking:

Active, persistent and careful consideration of any belief or supposed form of knowledge in the light of the grounds that support it and the further conclusions to which it tends constitutes reflective thought. (Dewey, 1933, p. 9.)

The issue here is control. In Dewey's view the development of reflective thought is the most important goal of education and enables the individual to take control of and responsibility for their own thinking in order to participate effectively as a member of a democratic society. Paradoxically it is the teacher's role to develop this thinking: in the various frameworks and taxonomies which follow, the roles of the teacher and the roles of the learner are not always made explicit. In some, the purpose of the classification is for the teacher to ensure more effective planning, delivery or assessment of a curriculum, but without the explicit and active engagement of the learner in being made aware of the specified thinking processes. In others, the role of the learner is acknowledged as central to this task. Both the philosophy and sociology of education have wrestled with the problems of indoctrination and empowerment. Contemporary work in psychology of education has identified the role of metacognition and self-regulation as of crucial importance. We see the apparently competing disciplines as offering complementary perspectives which are of value to learners and educators.

Metacognition and self-regulation

There is considerable debate about the meaning of the term 'metacognition' in the research literature. Perry (1970) spoke about 'meta-reason' and 'meta-thought' but the coining of the term 'metacognition' is usually attributed to Flavell (1976):

Metacognition refers to one's knowledge concerning one's own cognitive processes and products or anything related to them . . . For example, I am engaging in metacognition (metamemory, metalearning, metaattention, metalanguage, or whatever) if I notice that I am having more trouble learning A than B; if it strikes me that I should double-check C before accepting it as a fact . . . if I sense that I had better make a note of D because I may forget it . . . Metacognition refers, among other things, to the active monitoring and consequent regulation and orchestration of these processes . . . usually in the service of some concrete goal or objective. (Flavell, 1976, p. 232.)

Metacognition involves two major dimensions (Boekaerts and Simons, 1993). Firstly, it involves an awareness of one's own cognitive functioning (metacognitive knowledge) and secondly, application of one's cognitive resources for learning or problem-solving; described by Hacker (1998) as two components, metacognitive monitoring and metacognitive regulation.

There is some confusion between the terms *self-regulation* and *metacognition* and, across theories, definitions often overlap (Zeidner, Boekaerts and Pintrich, 2000). For some (Ashman and Conway, 1997) self-regulation is seen as one part of metacognition with the latter including knowledge in the form of awareness of one's own cognitive strengths and weaknesses (although they also see metacognition as a component of self-regulation). Others (e.g. Zimmerman, 2000) would include such self-knowledge within self-regulation. In similar vein, Demetriou (2000) similarly considers self-regulation to be the more comprehensive term not only encompassing metacognitive (or, for Demetriou 'hypercognitive') knowledge and skills but also the conscious control of motivational, affective and behavioural processes. It is important to note that metacognition is used narrowly by some and much more broadly by others. However, there are dangers in rendering such terms in increasingly all-encompassing fashion and the expansion of the term metacognition to include the student's theories of self, learning and learning environments can result in a weakening of such a construct's explanatory power (Boekaerts, 1997).

An important aspect of self-regulation is a sense of personal agency. Some see self-efficacy as integral to self-regulation, on the grounds that not only must the individual have knowledge of skills for appropriate functioning but they must also believe that they can perform these skills in the attainment of desired ends (Creer, 2000). Others, (e.g. Endler and Kocovski, 2000) see self-efficacy as an important factor in self-regulation, but do not conceive this as a subordinate or componential element. Despite their different theoretical and conceptual positions, most researchers appear to agree that self-regulation should be viewed as a systematic process involving the setting of personal goals and the subsequent channelling of one's behaviour towards their achievement. Zimmerman (1995, 2000) points out that an emphasis upon personal agency helps us to distinguish between metacognition that 'emphasises only knowledge states and deductive reasoning when, for example, choosing cognitive strategies' (2000, p. 14) and self-regulation that also includes self-beliefs and affective reactions with regard to specific performance contexts. Self-regulation involves cognitive, motivational, affective and behavioural components that enable individuals to adjust their actions and/or their goals in order to achieve desired results in changing environmental circumstances.

As one might anticipate, many classroom interventions, based upon theories of self-regulation, emphasise the importance of helping students develop a positive orientation to learning and a belief that they are capable of succeeding if they work hard and apply appropriate strategies. While such elements are also key to many thinking skills programmes, these often tend to be less theoretically explicit and subsidiary to the primary emphasis upon analytical reasoning and other problem-solving processes.

Psychological perspectives

Since the pioneering work of Bloom and his associates (1956), psychologists and educationalists have sought to conceptualise a multitude of cognitive processes as a means of improving teaching, learning and assessment. However, it is only during the past decade that the huge interest in the teaching of thinking has seen such work proliferate in everyday educational practices. Many initiatives originate from Western psychology and education, particularly the US and the UK. Various reasons have been adduced, such as relatively poor performance on international comparisons of educational attainment and a recognition that mature economies require more sophisticated learners and problem-solvers. This has led to a search for new curricula and pedagogies that will stimulate more productive thinking. However, interest in cognitive enhancement has become a worldwide phenomenon. Many in countries performing low on international measures of performance, such as South Africa, see the teaching of thinking as a valuable means of raising educational levels and developing social inclusion. Others, in countries that appear to be high-achieving on such traditional measures, such as Singapore and China, believe that such approaches may address students' limited creative and problem-solving abilities in order to develop better productivity in the global economy.

Cognitive psychologists typically study thinking in other people – a third-person perspective in which the metaphor of the brain as a computer has been dominant. In this view, the higher levels of the brain make a model of the actual world, a mental picture that parallels the world, though no doubt with distortions (Craik, 1943; Zangwill, 1980; Nathan, 1987). Thinking is an internal, mental process that constructs and operates on mental representations of information. Thagard describes six approaches to modelling the mind, involving: logic, rules, concepts, analogies, images, and neural connections (Thagard, 1996, p. 19). Thagard writes that 'thinking can best be understood in terms of representational structures in the mind and computational procedures that operate on those structures . . . There is much disagreement about the nature of the representations and computations that constitute thinking' (p. 10). Thagard draws an analogy between the mind and a computer program, where the mental representations in the mind are like the organisation of stored data and the algorithms that are then executed by the software correspond to the thinking procedures in the mind. Seductive though this analogy may be, it does not capture some of the complexity, and particularly the quality of thinking that can be described by an individual. First-person introspective accounts of thinking have a different feel about them, since we all have the impression that we can consciously control our thoughts and actions. We experience wanting, will, effort and emotion in a holistic manner as we think, and it is only through subsequent analytical reflection that we can view these aspects dispassionately and identify some patterns or regularities in our experience.

Indeed a case can be made that while we are thinking (with our attention focused on certain elements) we are not aware of the thinking process itself (much of which is unconscious). It is only after the event that we can reflect on the products of our thinking and to a certain extent reconstruct and analyse the process. Like Velmans (2000) we take the view that first-person and third-person accounts of thinking are complementary and that one cannot be reduced to the other.

A teacher necessarily has a third-person perspective on the learner's thinking and can only make inferences about it on the basis of what the learner does. Some earlier approaches to instructional design have focused on precisely formulated, externally-imposed behavioural objectives in place of goals which learners set for themselves or agree with others. First-person goal setting may be desirable in some contexts and with certain types of content, whereas group negotiation of goals may be preferred in other contexts and teacher or other externally-driven instruction may be most effective in yet other contexts, particularly where masterly learning and accurate performance is expected. This argument applies just as much to the development of thinking skills as to any other kind of learning.

Sociological perspectives

One of Auguste Comte's aims in his *Cours de Philosophie Positive* was a scientific account of social aspects of human life which might account for the nature of society in the same way that natural sciences had described the physical world. Whilst this quest eluded him, it provides the grail of the subsequent academic tradition of sociology which he had effectively founded (Lawton and Gordon, 2002, p. 149). Sociological concepts and descriptions have been productively applied to education. For example, Durkheim's analysis of social solidarity and the transition from simple communities based on common interest to the interdependence of difference in modern society resonates with contemporary educational concerns. His belief in the power of education as a solution to this problem is repeated by thinkers in other traditions and has now become a commonplace for politicians across the spectrum. The work of the Frankfurt School and its key figures in Horkheimer, Adorno and Marcuse, through to Habermas' efforts to establish a communicative rationality and 'knowledge-constitutive interest' all have a bearing on socialisation and the place of the individual in society and their thinking (see Illeris, 2004, Chapters 5–6 for a synthesis of the impact of these approaches for our understanding of learning).

Nisbet (1966) argues that the key features of a sociological perspective are the notions of community, authority, status, the sacred and alienation. Whilst these terms are relevant to aspects of educational systems and practices, their bearing upon aspects of the frameworks reviewed in this book are less direct. The terminology and concepts they embody are relevant, however, in the way that the individual relates to a wider society and the customs and practices that restrict and inhibit some behaviours and support and foster others. These ideas can perhaps be regarded as setting limits on how widely applicable the more abstract terminology of the frameworks are to particular individuals as they 'participate' (Wenger, 1998) in particular contexts. This is of course a complex and reciprocal relationship where the individual 'acts back' (Jarvis, 1992) on the social:

When children are born, they are born into a society whose culture preceded them and will almost certainly continue after their lives are over. Culture therefore appears to be objective and external. But the children have inherited no, or minimal, instincts to help them live within society and conform to its culture; thus they have to acquire that culture. In the first instance, then, learning is a matter of internalizing and transforming something that is apparently objective to the individual . . . However, there comes a time when they begin to think for themselves, ask questions and generally experiment . . . Children gradually become more independent; they usually develop a mind of their own and then process the external cultural stimuli and respond to them in a variety of ways. Individuals begin to act back on the social world that has formed them. (Jarvis, 1992, pp. 22–23.)

The issue is perhaps one of perspective. As Illeris (2004) notes in his integrative account of learning encompassing the social, cognitive and emotional domains:

For the internal psychological dimensions, the individual is the setting, while the action takes place through the individual's meetings with the surrounding world. For the interaction dimension, it is the surrounding world that is the setting, and the action is the individual's deeds in relation to this surrounding world. (Illeris, 2004, pp. 117–118.)

Thinking always takes place in a context which has social influences and interactions whether direct or indirect, and the individual's thinking is affected by the various affordances and constraints of different contexts. The strategies that learners use in different situations suggest Vygotsky's 'functional learning systems' which Cole and Scribner (1974) describe as 'flexible and variable organisations of cognitive processes' (p. 193) and suggest that 'socio-cultural factors play a role in influencing which of possible alternative processes are evoked in a given situation and what role they play in total performance' (p. 193). We acknowledge the strength of these concerns, but suggest that it is still worth looking for features of thinking that recur across contexts. Identifying such similarities or regularities may have benefits for the educator by enabling teaching to build on different experiences and develop complementary teaching approaches. Awareness of aspects of thinking which can be applied in different contexts may also be of benefit to learners who can see that aspects of their own experience may be relevant in a new situation.

Philosophical perspectives

A number of philosophical issues have a bearing upon the aspects of thinking and learning covered in this book. In particular, aspects of epistemology, the philosophy of mind, the philosophy of language and related theories of meaning are relevant to an understanding of the way we think, know and learn. Educational philosophy has tended to view these issues in terms of learning to know or the development of knowledge: a genetic perspective. Indeed this forms the basis of the work of Jean Piaget (see pages 189–195). In contemporary educational philosophy the most pertinent debate is how general aspects of thinking can be identified in different contexts. On one side of the debate proponents of thinking skills, such as Ennis (1989, 1991) argue that there are important general thinking skills (or general critical thinking skills) that can be used or applied across different contexts. On the other, those like McPeck (1981) argue that thinking is always context specific in what appears like a philosophical echo of some of the proponents of situated learning (e.g. Lave and Wenger, 1991) or 'situation specificity' in social learning (Burr, 1995, p. 25).

Descriptive or normative?

Differences become apparent in the various conceptions of thinking and critical thinking outlined in some of the taxonomies and frameworks. Two broad groups can be identified in these accounts which can be described as descriptive and normative versions. Descriptive definitions of thinking tend to be psychological in origin. They specify cognitive skills and the mental processes or procedures involved in different aspects of thinking. Implicit in this model is that being good at thinking is being proficient at particular mental processes such as classifying, inferring, and evaluating. This procedural view is often taken to imply that thinking and problem-solving can be undertaken by practising a series of steps or procedures. The appeal of this approach is that it seems possible to scrutinise aspects of a curriculum for planning or teaching using selected key terms, so as to develop particular thinking skills.

By contrast, philosophers argue for a normative definition. By this they mean that critical thinking is inextricably connected with values and it essentially means 'good thinking'. From this perspective, a purely descriptive account omits the central issue of the quality of the thinking. So, for example, consider making a decision about whether or not to adopt a local recycling scheme. From a descriptive perspective, critical thinking would involve analysing the issue, generating possible resolutions, evaluating these potential solutions and synthesising the information to reach a decision. However it would be possible to analyse the issue from superficial perspectives (such as residents do not have space for a second rubbish bin or that they might get confused about which bin to put different kinds of waste in) or to evaluate some options from a biased perspective (the local factory which makes recycling bins argues for each household to have a bin for each kind of recyclable rubbish). So a check-list of thinking skills used in a partial analysis or from a biased perspective may well involve most of the types of thinking in a descriptive list.

Thinking skills and critical thinking

Of course the philosophical perspective itself has difficulties. There is no clear consensus from philosophers about a definition of critical thinking. Critical thinking has been an important movement in the education system in the US for a number of years, so much so that in 1987 an expert panel was convened by the American Philosophical Association to undertake a systematic enquiry into the current situation in education and assessment. The report includes a consensus statement regarding critical thinking and the ideal critical thinker, which begins:

We understand critical thinking to be purposeful, self-regulatory judgment which results in interpretation, analysis, evaluation, and inference, as well as explanation of the evidential, conceptual, methodological, criteriological, or contextual considerations upon which that judgment is based. CT (critical thinking) is essential as a tool of inquiry. As such, CT is a liberating force in education and a powerful resource in one's personal and civic life. Whilst not synonymous with good thinking, CT is a pervasive and self-rectifying human phenomenon. (Facione, 1990.)

Despite the ponderous tone of the statement, inevitable perhaps when a panel of experts is asked to reach a consensus on something so complex, the report provides a useful overview of what is understood by the term *critical thinking*. The concern with identifying rigorous and appropriate criteria for the formulation of judgments and the need to achieve a sound basis for belief and action as a key principle are evident. Ennis encapsulates this more succinctly when he describes critical thinking as 'reasonable, reflective thinking that is focused on deciding what to believe or do' (Ennis, 1985, see pages 152–157). In the UK, critical thinking has been gaining more attention since the introduction of the AS Level in Critical Thinking in 1999.

We have collected nearly 40 definitions of critical thinking, a term which has wider currency in the USA than in the UK. The literature on critical thinking is extensive: a search using this term on ERIC, a US-based electronic database, results in over 2000 references to articles alone. The term is used in different ways and has developed over time (see, for example, the review by Pithers and Soden, 2000). In the US 'critical thinking' is often considered to be synonymous with 'thinking skills'. There are a number of key issues in understanding critical thinking and how it relates to teaching and learning in various curricula which it may be helpful to outline. First is the nature of definitions of critical thinking and how these relate to what might be categorised as psychological and philosophical perspectives. Second, there are some identified distinctions in different philosophical positions, which relate to the nature of thinking and thinking skills which need to be outlined because of the implications for teaching. Third is the issue of assessment and how critical thinking relates to teaching and a curriculum.

Ennis believes that critical thinking depends essentially on two over-arching dispositions: caring to 'get it right' to the extent possible and caring to present positions honestly and clearly. It also depends on the process of evaluation (applying criteria to judge possible answers), a process implicit or explicit in most of the essential critical thinking abilities listed by Ennis (1987). The idea of evaluation is common to most, but not all, of the definitions we have found, but the overall impression is one of diversity and subjectivity rather than clarity. Each writer seems to have an individual conception of 'good' (i.e. 'critical') thinking, if not of 'reason' and 'truth'.

McPeck (1981) defines it as 'the appropriate use of reflective skepticism within the problem area under consideration' and closely identifies these problem areas with subject disciplines. In order to develop expertise in a subject discipline what you need, he argues, is more knowledge of that discipline, because thinking critically about something is thinking about that specific subject content. However, without going into the debate about subject specificity and general thinking skills in detail, this seems too extreme a position (Smith, 2002). It is not clear that it is only more subject content knowledge that an expert thinker needs. It seems likely that some tools in the critical thinking arsenal may well be useful across academic domains and beyond, and that these skills (or attitudes and dispositions) may be particularly useful as learners develop expertise. Such analysis has come from the use of argument and informal logic in reasoning broadly (e.g. Govier, 1988) or from a teaching and learning perspective, where making connections for learners to see similarities in what (and how) they are learning might usefully take a 'thinking' perspective (Higgins and

Baumfield, 1998). However it must be acknowledged that the use of the term 'thinking skills' is problematic. It seems to imply that teaching thinking skills can be successful without also developing attitudes or fostering dispositions or without being applied to specific contexts. Smith (2002) points to the negative connotations of specific schemes and approaches as well as to a lack of conceptual clarity.

Ennis' understanding of critical thinking is that it is 'reasonable reflective thinking that is focused on deciding what to believe and do' (Ennis, 1985, p. 45). Although he developed a taxonomy, he makes the point forcefully that the components cannot be so 'criterionized so that judgments can be made mechanically'. This is a crucial point about how critical thinking relates to teaching and learning and is taken up by Paul. Paul distinguishes two senses of critical thinking (1982): a weak sense in which a range of skills can be used to detect mistaken reasoning and a strong sense in which the complexity of most situations is acknowledged and 'precise identification and definition depends upon some arguable choice among alternative frames of reference'. This means that effective critical thinking involves judgment which is context dependent. Paul further argues (1987) that one of the purposes of critical thinking is to develop learners' perspectives, and argues for dialogue or 'dialectical experience' as an essential ingredient in helping to develop judgment about how and where particular skills can best be used. A further perspective comes from Lipman and the Philosophy for Children movement in school education. Although this was not intended to be a critical thinking programme, it has been interpreted as such and is widely used around the world in a range of educational contexts to achieve critical thinking aims. One key feature of the programme is that it cuts across subject boundaries, arguing for a position where learners develop connections between their areas of learning in order to draw on their experience and knowledge more broadly.

Each of these perspectives on critical thinking entails differences in a critical thinking curriculum. If McPeck's position is accepted, then each disciplinary area will need to identify its own distinctive rules carried out within that specific subject area. Students will learn knowledge about the subject and teaching critical thinking will form a part of this subject teaching, as a means of developing subject expertise.

On the other hand, other approaches, such as Lipman's, argue for a separate timetable slot where students learn and apply their thinking within a special pedagogical framework. The 'community of enquiry' structure is essential to Lipman's approach. McPeck, Paul and Ennis do not have published curricula that can be developed for different educational settings. Lipman has such material, and his work has been adapted internationally (Splitter and Sharp, 1995) for learners of different ages, from nursery children (e.g. Murris and Haynes, 2001) to post-16 contexts (e.g. Gregson, 2003).

From both philosophical and psychological perspectives, the assessment of critical thinking is challenging. It is not possible to assess single aspects of critical thinking or discrete skills without the risk of these separate assessments failing to capture either the quality of that thinking or the relation of the identified thinking skill to the task which aims to assess it. An example here might be learning to drive. Whilst it is possible to learn aspects of driving in a classroom or in a practice environment and become skilful, assessment by a qualified tester takes place in a real environment. The tester has criteria, but also needs to make a judgment about how well a learner has fitted together their observational and physical skills and evaluate whether or not their driving is good enough.

A synthesis of descriptive and normative approaches can be proposed. This involves taking in the strengths of each perspective. So a descriptive analysis is useful in identifying how particular aspects of thinking are valuable for a particular subject or in a curriculum in order to ensure that the teaching or elements of the course cover a range of thinking 'skills', though these may need to be taught through appropriate and relevant contexts. However the implications for the assessment of such skills from the normative perspective is that it needs to take into account not just whether a student shows such thinking, but that it is appropriate in the context or meets particular requirements to ensure its quality, needing some judgment on the part of an assessor.

Thinking skills in education

In educational discourse, 'teaching thinking' or 'teaching thinking skills' is often used to refer to pedagogic approaches through which specific strategies and procedures may be taught and used by learners in a controlled, conscious way to make their learning more effective. These strategies and procedures may be what some use spontaneously and/or they may be otherwise contrived. Many such skills and abilities have been suggested, specific, broad, or general in nature. Ashman and Conway (1997) conclude that thinking skills programmes typically involve six related types of thinking:

- metacognition
- critical thinking
- creative thinking
- cognitive processes (such as problem-solving and decision-making)
- core thinking skills (such as representation and summarising)
- understanding the role of content knowledge.

For the purposes of this book we have conceptualised 'thinking skills approaches' as courses or organised activities which identify for learners translatable mental processes and/or which require learners to plan, describe and evaluate their thinking and learning. This usage of the term 'thinking skills' implies that there are learning and teaching situations that can induce processes which produce desired mental activity. It is underpinned by a judgment that thinking can be improved with practice particularly through the skilled intervention of a teacher. It also implies the use of mental processes to plan, describe and evaluate thinking and learning. One way of looking at this metacognitive aspect is to consider thinking skills as ways of managing working memory so that conscious and unconscious processes together are more likely to produce desired outcomes (Newton, 2000).

Without downplaying the importance of unconscious and social processes, we believe that thinking skills approaches or pedagogies which make aspects of thinking explicit to the teacher and learners will focus attention on self-aware goal-directed thinking, in which there can then be strategic management of attention and working memory, supported by various 'habits of mind', including critical reflection. The goals of thinking and learning may be concerned with information-gathering, with building understanding, with thinking that generates productive outcomes, or with dynamic combinations of all three. Directing attention by clarifying the language of thinking as the taxonomies and frameworks in this book all attempt will be of help to those who wish to achieve this in their teaching or their learning.

Emphasis upon instruction in cognition is the product of many influences. Some of the main influences can be identified.

On the one hand, not many teachers are enthused by what are widely regarded as simplistic behaviourist models, in which the focus of teaching is primarily observable behaviours rather than mental processing. The behavioural objectives movement has been particularly influential in special education (Ainscow and Tweddle, 1988), and in mainstream practice there has also been a trend towards setting and assessing precise learning goals and targets. The sterility and mechanistic nature of such approaches, however, has resulted in renewed interest in cognitive processes that appear to underpin learning (Elliott, 2000).

There has also been recognition that developmental stage theories, such as those of Piaget, where the individual passes through a series of stages reflecting superior levels of thinking, do not necessarily lead to a 'deterministic trap' (Adey and Shayer, 1994, p. 6) in which environmental inputs might be seen as capable of limited influence. Following the widespead interest in Vygotskian theory in recent decades, it has been increasingly accepted that educators should try to help learners engage in thinking at higher levels than might be possible without highly structured assistance. Vygotskian theory has been complemented by Bruner's work, in particular, the notion of scaffolding (Wood, Bruner and Ross, 1976). Many teachers are attracted by the idea of *cognitive apprenticeship*, a term that refers to a process whereby the 'expert' (teacher) structures the conditions of learning a task in such a fashion that the 'novice' (learner) is progressively given less support as he or she gains in the capacity to complete it independently (Rogoff, 1990).

A proliferation of thinking skills programmes, approaches and initiatives have emerged in education, especially for use by teachers in schools. In some cases, these take the form of highly structured and discrete programmes (such as Feuerstein's *Instrumental Enrichment*); in others, principles from cognitive education are drawn upon and used with existing curricula (such as *Cognitive Acceleration Through Science Education* by Adey, Shayer and Yates, 1989). Further educational initiatives take ideas from philosophy (such as Matthew Lipman's *Philosophy for Children* and can perhaps be better described as a pedagogy to support thinking rather than a thinking skills programme. Many are more eclectic and draw upon diverse perspectives, ranging from psychology to popular neuroscience. Wallace and Adams' *Thinking Actively in a Social Context (TASC)* (Wallace et al., 1993) has an eclectic, but coherent, theoretical foundation, drawing on psychological, philosophical, social and pedagogical sources. However, some of these initiatives are based upon such differing theoretical and conceptual perspectives that they bear little relationship to each other. Indeed, the same concept is often used to describe rather different cognitive processes. Given the lack of any unifying or overarching theory, the approaches, models and concepts are frequently adopted with little significant grasp of where these are located within the broader field of (albeit contested) knowledge.

It is hardly surprising that programmes to teach thinking have become plentiful (cf. Hamers and Overtoom, 1997). They often have powerful resonance with teachers and have been shown to have a generally beneficial effect (Higgins et al., 2004). While some maintain that their task is the delivery of a school or college subject, many others emphasise that they are trying to teach more generally applicable or 'translatable' skills or processes through the problem-solving elements of the curriculum, as well as encouraging learners to become thoughtful and reflective.

Teaching thinking: programmes and approaches

Widespread publicity is attached to highly charismatic and persuasive advocates of specific thinking skills programmes. One of these is de Bono, whose articulation of a set of thinking strategies, such as those set out in his Cognitive Research Trust (CoRT) programme, has been widely applied in both educational and vocational contexts.

The work of Lipman (see pages 157–164) has also received much attention. A teacher of philosophy in one of the USA's most prestigious universities, Lipman despaired at what he considered to be the widespread inability of his students to engage in high-quality thinking. As a consequence, he advocates the use of philosophical reasoning and argument with learners from as young as seven. He seeks to create 'communities of enquiry' in educational contexts that encourage listening carefully to the views of others and setting out and justifying one's own opinions and responses by recourse to logical argument.

In the 1970s there was a general interest in the field of special education in various 'psycholinguistic' programmes which sought to remediate weak or faulty psychological processing in perceptual and cognitive areas, such as visual perception, auditory sequencing, visual–motor processing, and concept formation. The theory behind interventions based upon such analyses was that tackling processing deficits would result in raised academic performance in other areas such as reading and mathematics (Swanson, 1999). However, empirical studies failed to support such notions, with transfer proving particularly problematic (Arter and Jenkins, 1979; Kavale and Forness, 1987). More recent work has focused on specific cognitive processes, such as inductive reasoning, apparently with more positive results (Klauer and Phye, 1994; Büchel, Schlatter and Scharnhorst, 1997).

Proving highly durable over several decades, Feuerstein's 'Instrumental Enrichment' (see pages 55–62 for an analysis) has been largely applied to learners with various forms of special educational need. Feuerstein's optimistic views of the capacity of all learners to make progress, his highly detailed and comprehensive description of specific cognitive processes that were often deficient in poor learners, together with the articulation of a comprehensive intervention programme, have resulted in much teacher interest across the world and a number of derivatives (e.g. Blagg et al., 1988).

As attractive as such programmes as Feuerstein's were to many teachers, in the UK there has been an increasing movement to undertake thinking programmes in discrete academic subject areas. The strong subject discipline emphasis of the National Curriculum; a heavy inspection regime in which the appropriateness of 'esoteric' courses might be questioned; the costs involved in getting the required training; and inconsistent research findings have limited the take-up of stand-alone programmes. However, approaches that embed thinking skills interventions within a specific curriculum subject, and which appear to result in significant attainment gains in that subject (Adey and Shayer, 1994) have a greater appeal.

Starting in science with the Cognitive Acceleration through Science Education (CASE) programme (Adey, Shayer and Yates, 1989), a similar approach has been applied in mathematics, technology and the arts (Shayer and Adey, 2002). An innovative curriculum development project called Thinking through Geography (Leat, 1998) was designed around a list of 'big' concepts which are important for geography teaching. The approach has been expanded to history, Religious Education, English, Modern Foreign Languages and primary education. It focuses on the use of 'powerful pedagogical strategies' (Leat and Higgins, 2002) to support teachers in developing their pupils' thinking. Another example of the 'infusion' approach for developing thinking skills can also be seen in the ACTS project (Activating Children's Thinking Skills) for upper primary level (McGuinness et al., 1997). As in Swartz and Parks' infusion approach in the US (1994), teachers trained in the ACTS methodology develop a range of thinking skills across the Northern Ireland curriculum at Key Stage 2 by focusing on specific strategies. Other subject-specific work showing evidence of impact is in the area of collaborative talk and thinking. When primary-age pupils are taught to follow agreed 'talk rules', their attainment in mathematics and science (Mercer et al., 2002) has been shown to improve. This 'Thinking Together' approach is also being extended to other subjects and age groups. Similar theoretical concerns underpin other programmes such as Wallace's TASC 'Thinking Actively in a Social Context' (Adams and Wallace, 1990; Wallace, 2001).

Also involved in the development of 'thinking' approaches to learning and teaching across the curriculum has been a strong orientation to the teaching of strategies for learning in an explicit fashion. Research studies have highlighted the gains that can be achieved when specific cognitive and metacognitive strategies are embedded in the teaching of academic subjects such as reading and mathematics (e.g. de Corte, Verschaffel and van de Ven, 2001; Fuchs et al., 2003). Much early work in this area was undertaken in the fields of memory (Cohen and Nealon, 1979) and reading comprehension (Palincsar and Brown, 1984; Meyer et al., 1989). Such 'learning to learn' initiatives were greatly strengthened by increasing teacher familiarity with the constructs of *metacognition* and *self-regulation*. As a result, the importance for learners of considering about how best to approach tasks involving such cognitive processes as memorising, problem-solving, and applying existing knowledge and skills to new areas (transfer), has become widely recognised by educators. Although metastrategic or metacognitive processes form a key part of most thinking skills programmes, they also now feature more independently in everyday teaching practices.

Cognitive forms of intervention have been influenced by several studies demonstrating that those with learning difficulties experience particular problems with metacognitive and self-regulatory functioning involving, for example, checking, planning, monitoring, reviewing, predicting and evaluating (Wong and Jones, 1982). Cognitive and metacognitive interventions in the US to help children with learning disabilities use a range of tactics and strategies (Swanson, 1999, 2000). These include: the use of advanced organisers (statements in learning materials that remind learners of procedures that they should employ in order to be more strategic in their approach); elaboration (in which students are actively encouraged to link material to be learned to information or ideas which they already have in mind); attributions (in which the reasons for a strategy succeeding or failing are considered); and thinking about and controlling one's thinking process (metacognition). The importance of metastrategic knowledge (knowledge of task objectives and knowledge of strategies) for all children is now widely accepted (Kuhn and Pearsall, 1998).

Developments in instructional design

Programmes and approaches for teaching thinking are located within the broader field of instructional design. Aims and objectives are required for any educational enterprise or training programme, as well as methods for achieving them. These can be expressed in global and/or specific terms, and with an emphasis on the learner and the learning process, and/or on the teacher and coverage of content. It is widely accepted that learners need to become skilled in accessing and using knowledge productively rather than learning factual content as a memory-based exercise (Resnick, 1989). Learning objectives usually focus on knowledge and skills, but long-term objectives are formulated in terms of attitudes and dispositions to behave in certain ways.

The instructional design community has undergone significant changes over the past 50 years. Eliasmith (1996) argues that the main reason for the failure of behaviourist theories of cognition was their rejection of the role of representation in animal and human thinking. The same author goes on to show how subsequently two main paradigms of cognitive science have gained prominence: 'connectionism', which sees cognition in terms of connectionist processing; and 'symbolicism', which argues that cognition is best understood as symbolic manipulation.

Other important new developments in instructional design theory are emerging. For example, Eliasmith points to the many powerful criticisms which have more recently been levelled against connectionist and symbolicist paradigms of cognitive science (Thelen and Smith, 1994; van Gelder, 1995; van Gelder and Port, 1995), particularly in relation to their inherent linear and unidirectional representation of thought processes and learning and their inability to explain the dynamic and socially and culturally situated nature of the complexities of human thinking.

De Corte (2000), Corno and Randi (1999) and Jonassen (1999) also draw attention to different fundamental problems in traditional approaches to instructional design and suggest how these shortcomings may be overcome. For example, de Corte (2000) points out that although recent research on learning and instruction has improved our understanding of how we think and learn, this has not resulted in proportional improvements and innovation in classroom practice.

He makes a distinction between a disciplinary orientation and an educational orientation in educational psychology. From the disciplinary orientation, educational psychology is considered as a branch of psychology, which is chiefly concerned with the development of theory, while the education orientation focuses upon developing a better understanding of education as a basis for improving educational practices. He argues that the disciplinary orientation effectively dominated 20th century research and is still alive in instructional psychology in the 21st century. He goes on to claim that this has led to 'the study of psychological variables and processes in isolation, and of individual learners independent of their social and cultural environment' (2000, p. 252).

Conducting research in this way, de Corte contends, not only runs the risk that educationally important aspects of learning are in danger of being overlooked, but also carries with it the assumption that 'in vitro' laboratory experiments can be extrapolated from the laboratory to the classroom. He points out how a lack of good communication between researchers and teachers has served to compound this problem and has culminated in a theory–practice gap. He illustrates how teachers tend to adapt rather than adopt educational innovations and it is for this reason that merely providing accessible and digestible research information or curriculum materials will simply not be enough to guarantee their translation into effective classroom practice.

Corno and Randi (1999) make an important and related point in a study of design theory for classroom instruction in self-regulation where they argue:

> If teachers are to help students become self-regulated learners, their own self-regulation has to be unleashed as well. Traditional design theories of instruction run the risk of interfering with rather than supporting this goal.
>
> (Corno and Randi, 1999, p. 296.)

De Corte emphasises how the education orientation, which developed from the work of Ausubel's criticism of the prevalence of the discipline orientation in the 1960s (Ausubel and Robinson, 1969), together with more recent research studies which have focused upon the design of new and powerful teaching–learning environments, has already resulted in an empirically underpinned knowledge base which can not only guide the analysis of the effectiveness and quality of teaching, but also serves to support the formulation and development of a practical and research-based theory of learning and instruction.

From a different starting point, Reigeluth (1999) arrives at a similar conclusion to de Corte. He distinguishes between descriptive theory (learning theory) and instructional design theory (theories or models of effective methods of instruction). He argues that the improvement of descriptive theory revolves around validity, whereas the improvement of design theories revolves around 'preferability' (which methods are better than their alternatives given a particular teacher's goals and values).

In contrast to de Corte, he claims that different kinds of research methodologies are required for improving each kind of theory and that most of the research methodologies developed to date were designed to advance descriptive theory. Through the work of Corno and Randi (1999) among others, he concurs with de Corte where he advocates a kind of formative research. By this he means a kind of developmental or action research that is intended to improve design theory for design and instructional practices or processes. Through the application of 'design experiments' he urges teachers and researchers to collaborate in the design, implementation and analysis of instructional design curriculum interventions in order to develop and refine instructional design theories. Reigeluth's underlying logic here is that, through the rigorous implementation and testing of an instructional design theory by teachers, any weaknesses found in implementation might reflect weaknesses in the theory. Conversely any improvements identified for the application may indicate ways to improve the theory. This resonates closely with the practical interests of teachers in actively investigating the impact of innovative approaches as a means both to develop their own practice, whilst at the same time testing the robustness of the theoretical and pedagogical design (Baumfield et al., 2002).

The instructional design community has come a long way since the pioneering work of Bloom and his associates. In the early 21st century it still struggles to balance the legacy of behaviourist theory with the sociocultural, multi-dimensional, multi-directional and dynamic nature of human thinking and learning. However, conceptions which emphasise sociocultural aspects of cognitive development are not always easily contextualised to classroom learning (Gruber, Law, Mandl and Renkl, 1999). Coaching individuals and small groups is not the same as trying to introduce concepts such as mediated learning and cognitive apprenticeship (Rogoff, 1990) into a class of 30 pupils. It remains to be seen how the research community and its counterparts in the teaching community will respond to the challenges of de Corte and Reigeluth to work together to develop ways of unifying theory-building and improving practice.

2

Lists, inventories, groups, taxonomies and frameworks

Bringing order to chaos

The world presents us with a confusion of objects. We seem inclined to order these objects according to their similarities. So, for instance, we divide people into men and women; events into past, present and future; and cutlery into knives, forks and spoons. Organising the world like this reduces its complexity, enables a more parsimonious description of it, and reduces the burden of thought to what can be managed.

Organising the world's objects may be something we are inclined to do, but objects can be organised in a variety of ways. Cutlery, for instance, can be sorted into plastic, metal and wooden items, long and short items, or knives, forks and spoons. Which is best? The answer, of course, depends on what you want to do. If you want to turn a hot coal, the first would be relevant; if you want to prise the lid from a can, the second would apply; if you want to eat dinner, the last would be appropriate. In other words, organisation and purpose go hand-in-hand (Bailey, 1994). An organisation that helps you do what you want is useful and can have survival value.

Here, we are concerned with kinds of thinking and how they have been organised. A particular aim is to assess the potential of these organisations for supporting thought about thinking, especially amongst those who want students to develop some proficiency in thinking. In practice, kinds of thinking have been organised in various ways, ranging from more or less orderly lists to elaborate taxonomies. Some were constructed to help teachers with an interest in developing thinking skills in their students. Others arose from, for instance, a desire to understand the elements of thinking and how they relate to one another. Despite being designed for different purposes, they may contribute something useful to our endeavour. However, lists and taxonomies are not the same. A few words about the various kinds of organisation we have met and their general strengths and weaknesses are relevant at this point.

Objects of study

In what follows, objects of study refer to the entities being collected, sorted, or grouped. Stamps in a stamp collection could be objects of study. They are discrete entities of the same kind. In educational practice, it is not always clear whether entities are discrete objects or exist at a higher level of abstraction.

Frameworks

A framework is a general term for a structure that provides support. In this context, it has to provide support for thinking about thinking. On this basis, lists, groups and taxonomies are frameworks that may support such thought, although the frames they offer may vary from a stick to an edifice. For Anderson (1983, pp. 12–13), 'a framework is a general pool of constructs for understanding a domain but it is not tightly enough organised to constitute a predictive theory'. It is not, however, the tightness of the organisation that makes a predictive theory, so much as the nature of the relationships in that organisation. The term *framework* covers a wide variety of structures.

Lists

A list is a device that presents the content of a collection or assemblage. The list may be unordered or ordered. An organising principle, if apparent, may make a list easier to use, as with an alphabetical index or a chronology of events. More than one organising principle can be present, as when a list reflects divisions in the collection and presents items alphabetically within each division. A list of the contents of a supposedly exhaustive collection may be described as an inventory.

Consider a list of words that denote thought, culled from a dictionary and presented in alphabetical order:

assume, brood, calculate, cerebrate, cogitate, conceive, conclude, consider, contemplate, deem, deliberate, design, determine, envisage, estimate, imagine, judge, muse, ponder, presume, reason, recall, recollect, reflect, remember, ruminate, suppose, surmise.

On the positive side, such a list may serve as a menu or check list. For instance, it could be an *aide-memoire* that reminds teachers what they have had their students do and have yet to do. Lists can be easy to use for checking that each item has been given attention.

However, the list of words above does not indicate relationships between entries and it does not show whether particular items are subsumed by others (i.e. are of a different rank). If such a list is intended to be a menu, there may be no basis for making a balanced or representative selection from it (or, conversely, a justifiably unbalanced selection). At its least helpful, a list could be a miscellany of unrelated items that does little for further thought.

Groups

A group is a collection of items that are related in some way. An entire collection of objects of study is itself a group, often referred to as the field. The field may be subdivided into smaller groups according to more specific similarities and differences amongst the objects of study. 'In its simplest form, classification is merely defined as the ordering of entities into groups or classes on the basis of their similarity' (Bowler, 1992, p. 165). The Russian chemist, Mendeleev, placed the then-known chemical elements into seven groups according to their behaviour and properties. For instance, he placed lithium, sodium and potassium in Group I and fluorine, chlorine and bromine in Group VII. These are discrete groups of the objects of study (the elements). The elements within these groups are more alike than the elements in different groups. In the list of 'thinking' words above, several are to do with bringing knowledge out of mental storage (e.g. recall, recollect, remember). These could be grouped together and labelled, say, 'retrieval processes'. This process of grouping may shorten the list, particularly when a word can be allocated clearly to a group. This is not always easy. 'Brood', for instance, has connotations of contemplation combined with dark emotion and 'contemplation' sounds like a passive review of recalled events but is it ever entirely passive?

On the positive side, groups can impose order on the world and make large amounts of data more manageable, especially if the groups are named. In other words, they are economical devices that can reduce the burden of thinking.

On the other hand, as with a list of words, a list of groups may be no more than a checklist or menu, albeit a shorter one than before. At the same time, placing an object of study in a group can seduce people to ignore its other attributes. The weather, for instance, can be categorised as calm, breezy, and stormy, but the division between a very strong breeze and a light stormy wind may not exist. Similarly, a sunny day can be also a windy day and critical thinking can be creative thinking and both can involve recall from memory.

Taxonomies

Groups may stand apart or be contained within other groups (see figure 2.1) or be some combination of these. Subsuming groups within others amounts to creating ranks of organisation. This is a common feature of taxonomies.

The term *taxonomy* comes from the Greek, *taxis* (arrangement) and *nomos* (law). A taxonomy comprises groups (taxa) of objects of study sorted according to their similarities and differences (Bowler, 1992, p. 52). The principle or basis of the classification (the law) can be, for example, similarities and differences in structure, behaviour and

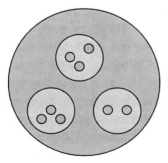

Fig. 2.1. Groups within groups within a field.

function. The verb *taxonomise* refers to the process of classification; a *taxonomy* is the product of that classification.

The process of sorting objects of study into groups can amount to a direct, empirical comparison in which similarities and differences are noted. This is sometimes referred to as a qualitative approach to taxonomy. Social scientists also use a quantitative approach to cluster objects of study into groups. In this approach, 'statistically speaking, we seek to minimise the within-group variance while maximising the between-group variance' (Bailey, 1994, p. 1). Both approaches commonly seek to arrange objects of study into groups so that each group is as different as possible from all other groups, but each group is as homogeneous as possible.

For example, biologists have constructed a taxonomy of living things which sorts them into a hierarchy to show their relationships. The hierarchy of ranks in this taxonomy is: Kingdom, Phylum, Class, Order, Family, Genus, and Species. Figure 2.2 illustrates a small part of the taxonomy, beginning with a kingdom and ending with a species. This taxonomy has the function of locating all organisms according to their genealogical relationships, a task that is carried out according to internationally agreed codes of practice. It supports the description of these organisms and, biologists claim, it affords a basis for making hypotheses, predictions and generalisations about evolutionary history, attributes and processes (Smith, 1979).

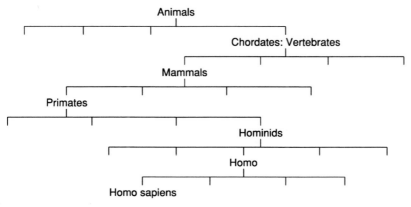

Fig. 2.2. A part of a biological taxonomy of organisms.

The support for thought that a taxonomy might give is well illustrated by Mendeleev's grouping of elements, mentioned above. He went on to sort the elements within each group and produced a two-dimensional array now known as the Periodic Table. This array had gaps, which led Mendeleev to predict undiscovered elements and describe their properties. Nevertheless, taxonomies are primarily descriptive devices and do not offer causal explanations, although, of course, they can provide information that supports speculation and the construction of theories. In the behavioural sciences, for instance, Stott and his co-workers define maladjusted behaviour as 'that which is disadvantageous to the agent' (Stott et al., 1975, p. 160) and then constructed a taxonomy of behavioural disturbance (see figure 2.3). While it gives psychologists concepts to think with, the taxonomy does not, in itself, explain why the groups are related or why people exhibit maladjusted behaviour.

In a taxonomy, the objects of study may be sorted into groups on one basis (a unidimensional taxonomy) or on more than one basis at the same time (a multidimensional taxonomy). For example, loaves of bread can be sorted into a two-dimensional taxonomy according to bread colour (brown or white) and state (cut or uncut). This forms what has been called a property space. Property spaces can, of course, have more than two dimensions. Bailey (1994, p. 78) describes a taxonomy of class structure with property, authority and expertise dimensions. A multidimensional, conceptual taxonomy may be referred to as a *typology* by social scientists, although many do not make this distinction.

The term *taxonomy* is usually reserved for a collection of groups that form some coherent whole. Thus, the groups, *writing implements, kitchen utensils, transport devices,* and *weeds* are mutually exclusive

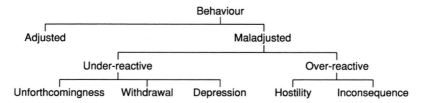

Fig. 2.3. A taxonomy of behavioural disturbances.

groups drawn from objects in the real world but they lack (at least, for us) a common theme. On the other hand, *igneous, sedimentary,* and *metamorphic* are mutually exclusive geological groups of the same objects of study, *rocks*. (In this instance, the taxonomy is also comprehensive in that it describes all naturally-occurring rocks.) On this basis, a taxonomy is a strong form of grouping in which the groups clearly relate to one another. 'Taxonomy (classification) consists of working out a system of mental pigeon holes in which every conceivable species [of thinking] would have an appropriate place' (Bowler, 1992, p. 102).

A taxonomy is useful because it can facilitate the mental representation of a field. In doing so, it aids study by dividing a field into units that can be related to other units (Bowler, 1992, p. 93) and a comprehensive taxonomy 'is the best inventory tool a researcher has' (Bailey, 1994, p. 12).

There are, however, some caveats. A taxonomy is manufactured and may not reflect reality, nor may it be the only useful way of classifying the objects of study. Objects of study can be classified in many ways and it is not always clear which way is 'best'. On occasions, objects of study may be entirely discrete, so that the divisions between the groups are sharp. But, with many groups, the divisions between them may be arbitrary and this can be overlooked. Taxonomies may seduce people into thinking in terms of sharp divisions between its groups. While taxonomies reduce a field to manageable proportions (for thinking), when they reduce the field to a very small number of groups, they can be simplistic. On the other hand, a large number of groups may reflect reality better but can be unmanageable. Finally, to classify is not to explain.

Utility

Provided that the caveats are kept in mind, taxonomies can be useful. To be useful, a classification or arrangement of any kind needs to suit its purpose. For instance, classification in biology is used for two different purposes: identification and making natural groups. The modern system of classifying species by grouping together those which display a clear relationship to one another was developed by

Ray, Linnaeus and others. A taxonomist in biology 'sees' generic attributes and differences of a specimen and allocates it to a group of like organisms (Losee, 1993, p. 8). The description serves to identify other specimens. Exemplars drawn from the group help to locate other organisms in the taxonomy. Unlike organisms, thinking skills, learning outcomes and teaching objectives are intangible. The first problem is to identify what sorts them in a meaningful way that is also useful to, for instance, teachers, curriculum planners and test developers.

Taxonomists may begin with a vast array of objects of study and progressively sort them into groups. This might be done empirically, trying different attributes until ones that discriminate between the objects are found. This process of group finding may be supported by, for example, cluster analysis. Another approach is to have theory or informed conjecture predict groups and then to see if they work. In the social sciences, however, constructs and concepts are such that meaningful groups that are entirely distinct do not always arise. From a practical point of view, this is not always a problem, as these groups can still be useful.

Taxonomies and models

Although a taxonomy alone is a descriptive framework, when it is shaped by a *model*, it can become a theoretical framework that explains and predicts. An explanatory model is a construct that behaves in some way like the phenomenon it represents. For example, the telephone exchange and the digital computer have provided explanatory models of the mind (see Gregory, 1987). In a real sense, a model brings a theory to the phenomenon under study (Anderson, 1983, pp. 12–13). In instructional technology, Hannafin and Hooper (1989) constructed a model to support the design of computer-based instruction. In essence, it focuses the designer's thoughts on retrieval, orientation, presentation, encoding, sequencing and context. Underpinning this with a taxonomy that relates the concepts makes a theoretical framework with practical application. Similarly, Gagné drew together a classification of types of learning (as outcomes) and a conceptual structure (the internal and external conditions of instruction) to produce a theoretical framework to guide instructional design (see Seels, 1997).

Maps, charts and diagrams

Various other terms have been used, sometimes loosely or metaphorically, to denote the fabric of a domain or field. For instance, a *map* can indicate relationships between categories by depicting a connection with a line. The strength of the connection may also be indicated by proximity or line density. Hence, various thinking skills may be depicted on paper and arranged so that they form clusters of related items. A map is a term applied to a wide range of depictions, pictorial and verbal, that may or may not constitute a taxonomy. Given the nature of a taxonomy, it would be perverse for a writer to call it something else unless it fell short of the mark. On the other hand, calling something a taxonomy does not make it one.

Examples

Some examples are now discussed to illustrate the processes involved in sorting, grouping and taxonomising educational objects of study.

Bloom's taxonomy

This taxonomy is particularly well known in educational circles, as its objects of study are educational objectives (Bloom, 1956). These are arranged into a hierarchy of six levels, with *knowledge* at the lowest and *evaluation* at the highest level. Between these are *comprehension* (level 2), *application* (level 3), *analysis* (level 4), and *synthesis* (level 5). It is claimed that nearly all cognitive educational objectives can be located in this hierarchy. However, users sometimes disagree about where to locate particular educational objectives in the hierarchy, a lack of reliability that seems to stem from the vagueness of the definitions (de Landsheere, 1989). Perhaps more seriously, the linear nature of Bloom's hierarchy is disputed. Madaus et al. (1973) presented evidence for a linear hierarchy comprising: *knowledge, comprehension,* and *application*. After this, the structure they found branches into *analysis* on the one hand and *evaluation and synthesis* on the other. Nevertheless, Bloom's taxonomy has been found to be very useful amongst teachers, curriculum planners and test developers, not least because its concepts relate directly to the work they do.

Guilford's structure of intellect model

Guilford's objects of study were 'intellectual factors', which he sorted along three dimensions: *operation, product* and *content* (Guilford, 1967). Each of these dimensions was subdivided into a hierarchy. So, for instance, *product* comprises *units, classes, relations, systems, transformations* and *implications*, with *unit* at the lowest level. Subdivisions in the other dimensions gave rise to a cube with space for 120 kinds of intellectual factor. This three-dimensional structure has greater precision than Bloom's taxonomy, but seems to have found less favour amongst educators, possibly due to its greater size. It fits the description of a typology.

Gerlach and Sullivan's taxonomy

For Gerlach and Sullivan, the objects of study were not educational objectives or intellectual factors but *observable behaviours*. They listed hundreds of learning behaviours and sorted them empirically into six categories (Gerlach and Sullivan, 1967). These categories were then placed in order of increasing complexity of behaviour: *identify, name, describe, construct, order,* and *demonstrate*. Gerlach and Sullivan point out that this is not a rigorous hierarchy and their groups do not, strictly speaking, form a true taxonomy. Further, creative production and transfer are not included. Gerlach and Sullivan see it more as a meaningful checklist to help educators ensure adequate provision for these behaviours and this gives it its utility.

Conclusion

Lists, simple groups and comprehensive, related groups (in taxonomies and typologies) impose order on a field of study. They can be economical, descriptive devices with some potential to support thought and action. Just how much potential depends on their nature, how exhaustive they are, how relevant they are to the task in hand, and how readily they can be related to the observed world. The examples serve to warn us that:

1. not everything called a taxonomy is a taxonomy
2. categories may not be mutually exclusive

3. definitions of categories may be vague, making classification difficult
4. classifiers are not always consistent in their application of sorting principles
5. the structures may not be entirely sound
6. small structures (linear and with fewer categories) can be easier to grasp and use but this gain can be at the expense of content validity
7. large structures (several dimensions and with many categories) can be more precise, but this gain can be at the expense of meaningfulness and ease of use.

In spite of their shortcomings, such structures can be useful to the practitioner (e.g. the teacher, test developer, programme constructor) and the researcher (e.g. in education and in educational psychology). Which are useful depends on how well they fit the task or suit their purpose.

3

Frameworks dealing with instructional design

Introduction

Every instructional design system is underpinned in some way or other by a theory of learning and a way of 'knowing' or 'seeing' the world. While learning theory describes and attempts to explain how people learn, the main aim of instructional design is to provide guidance on the practical task of designing learning experiences. Placing instructional design theorists on an epistemological continuum, behaviourist systems lie towards the positivist end of the scale and the post-modernist concern with critical theory at the opposite pole. Nearer the centre, but still on the positivist side, are the cognitivists, with their combination of positivism and interpretation. Close by, but nearer to the post-modern end of the scale, are the constructivists, with their orientation towards interpretation and criticism. While 'behavioural objectivists' see learning largely in terms of response strengthening, 'cognitivists' tend to explain it in terms of knowledge acquisition, and 'constructivists' construe learning in terms of the dialogic generation of 'constructions'.

It is interesting to note that it was the more behaviouristic branches of instructional design which held most immediate appeal for the early–mid twentieth-century industrialists and educational policy-makers. One of the most popular branches of this approach to instructional design became known as 'programmed instruction'. This reached its peak in the 1960s – 70s, a period when linear and branching programmes were designed for teaching machines. Hawley (1967, p. 277) echoes the dominant ideology of the time where he identifies the centrality of behaviourism to early instructional design in terms of the importance of 'preparing the material to be learned in such a way as it can be presented to the learner in a series of carefully planned sequential steps'. According to this approach to instructional design, these steps progress from simple to more complex levels of instruction and the student is tested after each step to measure competence. Knowledge and skills are seen as carefully designed, deconstructed objects, which can be programmed into the learner's head.

Early twenty-first-century systems of state education in the West are generally based on highly-prescribed programmes of instruction, which aim to prepare children for a world of work and shape the minds of the existing workforce in line with shifting political and economic priorities (Brown, 2002). It is important to note, however, that behaviouristic assumptions have been challenged from within the instructional design community itself. The dominant approach among educational technologists is now a cognitivist one. Educational theorists who concern themselves more with teacher-mediated than with computer-mediated instruction most commonly believe that learners actively construct meaning and acknowledge a debt to Piaget and/or Vygotsky. Feuerstein was one of the earliest to create an instructional system in which Vygotsky's ideas about socially and culturally mediated learning were combined with ideas about cognitive structure and function.

A towering figure in the field of instructional design is Benjamin Bloom, who set out to classify educational goals (or instructional objectives) across the cognitive, affective and psychomotor domains. By drawing attention to outcomes which require different kinds of thinking (especially 'higher-order' thinking), he and his colleagues hoped to influence curriculum design by ensuring that educators operate in ways which are likely to instil qualities such as intellectual honesty, creativity, independence of mind and personal integrity. Bloom's influence is evident in many of the frameworks included in this book, and his cognitive domain taxonomy has been recently updated and extended by Anderson and Krathwohl (2001).

What all of the frameworks in this chapter have in common is that they are intended to influence classroom practice, by focusing attention on instructional goals, which always include, but are not confined to, the gathering of information and the building of understanding. These goals range from simple to complex, from specific to very broad and from short-term to long-term. They may extend across more than one domain of experience and they may or may not cover goals expressed in terms of metacognition and self-regulation.

Our grouping of frameworks into families inevitably leads to overlap. Productive thinking goals and broad aims about desirable 'habits of mind' or dispositions are cases in point, since these appear in every one of our families. Neverthess, we believe that there is some value in comparing like with like. Instructional design frameworks are intended for use in curriculum planning and assessment as well as at the level of a single lesson. These framework designers are influenced by pragmatic more than academic concerns and all write with teachers in mind. Instructional design is a field in which both educators and educational psychologists have been active, and that balance is reflected here.

Teachers and instructors can only benefit from advances in theory and knowledge about how we think and learn. However, instructional designers compete in their attempts to describe how and why their particular approach to instructional design works. They offer different perspectives on the learning process and make different assumptions about how to engender learning. Each is supported by differing degrees of empirical evidence. Yet the exercise of comparing them reveals similarities as well as differences and may help achieve new syntheses. It may well be the case, as Gagné (1985) argued, that different kinds of learning are best achieved in different ways.

Although some systems of instructional design appear to have been developed to be 'teacher-proof', all of them rely upon teachers and instructors to put them into practice. If teachers and instructors don't understand them, or if the learning theory upon which they are based is underdeveloped or inappropriate, they are unlikely to have a positive influence upon teaching, training and learning.

The following section of this chapter offers a review of 13 instructional design frameworks and shows how the intentions of different instructional designers have operated to influence the design and utility of respective systems.

Time sequence of the instructional design frameworks

Bloom's taxonomy of educational objectives (cognitive domain) (1956)

This framework is a way of classifying educational goals in terms of complexity. The intellectual abilities and skills of comprehension, application, analysis, synthesis and evaluation are applied to, and help build, knowledge.

Feuerstein's theory of mediated learning through Instrumental Enrichment (1957)

Building on his belief in cognitive modifiability, Feuerstein developed the concept of a mediated-learning experience in which the mediator uses prescribed tasks to promote thinking rather than rote learning.

Gagné's eight types of learning and five types of learned capability (1965)

Gagné set out an eight-level hierarchy of learning types, with problem-solving at the top. He also identified five domains of learning: motor skills, verbal information, intellectual skills, cognitive strategies and attitudes.

Ausubel and Robinson's six hierarchically-ordered categories (1969)

These are: representational learning; concept learning; propositional learning; application; problem-solving; and creativity.

Williams' model for developing thinking and feeling processes (1970)

This three-dimensional cross-curricular model seeks to encourage creativity. Teachers can use 18 teaching modes to promote fluency, flexibility, originality, elaboration, curiosity, risk taking, complexity and imagination.

Hannah and Michaelis' comprehensive framework for instructional objectives (1977)

The cognitive, psychomotor and affective domains are covered. Interpreting, comparing, classifying, generalising, inferring, analysing, synthesising, hypothesising, predicting and evaluating are listed as intellectual processes.

Stahl and Murphy's domain of cognition taxonomic system (1981)

These authors set out a multi-stage model of information processing from *preparation* to *generation*. They also identify 21 cognitive processes (e.g. classifying, organising, selecting, utilising, verifying), which may be used singly or in combinations at different levels.

Biggs and Collis' SOLO taxonomy (1982)

This is an assessment tool looking at the structure of the observed learning outcome. *Prestructural* responses betray limited understanding compared with *unistructural* and *multistructural* responses. *Relational* and *extended abstract* responses are qualitatively superior. Learners move through these response levels at each of five developmental stages.

Quellmalz's framework of thinking skills (1987)

This framework lists five cognitive processes (recall, analysis, comparison, inference/interpretation and evaluation) and three metacognitive processes (planning, monitoring and reviewing/revising).

Presseisen's models of essential, complex and metacognitive thinking skills (1991)

Presseisen lists five basic processes which are used in problem-solving, decision-making, critical thinking and creative thinking. She also lists six metacognitive thinking skills involved in strategy selection, understanding and monitoring.

Merrill's instructional transaction theory (1992)

Merrill identifies 13 cognitive transactions which aid in the construction of mental models: *identify, execute* and *interpret* relate to single knowledge frames; *judge, classify, generalise, decide* and *transfer* relate to an abstraction hierarchy; *propagate, analogise, substitute, design* and *discover* relate to meaningful links between frames.

Anderson and Krathwohl's revision of Bloom's taxonomy (2001)

Bloom's taxonomy (1956) has been refined and developed into a two-dimensional framework using six cognitive processes and four knowledge categories. There is an emphasis on aligning learning objectives with learning activities and assessment.

Gouge and Yates' Arts Project taxonomies of arts reasoning and thinking skills (2002)

A matrix of Piaget's levels (concrete, concrete transitional and formal operational thinking) and reasoning skills is used to create educational objectives for the visual arts, music and drama.

Description and evaluation of the instructional design frameworks

Bloom's taxonomy of educational objectives: cognitive domain

Description and intended use

This well-known taxonomy was produced in 1956 by a group of college and university examiners with the initial aims of promoting 'the exchange of test materials and ideas about testing' and of 'stimulating research on examining and on the relations between examining and education' (Bloom, 1956, p. 4). Broader aims of improving communication and practice among educators were also identified. The authors claimed that the taxonomy was a means of classifying intended behaviours 'related to mental acts or thinking' occurring 'as a result of educational experiences' (1956, p. 12). They intended it to be a useful tool for educators – readily communicable; comprehensive; capable of stimulating thought about educational problems; and widely accepted by curriculum designers, teachers, administrators and researchers.

Bloom's taxonomy consists of six major categories and has a varying amount of detail in the form of sub-categories. The basic structure is shown in table 3.1. Bloom's group provided many illustrative examples of actual test items within each category and sub-category, but these are not included here.

Table 3.1. Levels of detail in Bloom's taxonomy (cognitive domain)

Intellectual abilities and skills		
Evaluation:	judgments in terms of	*internal evidence* *external criteria*
Synthesis:	production of	*a unique communication* *a plan*
Analysis:	of	*a set of abstract notions* *elements* *organisational principles*
Application:		
Comprehension:	translation from	*one level of abstraction* * to another* *one symbolic form to another* * form or vice versa* *one verbal form to another*
	interpretation extrapolation	
Knowledge of:	specifics	*terminology* *specific facts*
	ways and means of dealing with specifics	*conventions* *trends and sequences* *classification and categories* *criteria* *methodology*
	the universals and abstracts in a field	*principles and generalisations* *theories and structures*

The starting point for the group's work was educational practice rather than educational or psychological theory. The group found that no single theory of learning 'accounted for the varieties of behaviours represented in the educational objectives we attempted to classify' (1956, p. 17). Nevertheless, they tried to order the major categories in terms of complexity and noted a possible association between levels of consciousness and complexity: 'it appears that as the behaviors become more complex, the individual is more aware of their existence' (1956, p. 19).

According to Bloom, the principle of ordering categories by complexity created a hierarchy in the sense that 'each classification within it demands the skills and abilities which are lower in the classification order'. For example, *application* is above *comprehension* in the hierarchy and 'to apply something requires "comprehension" of the method, theory, principle, or abstraction applied' (1956, p. 120). More fundamentally, the exercise of any intellectual ability or skill, whether it involves *comprehension, application, analysis, synthesis* or *evaluation*, logically depends on the availability of content in the form of knowledge.

Bloom's group worked according to the following guiding principles (1956, pp. 13–14):

- The major distinctions between classes should reflect . . . the distinctions teachers make among student behaviours.
- The taxonomy should be logically developed and internally consistent.
- The taxonomy should be consistent with our present understanding of psychological phenomena.
- The classification should be a purely descriptive scheme in which every type of educational goal can be represented in a relatively neutral fashion.

The group had initially planned to create 'a complete taxonomy in three major parts – the cognitive, the affective, and the psychomotor domains'. Their decision to limit their first published taxonomy to the cognitive domain was taken on largely pragmatic grounds. When the affective domain taxonomy was published in 1964, the authors acknowledged considerable overlap between the two taxonomies: 'The fact that we attempt to analyze the affective area separately from the cognitive is not intended to suggest that there is a fundamental separation. There is none' (Krathwohl, Bloom and Masia, 1964, p. 45). Nevertheless, there is (understandably) a strong emphasis on verbally expressed ideas throughout the cognitive taxonomy and an explicit exclusion of *synthesis* activities which 'emphasize expression of emotional impulses and physical movements, rather than organization of ideas' (Bloom, 1956, p. 165).

As can be seen in table 3.1, as well as by the number of pages devoted to it in Bloom (1956), the taxonomic category where least detail is provided is *application*. Bloom says that *application* is 'the use of abstractions in particular and concrete situations and may include general ideas, rules or procedures, generalised methods, technical principles, ideas, and theories which must be remembered and applied' (1956, p. 205). Bloom stresses that it cannot be assessed unless new and meaningful situations are provided in which the student has to restructure a problem, work out how best to respond and thereby demonstrate transfer.

It is worth asking whether metacognitive processes are included within the taxonomy, especially as the word 'metacognition' did not exist in 1956. This turns out not to be a problem. When the Bloom taxonomic categories are applied to self-knowledge and self-monitoring, the components of metacognition (such as analysing and evaluating one's own thinking) can be identified. Bloom does explicitly value self-regulation.

Evaluation

Bloom's taxonomy is based on clear definitions and provides a coherent framework for classifying thinking and learning outcomes, even though some category boundaries are fuzzy. Bloom and his team claimed to have achieved a high level of agreement through discussion, but Wood found that teachers using the taxonomy to classify examination questions found it difficult to make clear distinctions between the higher-order categories, especially between analysis and evaluation (Wood, 1977).

The taxonomy promotes the use of clear statements of educational objectives, even though a term like 'analysis' may mean different things in different contexts. Bloom did not intend the component processes identified by the taxonomy to convey the full meaning of complex tasks which require the orchestration of thinking, but believed that it is often helpful to draw attention to those processes.

The taxonomic categories are meant to reflect task complexity, albeit with considerable overlap between categories. Empirical work over the years has provided modest support for Bloom's proposed order of levels of complexity, although some studies have shown that 'evaluation' is not more complex than 'synthesis' (Kreitzer and Madaus, 1994). A number of authors have criticised the taxonomy for implying that evaluation is the most valuable (and most complex) type of human activity, whereas lower-level skills such as 'application' are less valuable to society. Indeed Ormell (1974) proposed that the idea of a cumulative hierarchy between categories should be abandoned and replaced by a set of six parallel taxonomic categories. It is reasonable to conclude that Bloom's taxonomy does not have a consistent hierarchical structure of intellectual skills and abilities, except for the dependence of all on memory.

Potentially, the taxonomy is applicable in all contexts of teaching and learning, including non-verbal as well as verbal areas. Feelings, movements and what is seen can be remembered, comprehended, applied, analysed, synthesised and evaluated just as much as ideas expressed in language. Both covert and overt 'behaviours' can be classified using Bloom's taxonomy.

As Bloom intended, the taxonomy is either neutral or explicit about educational values. When its authors are explicit about values they celebrate transferable learning, creative talent, freedom of thought and expression, self-regulation, intellectual honesty and wisdom.

Bloom's taxonomy is compatible with well-supported psychological knowledge and theory and has stimulated further theory-building and research. In some ways Bloom himself was taking important steps towards theory-building, by organising educational ideas in ways that help explain individual and group differences in thinking and learning. It is rather surprising that cognitive psychology has largely ignored him, even though large areas of the taxonomy have since become fashionable areas of psychological and neuroscientific research.

Paul (1985, p. 37) praises Bloom for encouraging critical thinking through 'mindful analysis, synthesis and evaluation', while taking him to task for implying that knowledge does not presuppose understanding and the active use of other critical thinking abilities. It is unfortunate that what Paul describes as 'a remarkable tour de force, a ground-breaking work filled with seminal insights into cognitive processes and their interrelations' (Paul, 1985, p. 39) has sometimes been interpreted and applied in one-dimensional and teacher-centred ways. This may in part be due to the author's decision to limit the first taxonomy to the cognitive domain. Bloom's cognitive domain taxonomy emphasises the structure of cognition rather than the processes of cognitive construction and the affective and social dimensions of learning. What seems to be missing from the pioneering cognitive, affective and psychomotor taxonomies produced by Bloom and his associates is a convincing explanation of how all three are integrated in the human experience of living, thinking, feeling and learning.

Yet Bloom wanted teachers to encourage creativity rather than reduce teaching to fragmented mechanical procedures. The shift in instructional practice away from reliance on simple transmission of facts towards higher-order thinking and problem-solving is one that still needs as much impetus as Bloom sought to give it in 1956.

The taxonomy has certainly proved to be meaningful and useful to teachers and other educational professionals, although its impact in curriculum planning, examining and research has probably been greater than its active use by teachers and very much greater than its explicit use by learners. It is not too complex for everyday classroom use. Hannah and Michaelis (1977) took the Bloom categories and provided lists of verbs for describing behaviours which can be classified under each heading: an approach which helps potential users understand the framework. The cognitive domain taxonomy still acts as an important stimulus to thinking about curriculum design, teaching, learning and assessment. Its categories can be recognised in many later adaptations and extensions, including the revision of Bloom's taxonomy by Anderson and Krathwohl (2001).

Summary: Bloom

Purpose and structure	Some key features	Relevance for teachers and learning
Main purpose(s): • to stimulate discussion and research about examining • to improve communication and practice among educators	**Terminology:** • clear definitions • easily understood	**Intended audience:** • curriculum planners • examiners • teachers

Domains addressed:	Presentation:	Contexts:
• cognitive	• logical and well structured • accessible summary • although some test items are dated, Bloom's writing is still relevant and accessible	• education
Broad categories covered:	**Theory base:**	**Pedagogical stance:**
• productive thinking • building understanding • information-gathering	• not based on a single psychological theory, but compatible with many • the importance of history and context are acknowledged • individuals creatively construct knowledge	• emphasis on transferable learning • enquiry-based learning and self-regulation are favoured • improve performance through the use of learning objectives that target higher-order thinking
Classification by:	**Values:**	**Practical illustrations for teachers:**
• type of knowledge • complexity of thought • level in a hierarchy of prerequisites for the use of a particular ability or skill	• the framework is meant to be either neutral or explicit • the authors value intellectual honesty, creativity, independent thought, decision-making, and personal integrity; all of which support a democratic way of life	• many examples of assessment items

Feuerstein's theory of mediated learning through Instrumental Enrichment

Description and intended use

In his studies of the mediated learning experience (MLE) the Israeli psychologist and educator Reuven Feuerstein identified specific parameters of mediation in human learning situations. Feuerstein and his associates argue that the presence of MLE is a crucial factor in helping individuals become independent learners, because it creates the conditions necessary for the acquisition of the 'psychological tools' needed for higher-order thinking (Kozulin, 1998, p. 4).

Instrumental Enrichment (IE) is an intervention programme developed from Feuerstein's early theory and research on cognitive modifiability (Richelle and Feuerstein, 1957). It was originally designed to be used with underachieving adolescents, but has since been implemented in a wide range of settings: for example, with gifted students; dyslexic students; and adult learners.

'Instrumental Enrichment is most simply described as a strategy for learning to learn. It uses abstract, content free, organisational, spatial, temporal and perceptual exercises that involve a wide range of mental operations and thought processes' (Begab, 1980, p. xv). According to Feuerstein, human beings are capable of altering the way they think, through the radical restructuring of the cognitive system. In his work with individuals facing genetic, developmental or socio-cultural challenges, Feuerstein has translated this belief into a number of educational strategies.

Mediated learning experience (MLE) depends on the quality of one-to-one interaction between the learner and the stimuli in the learner's environment, where this interaction is mediated by the presence of a more advanced individual who selects, emphasises, changes and interprets the stimuli for the learner. Feuerstein (1980) argues that an insufficient amount or inadequate type of parental or school-based teaching is responsible for the reduced learning potential of some individuals, and that the infusion of MLE into educational intervention is capable of significantly enhancing learning potential. Instrumental Enrichment emphasises the transfer ('bridging') of the principles discovered through MLE into other areas of learning and mediation of meaning.

Feuerstein's IE cognitive intervention programme targets those cognitive prerequisites of effective learning which, for whatever reason, have remained underdeveloped in an individual. These are addressed through a range of materials including 14 booklets of paper-and-pencil tasks with the following titles:

- *Organisation of dots*
- *Analytic perception*
- *Categorisation*
- *Temporal relations*
- *Transitive relations*
- *Illustrations*
- *Comparisons*
- *Instructions*
- *Numerical progressions*
- *Representational stencil design*
- *Orientation in space 1*
- *Family relationships*
- *Orientation in space 2*
- *Syllogisms.*

A list of the cognitive functions said to be tapped and developed through mediated learning with each instrument is provided by Feuerstein, Falik and Feuerstein (1998). There are more than 60 of these (including much duplication) and it is possible to classify them under the following eight headings:

- control of perception and attention
- comparison
- categorisation
- understanding relationships
- defining problems
- thinking hypothetically
- planning
- solving problems.

Feuerstein's theory of learning, instruction and cognitive modifiability has five interlinked aspects, but here we focus on the areas of thinking and problem-solving addressed in the Learning Propensity Assessment Device (LPAD) (Feuerstein, Falik and Feuerstein 1998). The LPAD (first produced by Feuerstein, Rand and Hoffmann in 1979) is designed to assess an individual's capacity to learn through 'dynamic assessment'. Individuals are not only given tasks, but also receive instruction based on the principles of MLE. The assessment takes into account the individual's response to mediation as well as the nature of the help provided.

There are thirteen instruments in the LPAD: four of these are said to assess perceptual–motor functions organised by cognitive components; four assess memory, with a learning component; and five assess higher-order cognitive processes and mental operations. What is striking is the heavy reliance on visual presentation, with only one orally-presented test making explicit demands on verbal reasoning. The types of task in the LPAD correspond very closely with those used in the IE teaching programme.

Skuy et al. (1991) provide a cognitive map (table 3.2) to guide the teacher to assess where difficulties in effective thinking may lie. The teacher can then plan the right combination of mediated learning experiences and interactions at the *input*, *elaboration* or *output* phases of the learning process.

A key strategy in overcoming learning failure for Feuerstein and his associates is the need to help learners to avoid impulsivity 'like the game of guessing what's in the teacher's head' and to take the time to consider options and alternatives more carefully' (Fisher, 1998, p. 16). The main intention here is for an adult or more competent peer to mediate the learner's experience of the learning environment, through the use of a system of specifically developed stimulating psychological tools, in such a way as to create a set of enabling sociocultural conditions designed to improve an individual's capacity to learn.

Evaluation

The cognitive tasks in the LPAD are derived from tasks in conventional tests of intelligence and visual perception, but with a greater emphasis on fluid than on crystallised abilities. No justification is offered for the inclusion of some tasks and the exclusion of others, but it is clear from the list of IE cognitive functions, which we have grouped into eight categories, that a broad range of thinking skills is covered. Planning skills are very strongly represented, with a greater emphasis on convergent than on divergent thinking. Memory is not emphasised, but understanding is.

The emphasis on non-verbal test formats reflects the fact that Feuerstein wanted Instrumental Enrichment to be accessible to learners with limited first- or second-language skills. However, this

Table 3.2. Map of cognitive strengths and weaknesses (adapted from Skuy et al., 1991)

Input

Clear perception/data gathering	Blurred and sweeping perception/ data gathering
Systematic exploration of a learning situation	Impulsive exploration of a learning situation
Precise and accurate receptive verbal tools	Impaired receptive verbal tools
Well-developed understanding of spatial concepts	Impaired understanding of spatial concepts
Well-developed understanding of temporal concepts	Impaired understanding of temporal concepts
Well-developed ability to conserve constancies	Impaired ability to conserve constancies
Precise and accurate data gathering	Impaired data gathering
Well-developed capacity to consider more than one source of information	Impaired capacity to consider more than one source of information

Elaboration

Accurate definition of the problem	Inaccurate definition of the problem
Ability to select relevant cues	Inability to select relevant cues
Ability to engage in spontaneous comparative behaviour	Inability to engage in spontaneous comparative behaviour
Broad mental field	Narrow and limited mental field
Can engage in spontaneous summative behaviour	Does not see need for spontaneous summative behaviour
Ability to project virtual relationships	Inability to project virtual relationships
Perceives need for logical evidence	Lack of need for logical evidence
Ability to internalise events	Inability to internalise events
Ability to use inferential/ hypothetical thinking	Inability to use inferential/ hypothetical thinking
Ability to use strategies for hypothesis testing	Inability to use strategies for hypothesis testing
Perceives need for planning behaviour	Lack of planning behaviour
Meaningful grasp of time and place	Episodic grasp of reality

Output

Mature communication	Immature communication
Participatory	Poor participation in discussion, etc
Worked-through responses	Trial-and-error responses
Adequate verbal tools	Inadequate verbal tools
Precise and accurate data output	Impaired data output
Accurate visual transport	Impaired visual transport
Appropriate behaviour	Inappropriate behaviour

presents major problems when learners are expected to bridge from (say) visuospatial tasks to verbal problem-solving.

Kozulin (1998, p. 5) claims that Instrumental Enrichment offers a comprehensive, systematically organised and rich assortment of symbolic tools which help learners internalise the psychological tools necessary for higher-order thinking. However, although the cognitive map shown in table 3.2 is organised within the potentially comprehensive framework of 'input', 'elaboration' and 'output', it consists of a mixture of skills, knowledge, ill-defined structural characteristics (e.g. 'mental field') and behaviour. The input items are all concerned with aspects of perception and understanding, linked in some cases with the application of a strategy. The elaboration items are far from comprehensive in their coverage of thinking skills. One item 'ability to use strategies for hypothesis testing' represents a complete problem-solving cycle, but, apart from this, little is said about higher-order thinking involving synthesis, evaluation and creativity. The output items add very little, as they are normative statements using imprecise qualifiers such as 'immature', 'adequate' and 'appropriate'.

Despite its wide scope, Feuerstein's theorising has been operationalised through what is really an ad hoc collection of instruments. However, these can be used to engage most of the areas of thinking covered in more systematic taxonomies and frameworks.

Feuerstein believes that, through IE, it is possible to teach generalisable cognitive skills on a one-to-one basis, using rather abstract decontextualised materials. However, the heavy reliance on paper-and-pencil tasks and visual presentation of material may restrict opportunities for collective learning and collaborative dialogue, and the selection and interpretation of stimuli by a more advanced individual may hold back the development of learner autonomy. Little is known about the efficacy of different approaches to bridging, but to date the empirical evidence for transfer as a result of IE is not strong (Romney and Samuels, 2001). Kozulin (2002) argues that greater attention needs to be paid to the pedagogy of content teaching that is supposed to be coordinated with the IE intervention.

Influenced by Vygotsky's (1962, 1978) sociocultural theory, Feuerstein believes that learning takes place where there is a very special relationship between teacher and learner in which both intellectual and emotional growth are encouraged and supported. One of the problems with Feuerstein's approach is his claim that the quality of mediated learning experiences can only be assessed subjectively.

Despite the fact that the key concept of a mediated learning experience is ill-defined, many psychologists and teachers have been trained in dynamic assessment and Instrumental Enrichment, seeing the idea of cognitive modifiability as offering more hope for learners than views of intelligence which emphasise its genetically determined nature. Other thinking skills packages have drawn on Feuerstein's theoretical framework, for example the Thinking Skills at Work modules, developed and described by Blagg et al. (1993). Kozulin (2002) reviews applications of Feuerstein's IE programme in different countries and with different populations of students. He also raises questions about how far the different goals of IE may require different pedagogical approaches.

Summary: Feuerstein

Purpose and structure	Some key features	Relevance for teachers and learning
Main purpose(s): • promoting a 'learning to learn' approach in assessment and teaching • to raise expectations concerning the learning potential of low-attaining groups	**Terminology:** • some psychological vocabulary and specially-defined terms are used • some theoretical concepts are ill-defined	**Intended audience:** • teachers • psychologists

Domains addressed:	Presentation:	Contexts:
• cognitive	• abstract in register	• education
	• prescriptive	• work (in a modified form)
Broad categories covered:	**Theory base:**	**Pedagogical stance:**
• productive thinking	• established models of intellectual and perceptual abilities	• belief in the special quality of one-to-one mediated learning
• building understanding		
• information-gathering		
• perception	• Vygotsky's theory of socially-mediated learning	• emphasis on process rather than subject-specific content
		• skilled 'bridging' is needed to ensure transfer
Classification by:	**Values:**	**Practical illustrations for teachers:**
• phase of learning process (input, elaboration, output)	• sociocultural elitism	
	• humanism	• special materials and training are offered

Gagné's eight types of learning and five types of learned capability

Description and intended use

Gagné (1985, p. xv) seeks to enable those with an interest in education to: 'acquire an organised schema of human learning as it occurs in situations of instruction . . . such a schema will be valuable as a referential model against which the complex events of teaching and learning can be compared and evaluated.'

He is concerned with the translation of psychological theory into the effective design of instruction. He believes that a better under-standing of how learning operates will facilitate planning for learning, managing learning and instructing. For Gagné, learning ability consists partly of trainable intellectual skills and partly of a strategic thinking capability that can only evolve as a function of experience and intelligence. He analyses learning in terms of the conditions of learning and learning outcomes. The conditions of learning are concerned with the external events that support different types of learned capability, as well as with internal processes.

According to Gagné, we first need to identify and classify learning outcomes. We then analyse the procedural components of learning to reveal prerequisites and to facilitate retrieval of previously learned material from long-term memory. Finally, we provide detailed task descriptions.

For Gagné, the factors that influence learning are chiefly determined by the environment, and many external conditions can be altered and controlled. It is, therefore, possible to study learning in a scientific manner. When analysing a learning task, it should be broken down into steps and a line drawn to indicate what the learner can already do (what is below the line), and what will be learned through the task (above the line). Essentially, Gagné subscribes to an information-processing model of learning, emphasising the mastery that can be achieved through learning and applying rules. His work has its roots in a behaviourist model, which he subsequently revised to address cognitive aspects of problem-solving.

Gagné considers prior learning to be extremely important, and this applies to the development of thinking skills. He argues that, as we cannot think in a vacuum, we always draw on acquired basic skills and knowledge. For Gagné, the time spent in formal school acquiring knowledge and intellectual skills does not mean that problem-solving and cognitive strategies are being neglected.

In his earlier work, Gagné (1965) identifies eight distinct types of learning, ordered here from simple to complex:

1. *signal learning* (classical Pavlovian conditioning)
2. *stimulus/response learning* (Skinner's operant conditioning)
3. *chaining* (learning sequences of actions through practice)
4. *verbal chaining* (learning sequences of words through practice)
5. *discrimination learning* (distinguishing similar items by their various features)
6. *concept learning* (the identity of classes)

7. *rule learning* (organising information using 'if, then' statements about concepts)
8. *problem-solving* (learning new rules or applying them to new situations).

Categories 2–8 are organised in what is claimed to be a hierarchy of prerequisite skills and abilities. For example, it is impossible to solve a problem without applying a rule. However, motor and verbal chaining provide an exception to the linear hierarchy, as they are at the same level and both have stimulus–response learning as prerequisite skills.

In his later work (Gagné, 1985), the eight categories are replaced by five varieties of learned capability (which can be presented in any order).

Intellectual skills

Intellectual skills (which are forms of procedural knowledge) are oriented towards aspects of the learner's environment and are used to solve problems. It is possible to identify organised sets of intellectual skills relevant to learning at the level of rules in specific domains, and these are 'learning hierarchies'. The skills of which the hierarchies are composed are: making discriminations, learning concepts, using rules, using higher-order rules and using procedures.

Cognitive strategies

These are defined as metacognitive and novel problem-solving processes – that is, processes of executive control. Thinking skills are included under cognitive strategies and Gagné talks about the possible existence of a 'master thinking skill' – a form of executive control that governs the management of other skills and strategies. He is of the opinion that this capability, which is essentially the ability to formulate situationally-relevant learning strategies, is a form of strategic problem-solving that cannot be taught effectively using traditional methods. It is generalised thinking ability – that is, processing ability not tied to a particular intellectual skill – and can only be inductively derived by students through incidental learning over years of practice. Consequently, metacognitive training can only be effective if it is accompanied by opportunities for frequent practice on a long-term basis within a curriculum that supplies an appropriate context for the development of executive control skills.

Verbal information

This is declarative knowledge and is dependent on the recall of internally-stored complexes of ideas which constitute meaningfully organised structures. Gagné contributed to the debate regarding the status of declarative and procedural knowledge by claiming that it is possible to be told how to do something (and then be able to do it well) without understanding the process. In fact, focusing too much on unpacking the processes can interfere with learning.

Motor skills

These are psychomotor chains.

Attitudes

Most attitudes are learned incidentally through modelling by key figures, rather than as a result of pre-planned instruction. Attitudes are influential in determining to what and how we pay attention.

Evaluation

Gagné's original work was based on concepts developed by experimental psychologists, such as paired-associate learning, serial learning, operant conditioning, concept learning and gestalt problem-solving. He later incorporated ideas from information-processing accounts of cognition and instructional design, but retained an analytic focus on the components of learning and a model of instruction in which learners are passive recipients.

According to his framework of learning, aspects of thinking skills, such as concept and rule formation, can be located in intellectual skills. Gagné's analysis of these can be a useful corrective for those who are over-dismissive of structured ways of teaching skills and concepts and procedures, as in direct instruction. Gagné is probably correct in believing that different instructional approaches are needed for different kinds of learning.

According to Gagné, problem finding, discovery learning and creative problem-solving depend on a sound knowledge base, extensive practice and general intelligence. Gagné expresses reservations regarding the amenability to instruction of the necessary cognitive strategies. This view is incompatible with the idea that young children are highly creative, not least in their play and developing use of language.

Gagné's emphasis on learning hierarchies, prerequisite knowledge and linking new learning to prior learning has had a major impact on instructional design (Gagné and Briggs, 1974). His influence has been strong in the design of computer-mediated instruction, for example integrated learning systems. However, an atomistic and linear approach to instruction is likely to encourage rote learning rather than the integration of components into meaningful wholes and the capacities to generalise and reframe.

Gagné's view of learning does not problematise what is to be learned, or seek to define good thinking. Its main focus is on efficiency in processing and on the retention of information.

Summary: Gagné

Purpose and structure	Some key features	Relevance for teachers and learning
Main purpose(s): • to help teachers understand learning and instruction • to identify the conditions of learning, particularly in terms of prerequisites and the sequencing of learning	**Terminology:** • clear • some psychological terms used	**Intended audience:** • designers of instruction and assessment • teachers
Domains addressed: • psychomotor • cognitive • affective	**Presentation:** • detailed breakdown of conditions for learning • clear guidelines on instructional design and practical issues	**Contexts:** • education • work • citizenship • recreation

Broad categories covered:	Theory base:	Pedagogical stance:
• executive control	• behaviourism	• teach according
• productive thinking	• cognitive	to the identification
• building understanding	information-processing	of the necessary steps
• information-gathering		for successful learning
• perception		• practise frequently
		• establish appropriate
		conditions for
		learning according
		to individual needs
		• Gagné is not convinced
		of the value of
		discovery learning
Classification by:	**Values:**	**Practical illustrations**
• degree of complexity	• concerned with the	**for teachers:**
in terms of required	efficiency of learning	• breakdown of
stages before learning	in terms of time spent	steps in learning
can take place	and desired outcomes	
• type of knowledge	• it is possible to	
	control the learning	
	environment to	
	achieve maximum	
	efficiency	

Ausubel and Robinson's six hierarchically-ordered categories

Description and intended use

Ausubel is best known for his theory of meaningful learning, developed in the 1960s (Ausubel, 1968). He proposed (1968, p. 10) that 'rotely and meaningfully learned materials are represented and organized quite differently in the student's psychological structure of knowledge.' He claimed that rote as opposed to meaningful learning is more likely to take place when:

- the material to be learned lacks logical meaning
- the learner lacks the relevant ideas in his/her cognitive structure
- the individual lacks a meaningful learning set (a disposition to link new concepts, propositions and examples to prior knowledge and experience).

Although he is not opposed to rote-learning techniques in, for example, the teaching of phonics, Ausubel sees the development of conceptual understanding as the goal of education. However, he asserts that much of what is termed conceptual understanding is actually the assimilation (rather than the formation) of concepts: 'Most of what anyone really knows consists of insights discovered by others that have been communicated to him or her in a meaningful fashion' (Ausubel, 1978, p. 530).

It is therefore important, in Ausubel's view, for teachers to present new learning in such a way that students can relate it to their existing knowledge, taking into account the complexity of the new learning and the cognitive development of the learners. Ausubel and Robinson (1969) use the following six hierarchically-ordered categories in their analysis of learning:

- representational learning
- concept learning
- propositional learning
- application
- problem-solving
- creativity.

As in Bloom's taxonomy (1956), here there is an emphasis on the need to build up a store of meaningful knowledge before operating with it at a more advanced level. Representational learning is equivalent to Bloom's *knowledge* category, while concept and propositional learning are equivalent to *comprehension*.

However, while Ausubel sees some value (especially at the secondary stage of education) in using problem-solving approaches within subject areas, he does not believe that the main purpose of education should be to develop generic thinking, enquiry and problem-solving skills. In his view (1978, p. 583), this idea is: 'little more than an illusory goal and a recurrently fashionable slogan in education. On theoretical and practical grounds it can never amount to more than a critical approach to the teaching of particular subject matter disciplines.'

Creativity and creative thinking fare no better under Ausubel's analysis. He regards genuine creativity as so rare that it is not worth pursuing in most educational contexts, where it is more democratic to use available resources to cater for the needs of the many rather than the few. He asks (1978, p. 546):

Would it not be more realistic to strive first to have each pupil respond meaningfully, actively and critically to good expository teaching before we endeavour to make him or her a creative thinker or even a good critical thinker and problem solver?

Ausubel believes that teacher-directed learning is more effective than learning by discovery, arguing that pupil enquiry can result in uncorrected errors and misconceptions and indeed, meaningless rote learning. Instead, teachers should 'provide ideational scaffolding', especially in the form of *advance organisers* (1967, p. 26). An advance organiser is 'material that is presented in advance of and at a higher level of generality, inclusiveness, and abstraction than the learning task itself' (Ausubel and Robinson, 1969, p. 606). This provides a framework, so that new learning material can be discriminated and integrated with previously learned, related ideas. To be most effective, the organisers should be formulated in terms of language and concepts already familiar to the learner and use appropriate illustrations and analogies.

Ausubel also proposes that big concepts should be presented first, as the adequacy of prior learning of key superordinate concepts is more important than age or IQ as a predictor of success:

Since subsumption of new information is generally much easier than acquisition of new superordinate concepts, curricula should be planned to introduce the major concepts or propositions early in the course to serve as a cognitive anchorage for subsequent learning. (Ausubel, 1978, p. 530)

He also urges teachers to order the sequence of subject matter by 'constructing its internal logic and organisation and arranging practice trials and feedback' (1967, p. 23). The aim is to facilitate 'integrative reconciliation'.

Evaluation

Ausubel and Robinson's basic intention is to help teachers to improve the structure and sequencing of their teaching in order to develop meaningful as opposed to rote learning. As with Bloom, the emphasis here is upon the need to help learners build up a store of meaningful knowledge, which they can relate to previous knowledge and experience and eventually use in higher-order thinking. This framework does usefully emphasise the importance of well-structured and carefully-sequenced expository teaching.

The focus here is upon making teachers more aware of the structure and content of learners' existing knowledge. However, learners are seen as more or less compliant recipients of new information, with the teacher rather than the learner as the chief architect of the cognitive construction process. Ausubel ignores Piaget's work on accommodation and the importance of cognitive restructuring after experiencing cognitive conflict.

Discovery learning is criticised on the grounds it might result in uncorrected errors. Rather than constructing understanding for themselves, learners are encouraged to learn what the teacher knows. The teaching of generic thinking is also criticised, but these criticisms are presented as ex cathedra judgments, rather than with empirical support. Ausubel seems blind to the idea that a positive attitude towards learning can be developed through giving pupils more opportunities to plan, monitor and evaluate their own learning.

From this predominantly teacher-led perspective it is perhaps not surprising to find that creative thinking is considered to be so rare that it is not worth pursuing. Here Ausubel seems to confuse the everyday creativity encouraged by active learning with being a creative genius.

Summary: Ausubel

Purpose and structure	Some key features	Relevance for teachers and learning
Main purpose(s): • to promote meaningful learning • to ensure education is informed by psychology	**Terminology:** • clear definitions and explanations of technical terms	**Intended audience:** • curriculum planners • examiners • teachers • students

Domains addressed:	Presentation:	Contexts:
• cognitive	• clear description of theory but academic in style	• education
Broad categories covered:	**Theory base:**	**Pedagogical stance:**
• productive thinking • building understanding • information-gathering	• draws upon Piaget and Vygotsky	• belief in the importance of presenting new learning in such a way as to relate prior knowledge to new knowledge • use of advance organisers to scaffold understanding • start with big concepts • teacher-structured learning rather than pupil enquiry
Classification by:	**Values:**	**Practical illustrations for teachers:**
• types of learning, which differ in structural complexity • superordinate and subordinate concepts	• rationalist • technological • all students can learn if taught well • opposes sentimentality regarding the critical/creative skills of young learners	• few examples of how to apply the theory

Williams' model for developing thinking and feeling processes

Description and intended use

In 1970, Williams published the first volume of his work on classroom ideas for encouraging thinking and feeling (Williams, 1970). He makes use of a three-dimensional model (figure 3.1) and argues that developing different teaching strategies and adopting different teaching roles across a range of subjects can bring about changes in students' cognitive and affective behaviours, moving them towards a higher level of creative thinking (see also Williams, 1972).

Williams describes 18 diverse teaching strategies which encourage not only thinking, but also the expression of feelings about both content and the learning process. He provides detailed lesson plans that envisage the three intersecting dimensions of subject content, teacher behaviour and pupil behaviours coming together to encourage creativity. Williams is striving towards an increase in student creative output, placing equal value on cognitive and affective aspects.

Creativity is a complex mental process that is difficult to define or measure. For Williams, it involves putting together new, different and unique ideas by employing the four cognitive and four affective behaviours shown in dimension three of the model in figure 3.1 and outlined below:

Cognitive behaviours
1. fluency – generating a large number of ideas
2. flexibility – being able to change categories
3. originality – being able to come up with a unique thought
4. elaboration – being able to take one idea and embellish it.

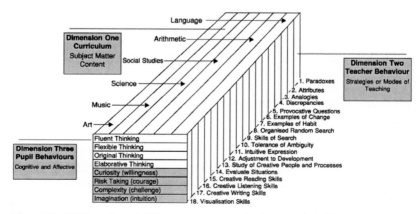

Fig. 3.1. Williams' model for encouraging thinking and feeling.

Affective behaviours
1. curiosity – willingness to explore and question
2. risk taking – courage to take a chance
3. complexity – facing the challenge of building order out of chaos
4. imagination – visualising and fantasising ideas.

It is worth noting that the four cognitive behaviours of *fluency, flexibility, originality* and *elaboration* are also to be found in the Torrance Tests of Creative Thinking (Torrance, 1966).

Williams originally intended his model to be used in elementary schools, but it seems to have found more resonance with those delivering programmes for gifted and talented pupils. In 1986, Williams developed the 'cognitive–affective intervention model for enriching gifted programs', but this appears to vary little from his original work. He has also produced an assessment tool, the Creativity Assessment Packet (CAP) (Williams, 1980).

Evaluation

Williams realises his intention to develop a cognitive–affective intervention model of learning and a range of strategies and roles which enable teachers to place equal value on cognitive and affective aspects of learning and help them to move students towards higher levels of creative thinking. He shows how teachers can plan to teach a curriculum subject in such a way as to develop creative thinking as well as positive dispositions to support learning. While he speaks of cognitive and affective *behaviours,* this serves largely to help teachers focus on the need for pupils to act, not simply to be passive recipients.

Williams achieves a balance between the need for pupils to demonstrate qualities such as willingness and courage and the need for teachers to provide them with a wide range of opportunites to do so. However, gaps can be detected in his lists of pupil and teacher behaviours. For example, he downplays the need for care in the planning and execution of creative work and does not explicitly refer to design or to drama. Despite this, there is a reasonable match beween his desired pupil behaviours, the critical thinking dispositions identified by Perkins and others (1993) and the creativity 'mindsets' of Petty (1997).

Some of Williams' categories of teaching behaviours and pupil behaviours are very general and certainly overlap. Nevertheless Williams' model and detailed lesson plans still provide a useful template for teachers interested in developing the creative thinking abilities of their students. His contribution is significant in its laudable attempt to represent the multi-dimensional nature of thinking, feeling and learning; and in the pragmatic way, through the use of actual examples and detailed lesson plans, in which he genuinely endeavours to make his work of use to teachers.

Friedman and Lee (1996) field-tested three gifted-education models and claim that Williams' cognitive–affective interaction model demonstrated the best results for increasing the cognitive complexity of classroom interactions and on-task behaviour of high-achieving pupils.

Summary: Williams

Purpose and structure	Some key features	Relevance for teachers and learning
Main purpose(s): • to encourage creative teaching and learning across the curriculum	**Terminology:** • clear • fairly simple	**Intended audience:** • teachers
Domains addressed: • cognitive • affective • conative	**Presentation:** • easily understood • addressed to practitioners	**Contexts:** • education
Broad categories covered: • self-engagement • productive thinking • building understanding • information-gathering	**Theory base:** • Guilford's *Structure of Intellect* model • Torrance's work on creativity	**Pedagogical stance:** • development of individual talents • interest in gifted education • cross-curricular emphasis

Classification by:	Values:	Practical illustrations for teachers:
• subject area • nature of learner behaviour (thinking and feeling)	• humanistic • individualistic	• several hundred in six curriculum areas • strategies are listed which are relevant for all age groups

Hannah and Michaelis' comprehensive framework for instructional objectives

Description and intended use

Acknowledging their debt to Bloom (1956) and Krathwohl, Bloom and Masia (1964), and drawing on relevant literature about perceptual and motor skills, Hannah and Michaelis (1977) were the first to realise Bloom's original aim of producing a comprehensive framework for the design and classification of educational objectives. They sought (1977, iii) to 'bring objectives back into teaching' by encouraging teachers to write lesson and course objectives 'so that students move from knowledge to operations on knowledge that involve increasingly more complex processes, to greater independence in the development of skills, and to higher levels of commitment insofar as attitudes and values are concerned'.

According to Hannah and Michaelis, the perceptual and knowledge base for learning is built up by data gathering (observing and/or remembering). As shown in figure 3.2, the availability of data is a prerequisite for all development. The authors illustrate (1977, p. 173) the interrelatedness of their categories in the following way:

a student with prior experience participating in an experiment may observe certain elements, recall prior learnings including a generalization, and quickly state an inference related to the experiment . . . Moreover, the student's feeling that she or he is a capable learner . . . influences both the receptivity to participation in experiment and the willingness to offer ideas. Mastered skills may have been involved in data collection during the experiment.

The categories of *intellectual processes*, *skills* and *attitudes and values* are independent but interacting dimensions, each of which is ordered

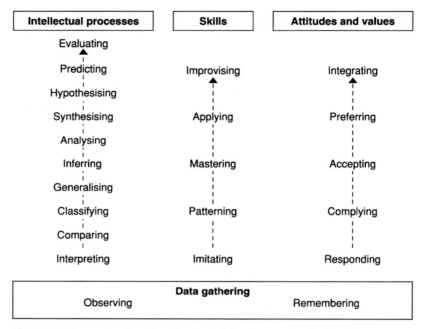

Fig. 3.2. The comprehensive framework for instructional objectives.

by a different principle (complexity, degree of learner independence and level of commitment, respectively). All the level headings used are clearly defined, as shown in the examples below:

- *Generalising* – the student expresses a conclusion drawn from the consideration of a number of specific instances.
- *Inferring* – the student uses appropriate generalisations to reach and express conclusions that go beyond the data studied.
- *Patterning* – the student practises a skill with assistance while progressing towards unassisted performance.
- *Integrating* – the student consistently demonstrates a pattern of value-based behaviour.

The scope of Hannah and Michaelis' framework is unrestricted, but it seems not to have been used outside the school-age range. The authors did not attempt a thorough academic justification for their framework, but instead put their energies into making it effective over a five-year period, working with teachers and administrators in the Elk Grove School District in California.

Evaluation

Hannah and Michaelis' primary intention was to encourage teachers to write lesson and course objectives in order to enable them to move students from lower levels to higher levels of thinking and to encourage them to become autonomous learners with a genuine commitment to learning. Their framework was developed with and field-tested by teachers. It uses many of the terms found in the work of Bloom and his associates and is compatible with several later frameworks. Although not aligned with a particular theoretical position, the authors were influenced by the behavioural objectives movement and drew on work in cognitive psychology, motivation and attitude development.

This initiative represents a significant development in the advancement of frameworks for thinking, in that it was one of the first attempts to integrate all of the three domains of learning identified by Bloom (i.e. the cognitive, affective and psychomotor domains). All types of skill (covert and overt) are encompassed by the *skills* category and the *attitudes and values* category is equally broad.

This comprehensive framework is descriptive rather than normative. While subscribing to democracy and human rights, Hannah and Michaelis are relatively neutral about which attitudes and values are worth developing. There is, for example, no explicit encouragement for learners to become more reflective or empathetic. At the same time, it is possible to detect the influence of a particular approach to pedagogy, as learning is largely portrayed as the responses of individuals to teacher instruction.

Hannah and Michaelis point out that while the categories of intellectual processes, skills and attitudes and values are independent, they are also interacting dimensions of learning. Their framework serves a useful purpose by raising questions for practitioners about how stages in one dimension may correspond to complementary stages in the others. However, they make unrealistic demands on teachers by expecting them to take all stages and dimensions into account when writing lesson objectives and making assessment decisions. This may lead some to over-plan and try to assess each lesson objective in excessive detail. However, for longer-term planning the framework has much to offer. It is expressed in simple language and has been worked out in considerable detail, with many illustrative objectives.

Despite the commendable multidimensionality of this framework, it seems to rest upon linear assumptions about the direction of learning in each dimension. Hannah and Michaelis also tend to emphasise the compliance of learners with the expectations and values of educators. Nonetheless, if interpreted flexibly, this framework clearly has considerable potential as a design tool and for a range of other uses, ranging from teacher education to programme evaluation.

Summary: Hannah and Michaelis

Purpose and structure	Some key features	Relevance for teachers and learning
Main purpose(s): • to guide teachers in writing and evaluating objectives • to provide a model of how students learn in order to align and improve planning, teaching and assessment	**Terminology:** • clear • simple	**Intended audience:** • teachers
Domains addressed: • cognitive • conative • affective • psychomotor	**Presentation:** • includes definitions, focusing questions and directions, illustrative objectives and assessment tools • teacher-friendly and not too complex	**Contexts:** • education • work • citizenship • recreation

Broad categories covered:	Theory base:	Pedagogical stance:
• self-engagement • productive thinking • building understanding • information-gathering • perception	• Bloom and other taxonomists of cognitive, affective, and psychomotor domains • compatible with behaviourist and cognitive theories	• teacher as guide • holistic in that most teaching addresses more than one category and level • promote skill development for mastery learning • support learner enquiry, critical thinking and creativity
Classification by: • complexity • degree of learner independence • level of commitment	**Values:** • either neutral or explicit in terms of educational values • democratic human rights	**Practical illustrations for teachers:** • many rich and detailed examples at primary and secondary level

Stahl and Murphy's domain of cognition taxonomic system

Description and intended use

Stahl and Murphy had the ambitious aim of producing a taxonomy based on the principle of a learning hierarchy of 'levels of cognitive-affect thinking and learning-related behaviours' (1981, p. 23). They were writing for teachers and teacher-educators and, as Marzano did 20 years later, based their taxonomy as far as possible on theory and research findings in cognitive psychology. They address memory, thinking and learning and are concerned with helping teachers to 'separate pre- and post-learning behaviours within classroom situations' (1981, p. 10). The taxonomy is intended to be used in instructional design and the authors assume that teachers can infer from pupil behaviour what mental processes are, or have been, taking place. It is located in a broad theoretical framework which includes a cognitive belief system (equivalent to Marzano's self system), but not a separate system dedicated to metacognition.

The levels and sub-levels of the domain of cognition system are shown in table 3.3, together with illustrative general instructional objectives. The same instructional objectives are repeated at different levels, as the levels represent no more than progress towards the internalisation and automatic use of new knowledge.

Stahl and Murphy identify 21 mental processes involved in thinking and learning, and claim that these may be used in different combinations at any of the following levels: *transformation, transfersion, incorporation, organisation* and *generation*. These processes are said to operate with all kinds of content, whether cognitive or affective. They are provided in list form, as follows:

1. *associating*: connecting items together
2. *classifying*: putting items into categories
3. *combining*: putting items into some single whole
4. *comparing*: identifying similarities and differences
5. *condensing*: producing a shortened version of information
6. *converting*: changing the features of an item or information
7. *describing*: reporting the features of an item or information
8. *designating*: assigning a name or exactness to an item
9. *discriminating*: treating some items or information differently
10. *extending*: providing information to fill a gap or gaps
11. *extracting*: focusing on parts, part–part and part–whole relationships
12. *interpreting*: making sense of information
13. *organising:* putting items in order or sequence to bring out their relationships
14. *proposing*: suggesting a probable way of dealing with a problem
15. *reconciliating*: putting opposing items together to make a consistent whole
16. *selecting*: making a preferred, imperative or needed choice
17. *separating*: taking things apart to identify distinct components
18. *translating*: putting information into a different form or version
19. *utilising*: demonstrating how things could be, are being or have been put to use
20. *valuating*: assigning value, a rating or priority to an item or information
21. *verifying*: specifying how information should be accepted as valid or true.

Table 3.3. The domain of cognition taxonomic system

Levels and sub-levels	Function	Illustrative instructional objectives
Preparation	Readying oneself to receive and/or be capable of accepting information	
Observation	Taking in and becoming aware of information and stimuli	
Reception Literation Recognition Recollection	Noticing and remembering information that has just been presented (during a lesson)	Understands information and facts Recognises details and data Knows verbal information Understands steps of a method Knows a formula or principle Recognises laws or theories
Transformation Personalisation Adaptation (rehearsal and 'field-testing')	Giving meaning to information that has just been received (during a lesson) Applying principles, using steps of a method, solving problems	Understands laws or theories Comprehends information Understands facts Knows the meaning of . . . Applies principles to a situation Uses steps of a method Solves problems Constructs examples of a graph
Information acquisition Encoding Storage Retrieval	Placing information and meanings into long-term storage	

Table 3.3 *(cont.)*

Levels and sub-levels	Function	Illustrative instructional objectives

Retention
  Recognition
  Recollection
	Identifying information retrieved from long-term storage (from previous lessons)	Understands information and facts
		Recognises verbal information
		Knows laws, principles or rules
		Understands steps of a method

Transfersion
  Replication
  Variation
	Using recalled information (guidelines and rules) to deal with new situations	Understands laws or theories
		Applies information
		Uses steps of a method
		Solves problems
		Applies principles or laws
		Understands how information is used

Incorporation	Automatically using fully internalised guidelines and rules	(Same as above)
Organisation	Interrelating and prioritising all previously understood information within one's cognitive belief system	Demonstrates consistent and predictable beliefs Provides consistent and defensible rationale Demonstrates commitment to a particular perspective Appreciates how a technique works Values a particular point of view or product
Generation	Synthesising previous information (guidelines and rules) to form new ideas and understandings	Formulates a new set of rules or principles Develops a new explanation Formulates a new way of solving a problem

Evaluation

Stahl and Murphy's taxonomic system is an ambitious attempt to create a framework for classifying instructional objectives, taking account of learning as well as thinking and extending from the reception of information to the creative synthesis of ideas and beliefs. The strengths of this taxonomy lie in its inclusion of affective as well as cognitive aspects of learning and its acknowledgement of the role of a system of ideas, beliefs and values in actively giving meaning to new information. However, they largely ignore social and cultural influences, do not deal with metacognition and treat feelings only as a source of additional information.

The 21 mental processes listed by Stahl and Murphy are not presented as a taxonomy and no claim is made for their completeness. However, nearly all the processes fit well within the six levels of Bloom's taxonomy, with 'proposing' and 'selecting' being possible exceptions.

The structure of the domain of cognition is said to be hierarchical in that thinking at a particular level cannot occur unless the relevant information has been processed at all of the lower levels. In general terms this appears to be a reasonable claim, but some counterexamples may be found. It is not always the case that new explanations or solutions can only be generated within a field where knowledge is fully internalised and its use almost unconscious. Neither is it obvious that rules can never be applied to deal with new situations unless they have been permanently established in memory.

Stahl and Murphy's hierarchical model of internalisation is not unlike that used by Krathwohl, Bloom and Masia (1964) in their taxonomy of educational objectives in the affective domain. The authors' focus of concern in their exposition of how people learn is establishing factual and procedural knowledge in long-term memory. The most valued level of thinking is 'generation', which is described as being the synthesis of rules understood as abstractions (such as Hegel's dialectic) and said to be 'a very sophisticated mental operation not utilised by most persons' (Stahl and Murphy, 1981, p. 34). This statement suggests an elitist, academically-biased value system.

The illustrative instructional objectives are expressed at a general level and leave the teacher or instructional designer with a formidable task if the system is intended for daily use in planning lessons. In view of its complexity, teachers will find the system impractical for monitoring the developing understanding of individual students, but they may derive value from Stahl and Murphy's description of how learners transform, internalise, organise, use and generate ideas. However, the terminology they use is far from simple and is certainly not accessible to students. Communicability is not assisted by the use of technical terms such as 'literation' and 'encoding', the neologism 'transfersion' and specially defined meanings, such as those for 'adaptation' and 'extracting'.

Throughout, these authors tend to reduce all content to information and rules, failing to provide a convincing account of attitudes, beliefs and systems. There is also a certain rigidity in their belief in a hierarchy of levels of thinking.

Summary: Stahl and Murphy

Purpose and structure	Some key features	Relevance for teachers and learning
Main purpose(s): • to help teachers and teacher-educators understand thinking and learning • a tool for use in instructional design and teaching	**Terminology:** • not easy to grasp • uses specially defined technical terms	**Intended audience:** • teachers and teacher-educators
Domains addressed: • cognitive • affective (but only as a source of information)	**Presentation:** • the complexity of lists, tables and graphics is offputting	**Contexts:** • education

Broad categories covered:	Theory base:	Pedagogical stance:
• self-engagement • productive thinking • building understanding • information-gathering	• psychological models of information-processing	• transmission of knowledge
Classification by:	Values:	Practical illustrations for teachers:
• levels of internalisation of information and rules	• not made explicit	• instructional objectives are used to illustrate the levels and sub-levels only, no curriculum examples are given

Biggs and Collis' SOLO taxonomy: Structure of the Observed Learning Outcome

Description and intended use

The taxonomy was devised by Biggs and Collis (Biggs and Collis 1982; Biggs, 1995; 1999). According to the authors it provides a systematic way of describing how a learner's performance grows in complexity and level of abstraction when mastering many tasks, particularly the sort of task undertaken in school. Collis and Biggs (1982) proposed that there are clear implications for how schools develop programmes. They argue for a general sequence in the growth of the structural complexity of many concepts and skills, and that sequence may then be used to identify specific targets or to help teachers assess particular outcomes. The SOLO taxonomy therefore attempts to describe the level of increasing complexity in a student's understanding of a subject, through five levels of response, and it is claimed to be applicable to any subject area. Not all students get through all five levels, and not all teaching (and even less 'training') is designed to take them all the way. The levels are described in outline below and with additional criteria in table 3.4.

Table 3.4. The SOLO taxonomy levels, with descriptors and criteria

SOLO description	Capacity	Relating operation	Consistency and closure
Pre-structural	Minimal: cue and response confused	Denial, tautology, transduction. Bound to specifics.	No need felt for consistency: closure without seeing the problem.
Unistructural	Low: cue and one relevant datum	Can generalise only in terms of one aspect.	No need felt for consistency: thus closed too quickly; jumps to conclusions so can be very inconsistent.
Multistructural	Medium: cue and isolated relevant data	Can generalise only in terms of a few limited and independent aspects.	Feeling for consistency: closure too soon on basis of isolated fixations so can reach different conclusions with same data.
Relational	High: cue and relevant data and interrelations	Induction: can generalise within given or experienced context using related aspects.	No inconsistency in given system, but closure is unique to given system.
Extended abstract	Maximal: cue and relevant data and interrelations and hypotheses	Deduction and induction: can generalise to situations not experienced.	Inconsistencies resolved: no need for closed decisions; conclusions held open or qualified to allow logically possible alternatives.

1. *Pre-structural:* here students are simply acquiring bits of unconnected information, which have no organisation and make no sense.
2. *Unistructural:* simple and obvious connections are made, but their significance is not grasped.
3. *Multistructural:* a number of connections may be made, but the meta-connections between them are missed, as is their significance for the whole.
4. *Relational:* the student is now able to appreciate the significance of the parts in relation to the whole.
5. *Extended abstract:* the student makes connections not only within the given subject area, but also beyond it, and is able to generalise and transfer the principles and ideas underlying the specific instance.

The taxonomy makes use of a modified Piagetian framework (Piaget, 1952) and the same progression through levels of response is said to be repeated at each of the following stages:

  i. sensorimotor (from birth)
 ii. iconic (from 18 months)
iii. concrete symbolic (from 6 years)
 iv. formal (from 16 years)
  v. post-formal (from 18 years).

Each level of response does not so much *replace* the previous one as *add* to the repertoire of available cognitive responses. In different situations, therefore, learners may 'regress' to an earlier level of response or utilise a higher cognitive function than is strictly required, adopting a 'multi-modal' approach to the task at hand (Biggs and Collis, 1991). The SOLO taxonomy is based on an analysis of the work of several hundred pupils of different ages across a range of subjects and the identification of recurring patterns in pupils' thinking. Biggs and Collis found a general age-related progression through secondary schooling, from multistructural to relational to extended abstract thinking (equivalent to Piaget's formal operations stage and not usually reached before the age of 16).

Each level of the SOLO taxonomy refers to a demand on the amount of working memory or attention span, since at higher levels there are not only more aspects of a situation to consider but also more relationships between aspects and between actual and hypothetical situations.

The purpose of the SOLO taxonomy is to provide a systematic way of describing how a learner's performance grows in structural complexity when tackling and mastering a range of tasks. It can therefore be used to identify and define curriculum objectives which describe performance goals or targets; as well as for evaluating learning outcomes, so that the levels that individual students are performing or operating at can be identified.

Evaluation

The SOLO taxonomy enables teachers to identify the complexity and quality of thinking expected of and produced by students. It is particularly helpful when applied to challenging aspects of learning such as the understanding of concepts and problem-solving (Collis and Romberg, 1991). Provided that the underlying logic of student responses can be reliably inferred by others, the taxonomy can be used to improve learning outcomes by enhancing the quality of feedback. When understood and internalised by students it can also be usefully applied when planning work and in self-assessment.

Biggs and Collis do not concern themselves with the social nature of interactions or with the influence of affective and conative factors on thinking, because their focus is on student performance (in particular contexts at particular times). SOLO taxononomy users must therefore assume that the tasks selected are understood by students and offer effective contexts for assessment.

The key SOLO terms and definitions have remained the same for over 20 years. The taxonomy sets out a developmental progression of a student's cognitive responses, based on Piaget's theory of genetic epistemology. It therefore makes implicit assumptions about the nature of knowledge and is open to some of the common criticisms of stage theories (in terms of the relationships between, and progression through, the stages). However the concept of 'multi-modal' thinking allows that learners may sometimes use a less sophisticated approach or perform at a higher cognitive level than the situation requires. While Biggs and Collis do not assume learning to be unidirectional they do consider it to be relatively predictable.

There are links between the approach of Biggs and Collis and other work on learning, such as Säljö's conceptions of learning (Säljö, 1979a; 1979b), and Bateson's levels of learning (Bateson, 1973). Unistructural and multistructural levels are equivalent to *surface level* and relational and extended abstract to *deep level* processing.

The SOLO taxonomy has proved effective as a means of planning and developing curricula based on the cognitive characteristics of the learners. It has been used in a wide range of studies to evaluate learning, from LOGO (Hawkins and Hedberg, 1986) to higher education (Boulton-Lewis, 1995); for an overview and summary of research see Prosser and Trigwell, 1999). The wide and effective application of the taxonomy by educational researchers, curriculum designers and teachers at all levels of education and across a wide range of subjects indicates its practical value and the ease with which it can be understood, especially in the context of assessment. With relatively little practice and feedback, most teachers can use at least the lower levels of the SOLO taxonomy to identify appropriate curriculum objectives which will help move students on to the next stage of their learning. However, those professionals whose own thinking and written expression is at the multistructural level or lower may struggle in applying it at relational or extended abstract levels.

Summary: Biggs and Collis

Purpose and structure	Some key features	Relevance for teachers and learning
Main purpose(s): • to assess the structural complexity of learning outcomes using five levels of development	**Terminology:** • clear definitions and explanations of technical terms	**Intended audience:** • curriculum planners • examiners • teachers and students
Domains addressed: • cognitive	**Presentation:** • accessible to a wide readership • good use of tables and graphs	**Contexts:** • education • work • citizenship • recreation

Broad categories covered:	Theory base:	Pedagogical stance:
• productive thinking	• Piaget's	• belief in improving
• building understanding	developmental stages	cognitive performance
• information-gathering	• levels of learning	through assessment and
		feedback
Classification by:	**Values:**	**Practical illustrations**
• structural complexity	• rational	**for teachers:**
from concrete to	• deep-level learning	• several (e.g. curriculum
abstract use of	• higher-level thinking	objectives, marking
organising principles		criteria and essays)
• developmental stage		

Quellmalz's framework of thinking skills

Description and intended use

Edys Quellmalz is an educational psychologist who produced an integrated thinking skills framework to help teachers and learners understand the strategies and processes used in problem-solving. She draws on work by philosophers such as Ennis, by psychologists such as Guilford and Sternberg, and on Bloom's taxonomy. Her framework (1987) is intended for use in the design of instructional and assessment tasks as well as in classroom practice. She wishes greater emphasis to be placed on higher-order skills, since these are needed in different subject areas as well as in solving real-life problems. She provides illustrations of analysing, comparing, inferring and evaluating in the subject domains of science, social science and literature (1987). Within subject areas, Quellmalz urges teachers to 'emphasise the use of a full problem-solving process, rather than drill on isolated components' (1987, p. 95).

The proposed framework is hierarchical only in that a distinction is made between lower- and higher-order thinking skills (Stiggins, Rubel and Quellmalz, 1988). It includes a lower-order category called *recall*, which is a combination of the Bloom categories of *knowledge* and *comprehension*. While *recall* is a means of gaining access to existing knowledge, *higher-order thinking* is about restructuring it. The higher-order thinking strategies and processes are all needed in problem-solving and are not seen as hierarchical in terms of difficulty or progression. The higher-order framework as presented in 1987 (see table 3.5)

Table 3.5. Quellmatz's higher-order thinking strategies and processes

Strategies

Students engage in purposeful, extended lines of thought where they:
 identify the task (or type of problem)
 define and clarify essential elements and terms
 gather, judge and connect relevant information
 evaluate the adequacy of information and procedures for drawing
  conclusions and/or solving problems.
 In addition, students will become self-conscious about their thinking
  and develop their self-monitoring problem-solving strategies.

Processes

Cognitive	*Metacognitive*
analysis	planning
comparison	monitoring
inference/interpretation	reviewing/revising
evaluation	

includes strategies in which demands are made on both cognitive and metacognitive processes (all of which are seen as teachable).

Stiggins, Rubel and Quellmalz (1988) provide definitions of the higher-order cognitive processes which we paraphrase as follows:

- *Analysis* involves restructuring knowledge by getting information from abstract visual representations, by classifying items, or in terms of whole-part or causal relationships.
- *Comparison* goes beyond whole-part relationships and involves explaining how things are similar and how they are different.
- *Inference* is deductive (moving from the general to the specific) or inductive (moving from details to a generalisation).
- *Evaluation* involves judging quality, credibility, worth or practicality using established criteria.

For each of these processes, trigger words and sample activities are provided, together with an indication of the corresponding Bloom taxonomy processes (e.g. *recall* requires knowledge and comprehension, and *inference* requires application and synthesis).

Evaluation

Quellmalz's framework is successful in that it accommodates reasoning skills identified by philosophers within the critical thinking tradition and cognitive skills identified by psychologists studying problem-solving. It encompasses both cognition and metacognition and the categories are applicable to both convergent and divergent thinking (although the examples provided suggest that she is more interested in the former). Quellmalz helpfully emphasises a 'plan-monitor-review' cycle which includes problem finding, but does not address affective, conative and social aspects of thinking. Dealing only with thinking skills, she does not refer to the dispositions which support critical thinking.

The definitions used by Quellmalz, while clear, do not always accord with common usage or with those used in other taxonomies. This problem is most acute with the very broad 'analysis' category. Whereas for Bloom and for Anderson, sorting and classifying as well as translating from one form of representation to another are indicators of understanding, for Quellmalz they fall under 'analysis'. 'Comparison' overlaps with every other category, so it is doubtful whether it should be treated separately. For Quellmalz 'inference/ interpretation' extends beyond deductive and inductive reasoning and is an umbrella term which also covers 'apply a rule', 'synthesise' and 'create'. It is not known to what extent teachers who use the framework are able to consistently classify questions and tasks.

Quellmalz worked with the Arkansas Department of Education to apply her framework across the curriculum in the form of a reading/ thinking/writing intervention, the McRAT (Multicultural Reading and Thinking) programme (Quellmaltz, 1987; Quellmalz and Hoskyn, 1988). This was designed to promote relective reading, the ability to back up opinions with evidence and effective written communication. Participating teachers received 18 days of training over two years and the approach yielded moderate effect sizes (up to 0.65) in a controlled trial (Fashola and Slavin, 1997).

Quellmalz believes that learners construct meaning in the context of project work where they are asked to solve problems in different curriculum areas. She values extended problem-solving activities, for example reading and discussion leading to extended writing. Her framework has the appeal of simplicity and highlights for teachers the importance of modelling and teaching metacognitive skills. Schools and school districts have successfully used it to infuse critical thinking across the curriculum.

Summary: Quellmalz

Purpose and structure	Some key features	Relevance for teachers and learning
Main purpose(s): • to encourage the teaching of problem-solving across the curriculum	**Terminology:** • clear definitions, but some do not accord with common usage	**Intended audience:** • designers of instruction and assessment • teachers • researchers
Domains addressed: • cognitive	**Presentation:** • teacher-friendly, easily understood • tabular format with trigger words and examples	**Contexts:** • education • citizenship • recreation
Broad categories covered: • self-engagement • reflective thinking • productive thinking • building understanding • information-gathering	**Theory base:** • cognitive psychology • learners construct meaning • philosophical accounts of critical thinking	**Pedagogical stance:** • model and teach metacognition • critical thinking can be infused across the curriculum through extended problem-solving activities
Classification by: • lower- or higher-order thinking • type of thinking process	**Values:** • learner autonomy • there is an implicit emphasis on convergent rather than divergent and creative thinking	**Practical illustrations for teachers:** • many provided, especially through the Multicultural Reading and Thinking programme

Presseisen's models of essential, complex and metacognitive thinking skills

Description and intended use

Presseisen presents a taxonomy of essential thinking skills, a model of complex thinking skills and a model of metacognitive thinking skills in a chapter in Costa's (2001) book *Developing Minds*. This is a revised version of similar material which she originally presented 10 years earlier (in Costa, 1991). She seeks to provide a common understanding of 'thinking' which will help teachers in their planning, teaching and assessment. The overriding aim is to improve students' cognitive performance. Presseisen (2001, p. 52) believes that a shared understanding of thinking will also 'help educators examine the kinds of material available to them to enhance thinking in the classroom'.

According to Presseisen (2001), there are at least five categories of thinking skill that have to be included in a taxonomy of essential thinking skills: *qualifying, classifying, finding relationships, transforming* and *drawing conclusions*. These are ordered from simple to more complex, as shown in table 3.6. The main use of such a taxonomy is in 'planning a curricular sequence' (2001, p. 49).

Essential skills are not enough, since they need to be orchestrated and used in different combinations for different purposes. Presseisen (2001, p. 58) stresses that it is important that 'educators develop and use a common design to link essential skills to higher-order, more complex operations'. She uses Cohen's (1971) macro-process strategies of *problem-solving, decision-making, critical thinking and creative thinking* to create a 4×3 matrix with *task, essential skills* and *yields*. This produces her model of complex thinking skills in which the elements of the taxonomy can be applied (see table 3.7).

In her model of metacognitive thinking skills, Presseisen acknowledges the importance of self-regulation. This has two main dimensions: *monitoring task performance* and *selecting appropriate strategies* (see table 3.8).

Presseisen ends her chapter with an overview called a 'Global view of thinking'. In addition to *cognition* and *metacognition*, this introduces two new components:

Table 3.6. Presseisen's taxonomy of essential thinking skills

Qualifying *(finding unique characteristics)*	• recognising units of basic identity • defining • gathering facts • recognising tasks/problems
Classifying *(determining common qualities)*	• recognising similarities and differences • grouping and sorting • comparing • making either/or distinctions
Finding relationships *(detecting regular operations)*	• relating parts and wholes • seeing patterns • analysing • synthesising • recognising sequences and order • making deductions
Transforming *(relating known to unknown)*	• making analogies • creating metaphors • making initial inductions
Drawing conclusions *(assessing)*	• identifying cause and effect • making distinctions • inferring • evaluating predictions

- *Epistemic cognition*: the skills associated with understanding the limits of knowing, as in particular subject matter and the nature of the problems that thinkers can address.
- *Conation*: the striving to think clearly, including personal disposition, and to develop and consistently use rational attitudes and practices.

No classificatory system is proposed for epistemic cognition and conation.

Evaluation

Presseisen's writing is influenced by her commitment (1988) to reduce student drop-out and improve the effectiveness of teaching in schools.

Table 3.7. Presseisen's model of complex thinking skills

	Problem-solving	Decision-making	Critical thinking	Creative thinking
Task	Resolve a known difficulty	Choose the best alternative	Understand particular meanings	Create novel or aesthetic ideas or products
Essential skills emphasised	Transforming; conclusions	Classifying; relationships	Relationships; transforming; conclusions	Qualifying; relationships; transforming
Yields	Solution Generalisation (potentially)	Assessment	Sound reasons Proof Theory	New meanings Pleasing products

Table 3.8. Presseisen's model of metacognitive thinking skills

Monitoring task performance (leads to more accurate performance of task)	• keeping place, sequence • detecting and correcting errors • pacing of work
Selecting and understanding **appropriate strategy** (leads to more powerful ability to complete thinking processes)	• focusing attention on what is needed • relating what is known to material to be learned • testing the correctness of a strategy

Here she achieves her aim to provide accessible models of thinking which are potentially useful to teachers. Her model of complex thinking skills is clearly expressed and sets 'essential' thinking skills in purposeful contexts. By dealing with metacognition in a separate model, she avoids the potential problem of an over-complex single structure, and conveys the key ideas very directly.

What Presseisen calls a taxonomy of essential thinking skills does seem to be ordered by a principle of complexity, albeit with fuzzy boundaries between categories. The categories resemble the product dimension of Guilford's (1967) Structure of Intellect model, but Presseisen combines Guilford's 'relations' and 'systems'. Her models of complex and metacognitive thinking skills have types of task and product as organising principles and are consistent with a wide range of literature and with established areas of psychological research. Presseisen takes an eclectic approach to theory, seeing value in a wide range of established and contemporary psychological and philosophical approaches.

These models are principally concerned with the cognitive domain and Presseisen has little to say about the emotional and social aspects of thinking, which many argue to be equally important in developing a shared understanding of the processes of cognitive construction. Presseisen does include a consideration of the role of dispositions in learning, but this receives little elaboration and it is not entirely clear how either dispositions or epistemic components relate to each other or to the three models.

Presseisen provides teachers and learners with a meaningful vocabulary with which to discuss the processes and products of thinking and learning from a rationalist perspective. Her 2003 chapter is an excellent theoretical introduction to the subject, but teachers wishing to apply her models will look for more concrete examples and case studies.

Summary: Presseisen

Purpose and structure	Some key features	Relevance for teachers and learning
Main purpose(s): • to outline a 'global view of thinking' • to improve thinking in the classroom • to have teachers plan instructional sequences	**Terminology:** • clear definitions and explanations of terms	**Intended audience:** • teachers and students
Domains addressed: • cognitive • conation (partial)	**Presentation:** • accessible to a wide readership, including learners	**Contexts:** • education
Broad categories covered: • self-regulation • reflective thinking • productive thinking • building understanding • information-gathering	**Theory base:** • Guilford • Bloom • an eclectic theoretical approach	**Pedagogical stance:** • thinking skills should be developed in meaningful contexts • pupils should be given more complex and challenging tasks
Classification by: • structural complexity of essential thinking skills • type of task and product	**Values:** • rationalist • strong belief that teaching thinking will improve the quality of education	**Practical illustrations for teachers:** • few examples given

Merrill's instructional transaction theory

Description and intended use

Merrill et al. (1990a; 1990b) define the aims of 'second generation instructional design' as building on Gagné's principle that different learning outcomes require different conditions of learning (Gagné, 1965; 1985), but with much greater attention to conditions which support learners in constructing mental models. He and his colleagues seek to help learners acquire integrated sets of knowledge and skills through interactive pedagogic strategies. They argue that both organisation and elaboration during learning lead to better understanding and retention, and that both are facilitated by instruction that explicitly organises and elaborates the knowledge being taught.

When Merrill speaks about knowledge frames he is referring to ways in which course information is organised, for example in the form of software. Knowledge frames are believed to correspond to mental models or schemas. There are three types of knowledge frame: entities (e.g. which draw attention to a name, feature or function); activities (e.g. where the learner executes steps); and processes external to the learner (e.g. where a causally-connected chain of events is presented).

For each type of knowledge frame there are three types of elaboration, each being designed to facilitate cognitive change through a type of instructional transaction. The three types (fully specified by Merrill, Jones and Zhongmin Li, 1992) are:

1. component transactions (corresponding to the internal structure of a single knowledge frame):
   - identify
   - execute
   - interpret
2. abstraction transactions (content from a class frame and two or more instance frames in an abstraction hierarchy):
   - judge
   - classify
   - generalise
   - decide
   - transfer

3. association transactions (meaningful links to other frames):
   - propagate (a tool or a method)
   - analogise
   - substitute
   - design
   - discover.

These transactions can take any form and include one-way transmission, discussions and conversations, tutoring, simulations and micro-worlds. Discovery learning can be accommodated, especially through the use of simulations and in microworlds, but Merrill believes that this approach has been over-used, especially where learners are already experienced in a related domain or have virtually no knowledge of a subject.

Here we have an outline specification for instructional design which uses the language of cognition. Although the aim is to produce an open and flexible computerised system capable of adapting strategically to the needs of learners (including their developing knowledge and level of motivation), Merrill acknowledges that human pedagogic expertise will still be required.

Evaluation

Merrill is a key figure in a tradition of instructional design in which Gagné and Reigeluth have also made major contributions. Gagné's early work on instructional prerequisites and conditions of learning (Gagné, 1965), Merrill's 'Component display theory' (Merrill, 1983) and Reigeluth's 'Elaboration Theory' (Reigeluth and Stein, 1983) were part of what Merrill et al. (1990a) describe as 'first generation instructional design'. A common feature of these approaches is detailed analysis of the components of content and instruction, with the learner often a passive recipient.

With 'second generation instructional design' Merrill claims to have embraced a cognitivist rather than a behavioural approach, a stance also taken by Reigeluth (1996; 1997) and van Merriënboer (1997). He shares many ideas with these theorists, as he acknowledges in a paper where he sets out five 'First Principles of Instruction' (Merrill, 2002). Learning is facilitated when students are given real-world problems, but especially when prior knowledge is activated and new knowledge demonstrated, before being applied and 'integrated into the learner's world' (p. 45). Yet the language used here is still in the passive voice for the learner, betraying the fact that it is the instructional designer who is active, constructing ever-more-complex multi-path systems behind the scenes. Indeed Merrill (Merrill et al., 1990b) admits that, as little is known about how cognitive structure is organised and elaborated, the instructional designer has to analyse knowledge in other ways.

Merrill's approach lies between Ausubel's 'meaningful learning' (Ausubel, 1978) and Jonassen's conception of constructivist learning environments (Jonassen, 1999). He does offer scope for creative thinking under the headings 'design' and 'discover', but does not portray the learner as being capable of self-regulation.

The three types of transaction appear to be distinguished in terms of complexity (as measured by the number of 'frames' involved). The cognitive process terminology used to classify 'transactions' is close to that used by many other theorists who have been influenced by Bloom (1956), and refers to components within various forms of knowledge utilisation more than to complete problem-solving processes. The selection appears to be arbitrary, with equivalents of Bloom's 'comprehension' being most strongly represented and 'analysis' appearing only under the term 'execute'.

Summary: Merrill

Purpose and structure	Some key features	Relevance for teachers and learning
Main purpose(s): • to help learners acquire integrated sets of knowledge and skills	Terminology: • clear definitions, but it is not always easy to determine whether Merrill is referring to mental models or to the content and process of instruction	Intended audience: • designers of instruction and assessment

Domains addressed:	Presentation:	Contexts:
• cognitive	• highly structured exposition	• education • work
Broad categories covered: • productive thinking • building understanding • information-gathering	**Theory base:** • behavioural and cognitive psychology, especially Gagné and Ausubel	**Pedagogical stance:** • a transmission model, with some room for discovery learning and creativity
Classification by: • cognitive complexity • type of thinking	**Values:** • interest is largely confined to achieving 'engineering' solutions	**Practical illustrations for teachers:** • course material has been produced

The practical value of instructional transaction theory has yet to be demonstrated, since the overall evidence for the effectiveness of even the most sophisticated computer-mediated instruction is far from overwhelming. The costs involved in bringing complex interactive and adaptive systems to the market are so high that the idea of modifying them in response to feedback from users and/or learning outcomes is rarely entertained.

Anderson and Krathwohl's revision of Bloom's taxonomy of educational objectives

Description and intended use

This revision of Bloom's framework for categorising educational objectives was undertaken to refocus attention on Bloom's cognitive domain taxonomy (1956) and to incorporate the many advances in knowledge since the original publication. The revision took account of international feedback and Bloom, together with several of his co-authors, contributed to several chapters in this work.

The original framework comprised the following six categories: *knowledge, comprehension, application, analysis, synthesis* and *evaluation.*

With the exception of *knowledge*, all categories were labelled as 'abilities and skills'; and for each of these, knowledge was deemed a prerequisite. The categories were presumed to constitute a cumulative hierarchy; that is, each category was conceived as building on and comprising a more advanced achievement than its predecessor.

The Anderson and Krathwohl revision (2001) retains six cognitive process categories: *remember, understand, apply, analyse, evaluate* and *create*. These correspond closely to the Bloom categories, and since the revision draws heavily on Bloom, it is worth identifying the changes incorporated into the revision.

Changes in emphasis

The revision emphasises the use of the taxonomy in course planning, instruction and assessment; and in aligning these three. The authors view this as a major shift from the original handbook, where the focus was on providing extensive examples of test items in each of the six categories. Other significant changes are listed below.

- While the original handbook was developed by college examiners, the revision is designed to be of use by elementary and high-school teachers.
- Sample assessment tasks contained within the revision are designed to illustrate and clarify the meaning of the various sub-categories. They are not included as model test items, as in the original handbook.
- The original handbook made use of test items to clarify the meaning of definitions; in the revision, meanings are clarified through extensive descriptions of sub-categories and case vignette illustrations.
- It is no longer claimed that the process categories form a cumulative hierarchy where the learner cannot move to a higher level without mastering all those below it.

Changes in terminology

- Educational objectives indicate that a student should be able to do something (verb) to or with something (noun). In the original framework, nouns were used to describe the knowledge categories (e.g. *application*). In the revision, the major categories in the cognitive process dimension have been relabelled with verb forms (e.g. *apply*). Knowledge as a cognitive process is renamed *remember*. Sub-categories in the cognitive process dimension have also been labelled with verbs, such as *checking* and *critiquing* (sub-categories of *evaluate*).

- The revision has renamed and reorganised the knowledge sub-categories as four types of knowledge: *factual*, *conceptual*, *procedural* and *metacognitive*.
- Two of the major categories in the original framework have been renamed: *comprehension* has become *understand* and *synthesis* has become *create*.

Changes in structure

Anderson and Krathwohl's taxonomy (2001) involves a two-dimensional table, with six cognitive processes and four types of knowledge. Figure 3.3 summarises the structural changes from Bloom's original framework; the examples of learning objectives, activities and assessment shown in table 3.9 illustrate why it is useful to separate the 'knowledge' and 'cognitive process' dimensions.

The revised framework orders the six cognitive process categories according to their degree of complexity. In the original framework, it was claimed that mastery of a more complex category required mastery of all the preceding, less complex categories. Anderson and Krathwohl state that empirical evidence only supports a cumulative hierarchy for Bloom's middle three categories of *comprehension, application* and *analysis*. However, they confirm that the revised framework remains hierarchical in overall complexity.

Throughout the book, the authors use four organising questions to show how the taxonomy framework can be used to support teachers in the classroom.

- *The learning question*: what is important for students to learn in the limited school and classroom time available?
- *The instruction question*: how does one plan and deliver instruction that will result in high levels of learning for large numbers of students?

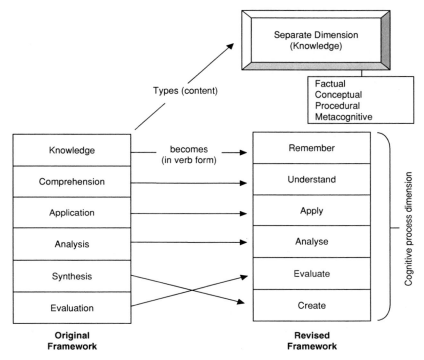

Fig. 3.3. Structural changes from Bloom to the Anderson and Krathwohl revision.

- *The assessment question:* how does one select or design assessment instruments and procedures that provide accurate information about how well students are learning?
- *The alignment question:* how does one ensure that objectives, instruction and assessment are consistent with one another?

A series of vignettes based on actual classroom practice is used to demonstrate how the taxonomy table can be used to aid understanding of the complex nature of classroom instruction. It is claimed that increased understanding of the framework can result in improving the quality of classroom instruction, not least by encouraging teachers to include more complex cognitive process categories in classroom instruction. First and foremost, the taxonomy table should be used as an analytical tool to enable teachers to conduct a deeper examination of the alignment of learning objectives, instruction and assessment.

Table 3.9. Taxonomy table with illustrative examples

Knowledge Dimension	Cognitive process dimension					
	Remember	**Understand**	**Apply**	**Analyse**	**Evaluate**	**Create**
	• Recognising • Recalling	• Interpreting • Exemplifying • Classifying • Summarising • Inferring • Comparing • Explaining	• Executing • Implementing	• Differentiating • Organising • Attributing	• Checking • Critiquing	• Generating • Planning • Producing
A. Factual Knowledge • knowledge of terminology • knowledge of specific details and elements	*Example assessment* Quiz on addition facts					*Example activity* Prepare and deliver a short talk about an aspect of a famous person's life

B. Conceptual Knowledge • knowledge of classifications and categories • knowledge of principles and generalisations • knowledge of theories, models and structures		*Example learning objective* Understand the theory of plate tectonics as an explanation for volcanoes	*Example learning objective* Select sources of information related to writing about a historical figure	*Example learning objective* Evaluate food commercials from a set of principles	*Example activity* Rewrite a scene from Macbeth in a modern idiom
C. Procedural Knowledge • knowledge of subject-specific skills and algorithms • knowledge of subject-specific techniques and methods • knowledge of criteria for determining when to use appropriate procedures	*Example learning objective* Gain a working knowledge of memorisation strategies				*Example learning objective* Create a commercial that reflects understanding of how commercials are designed to influence people

Table 3.9. (cont.)

Knowledge Dimension	Cognitive process dimension					
	Remember	Understand	Apply	Analyse	Evaluate	Create
D. Metacognitive Knowledge		*Example learning objective*			*Example learning objective*	
• strategic knowledge		Understand the efficiency of memorisation strategies (in certain circumstances)			Check the influences of commercials on students' 'senses'	
• knowledge about cognitive tasks, including appropriate contextual and conditional knowledge						
• self-knowledge						

Evaluation

This two-dimensional taxonomy is limited to the cognitive domain, despite the fact that one of its authors, David Krathwohl, played a part in extending the original work of Bloom and his team into the affective domain (Krathwohl, Bloom and Masia, 1964). While acknowledging that almost every cognitive objective involves an affective component, the present authors judged that inclusion of the affective domain would create an overly complex taxonomy, which would not, for that reason, become widely adopted. However, they consider that their revised cognitive domain taxonomy 'does contain some seeds for future affective development' in that *metacognitive knowledge* goes some way to bridging the cognitive and affective domains (Anderson and Krathwohl, 2001, p. 301). Mayer (2002) argues that in addition to the new category of *metacognition*, the revised taxonomy recognises the role of metacognitive and motivational processes, in that it clarifies their role within the cognitive process dimension, and in particular within the categories of *create* and *evaluate*.

The shortcomings of this taxonomy still lie in its over-emphasis of the cognitive domain to the neglect of the others and its absence of a convincing explanation of how all three domains might interact in the human experience of thinking, feeling and learning.

The widely used terms 'critical thinking' and 'problem-solving' have not been included as major categories within the taxonomy, since the authors view these terms as having similar characteristics to their category *understand*. However, they maintain that, unlike *understand*, critical thinking and problem-solving tend to involve cognitive processes in several categories across their cognitive process dimension.

The creation of a matrix whereby cognitive processes operate with different types of subject matter content (i.e. *knowledge*) provides teachers with a useful tool to help analyse their teaching objectives, activities and assessment. Classifying learning objectives within the framework is likely to increase a teacher's understanding of each objective and help them plan ways to ensure that pupils succeed. Classifying longer units of work allows teachers to make choices relating to coverage across both dimensions. We note, also, that this approach has been taken by several other theorists: Romiszowski, Jonassen and Tessmer, for example.

There is little to choose between Bloom and Anderson and Krathwohl in their treatment of types of knowledge. The revised term for Bloom's 'knowledge of specifics' is 'factual knowledge'. What Bloom calls 'knowledge of ways and means' is now called 'procedural knowledge', and Bloom's 'knowledge of the universals and abstractions in a field' is now labelled as 'conceptual knowledge'. However, while Bloom made implicit references to what we now call *metacognition*, Anderson and Krathwohl explicitly list 'metacognition' as a type of knowledge. But it is open to question whether the term 'metacognition' refers to knowledge of a different type. It is not uniquely distinguished by the processes involved (knowing that, knowing how and understanding ideas), rather by its content.

While Anderson and Krathwohl give weight to the separate classification of metacognitive *knowledge*, they do not explicitly address the monitoring, control and regulation of students' cognition, arguing that this involves 'different types of cognitive processes and therefore fits into the cognitive process dimension' (Anderson and Krathwohl, 2001, p. 43). When addressing metacognition within the knowledge dimension the authors provide a rationale for the inclusion of metacognitive knowledge, a comprehensive overview of each of the three types of metacognitive knowledge along with illustrative examples. Their treatment of metacognition within the cognitive process dimension attracts little attention and provides the reader with only two examples. This decision results in an inconsistent treatment of the two aspects of metacognition (knowledge and self-regulation).

Theoretical advances in educational psychology, and to a lesser extent in cognitive psychology, have contributed to this revision of Bloom's framework. The focus on knowledge types, and the delineation of process categories into specific cognitive processes, is based largely on 'an examination of other classification systems' (Anderson and Krathwohl, 2001, p. 66), dating from 1969 to 1998, and including Sternberg's model of 'successful intelligence' (Sternberg, 1998). While acknowledging that the framework should ideally be based on a single, widely accepted, and functional theory of learning, the authors note that, despite recent advances, we are still without a single psychological theory that adequately provides a basis for all learning. The framework reflects the authors' beliefs that knowledge is structured by the learner in line with a rationalist–constructivist tradition. They do not adhere to the idea that knowledge is organised in stages or in system-wide logical structures, as in traditional developmental stage models of thinking.

Anderson and Krathwohl claim their taxonomy is 'value neutral and therefore can be used by those operating from a variety of philosophical positions' (2001, p. 296). This is broadly true, despite the implication (equally present in Bloom's taxonomy) that more complex thinking is usually more highly valued.

The taxonomy was designed to help teachers understand and implement a standards-based curriculum. The authors expect the framework to be used mainly by teachers who are given a set of objectives, and are expected to deliver instruction that enables a large proportion of pupils to achieve the expected standard. However, Noble (2004) describes how, with support, 16 teachers successfully used a matrix which combined the revised Bloom taxonomy with Gardner's multiple intelligences in order to formulate their own differentiated curriculum objectives.

The dominant theme running throughout the Anderson and Krathwohl text is the alignment of learning objectives, instruction and assessment. The taxonomy encourages teachers to focus on coverage, thereby allowing students to experience learning opportunities across the cognitive domain. The purpose of the framework is to help teachers clarify and communicate what they intend their students to learn. The authors are less concerned with how teachers teach, since it is their view that most instructional decisions depend on the teacher's creativity, ingenuity and wisdom.

There are several reasons why the taxonomy may prove attractive to practitioners. It does not seek to radically change how they teach or challenge their beliefs about teaching and learning. The authors use language that teachers are familiar with, and exemplify use of the taxonomy with detailed case studies that reflect current classroom practice.

Summary: Anderson and Krathwohl

Purpose and structure	Some key features	Relevance for teachers and learning
Main purpose(s): • to support the delivery of a standards-based curriculum through the use of a revision of Bloom's taxonomy	**Terminology:** • clear definitions	**Intended audience:** • teachers • curriculum planners
Domains addressed: • cognitive	**Presentation:** • accessible to a wide readership • good use of tables and matrices	**Contexts:** • education
Broad categories covered: • reflective thinking • productive thinking • building understanding • information-gathering	**Theory base:** • not based on a single psychological theory, but compatible with many	**Pedagogical stance:** • belief in improving cognitive performance through the alignment of learning objectives, assessment and instruction
Classification by: • cognitive processes and types of knowledge	**Values:** • neutral, except for favouring higher-level thinking	**Practical illustrations for teachers:** • a series of vignettes illustrates key concepts and elements of the taxonomy table

Gouge and Yates' ARTS Project taxonomies of arts reasoning and thinking skills

Description and intended use

These taxonomies were devised by a cognitive acceleration project team seeking to develop a new approach to the teaching of thinking through the creative arts (visual arts, music and drama). The theories informing this approach are those of Piaget (1950) and Vygotsky (1978) [which also underpin the well-known CASE and CAME cognitive acceleration programmes in science (Adey, Shayer and Yates 1995) and mathematics (Adhami, Johnson and Shayer, 1998)]. Gouge and Yates (2002, p. 137) describe how three taxonomies were devised, using basically the same framework 'in order to provide a consistent structure for designing a programme of intervention lessons' for pupils aged 11–14.

In essence, Gouge and Yates have produced a framework for classifying the reasoning skills involved in creative thinking. They state (2002, p. 137) that creativity 'requires mental discipline, previous experience and a firm grounding in knowledge', and see dangers in the notion that the arts are all about 'fun' and free expression.

Three Piagetian levels of cognitive demand are used: *concrete, concrete transitional* and *formal operational thinking*. These are said to correspond with Peel's (1971) *restricted, circumstantial,* and *imaginative comprehensive* stages of adolescent judgement. Although 'formal operation thought can begin to develop at about the age of 12', Gouge and Yates claim (2002, p. 137) that even by the age of 16, few adolescents are 'deductive, rational and systematic' in their thinking, able to 'reason about hypothetical events that are not necessarily in accord with their direct experience'. Their aim is to accelerate adolescent cognitive development beyond the level where pupils can only 'make simple assumptions and deductions to offer imaginative explanations'.

Five reasoning patterns are common to all three taxonomies, but a sixth pattern (narrative seriation) is used in the taxonomy for drama. The common 3×5 matrix, within which sets of educational objectives are located, is illustrated in table 3.10.

The six reasoning patterns are based on unpublished work by Fusco (1983). They are not ordered by any principle and no claim is made as to their comprehensiveness. A summary is provided below:

- *classification* – the ability to group or order attributes or objects by one attribute or criterion
- *frames of reference* – dealing with relativity of thought by attempting to reconcile conflicting information and reach closure

- *symbolic reasoning* –the use of a wide range of visual and auditory symbols to create imagery and perspective and to communicate ideas
- *critical reflection* – the development of judgment, from restricted to imaginative and comprehensive forms
- *intention, causality and experimentation* – the act of making, including hypothesising and trialling
- *narrative seriation* – the ability to sequence and re-sequence actions to create a narrative and to manipulate components to give multiple meanings and layers of complexity.

Each cell in the taxonomy framework contains between two and four educational objectives. The distinctions between the Piagetian stage levels are expressed in several ways, including the number of variables or viewpoints involved, the level of abstraction and the use of argument to support diverse interpretations. Here is an illustrative example for the reasoning pattern *classification*, taken from the taxonomy for music:

> *Concrete*: identify similarities and differences in music; for example, mood and pace.
>
> *Concrete transitional*: compare and contrast pieces of music using more than two variables simultaneously.
>
> *Formal operational*: make rich comparisons of two or more pieces of music, identifying multiple variables such as context, style and instrumentation.

Gouge and Yates do not move beyond a Piagetian framework into a conception of 'post-formal' or 'post-logical' thought, although they do acknowledge that it is not always possible to arrive at firm conclusions on artistic matters. The overall impression is that they have tried to bring an analytic scientific perspective to bear on the creative arts in 'an attempt to deconstruct the neglected aspects of critical thinking which practising artists use intuitively, and which they usually have difficulty in articulating' (2002, p. 138).

Cognitive acceleration is based on the five pedagogical principles, with reasoning patterns being the focus of each lesson. These principles are as follows:

Table 3.10. The common framework used in the ARTS reasoning taxonomies

	Classification	Frames of reference	Symbolic reasoning	Critical reflection	Intention, causality and experimentation
Concrete					
Concrete transitional					
Formal operational thinking					

1. cognitive conflict within Vygotsky's 'zone of proximal development'
2. social construction of knowledge with teacher and peer mediation
3. preparation (including establishing a shared language) and 'bridging' (creating links to facilitate transfer to other domains of experience)
4. metacognition (thinking about one's own thinking)
5. reasoning patterns (in this case, the six patterns listed above).

Evaluation

Gouge and Yates have extended to the creative arts an established cognitive acceleration approach which was first developed for science and mathematics teaching. This appears to give pride of place to an analytic reasoned approach and the ability to handle complex abstractions in an area where other values (such as emphasising concrete experience and emotional resonance) often prevail. At the same time they include types of thinking and expression which are well established in the creative arts, notably imagery and narrative. Their initiative is intended to be a challenge to teachers 'to restructure their attitudes and behaviour as mediators of cognitive development' (2002, p. 138).

Some will undoubtedly welcome this approach, seeing it as providing a respectable and rigorous academic framework which can be used to defend the creative arts against attack by philistines. Others will feel that qualitatively different kinds of thinking are important in artistic expression and that formal operation thinking is too closely allied to traditional conceptions of working memory and intelligence. Some may see it as being inimical to creativity.

It remains to be seen how teachers will respond to cognitive acceleration in the arts. It lays down a challenge to those who believe that spontaneity is all and knowledge and skills relatively unimportant. It may well stimulate theorists and practitioners to achieve a new synthesis between the affective, motivational and cognitive aspects of their practice.

Summary: Gouge and Yates

Purpose and structure	Some key features	Relevance for teachers and learning
Main purpose(s): • to use the Arts as a vehicle for Cognitive Acceleration • to promote creative and critical thinking	**Terminology:** • clear • technical terms are explained	**Intended audience:** • teachers
Domains addressed: • cognitive • conative	**Presentation:** • one-page tabular format • well-structured and not too complex	**Contexts:** • education
Broad categories covered: • reflective thinking • productive thinking • building understanding • information-gathering	**Theory base:** • Piaget's genetic epistemology • Vygotsky	**Pedagogical stance:** • directive, but also facilitatory in enabling the mediation and construction of meaning • learning through peer-coaching and collaboration

Classification by:	Values:	Practical illustrations
• Piagetian cognitive level	• all learners are expected	for teachers:
• subject area	to be creative	• curricula for the
	• value is equated with	visual arts, music
	complexity of analysis	and drama have
	and appreciation	been developed
	• a rational approach	
	is expected	

Some issues for further investigation

- Which authors have clearly articulated a theory of learning?
- Which frameworks most clearly distinguish between different 'ways of knowing'?
- What kinds of learning are most clearly linear and which non-linear?
- Are there any general categories of cognitive process which are essentially too complex for some people to manage?
- Which frameworks describe the structure of cognition; which describe the processes through which cognition is constructed; and which do both?
- Do any of the authors concern themselves with the interplay between cognitive, emotional, social and societal dimensions of learning?
- Which later frameworks build most helpfully on the taxonomic efforts of Bloom and his co-authors?
- How has the work of each author been used, by whom and to what ends?
- Which frameworks can be used to support direct instruction as well as discovery learning?
- Which frameworks are most suitable for use in the context of assessment – and why?
- Which of these frameworks best accommodate learning situations in the social sciences and humanities?
- In what ways does the role of the teacher need to change when intensive use is made of computer-mediated learning?
- How do different authors envisage their framework of instruction design being put into practice and by whom?

- Which authors aim to advance theories of learning and instruction as well as to change classroom practice? What impact have they made?
- Which frameworks are most suitable for use in talking about thinking and learning with students?
- Are there pedagogical advantages in using several small frameworks (or in taking elements from different frameworks) instead of getting to grips with a more comprehensive framework?
- Which authors address the question: 'What role, if any, do teachers have in advancing instructional design theory and practice?'
- Which frameworks are best supported by empirical evidence about 'what works' in education?

4

Frameworks dealing with productive thinking

Introduction

The second family group consists of frameworks for understanding critical and creative thinking, which we subsume under the more general term *productive thinking*. By *productive thinking* (a term used by Romiszowski, 1981), we understand what Bloom refers to as *analysis*, *synthesis* and *evaluation* and various combinations of these and other processes, when they lead to deeper understanding, a defensible judgment or valued product. It may involve planning what to do and say, imagining situations, reasoning, solving problems, considering opinions, making decisions and judgments, or generating new perspectives. The phrase captures the idea that this kind of thinking is not confined to the analysis of existing arguments, but is also concerned with generating ideas and has consequences for action. It makes little sense to separate critical thinking from creative thinking, since in many situations they overlap and are interdependent.

Thinking as conceptualised within the frameworks included in this family is considered to involve more than cognition, since most theorists also specify dispositions which they believe to be extremely important in the development of productive thinking. Allen and colleagues who limit themselves to argument analysis (Allen, Feezel, and Kauffie, 1967) are exceptions to this generalisation. It should be noted that the role of dispositions was one of the issues which divided the American Philosophical Association's expert panel on critical thinking, although the majority (61%) did regard specific dispositions to be integral to the conceptualisation of critical thinking and 83% thought that *good* critical thinkers would have certain key dispositions (Facione, 1990). In stressing the importance of affective dispositions they called for the development of effective and equitable materials, pedagogies and assessment tools capable of cultivating and extending critical thinking beyond the narrow instructional setting to encourage the application of such 'habits of mind' to personal and civic life. Authors of critical thinking frameworks believe that critical thinking is improved by reflection and metacognition, but tend not to specify different kinds of objective (e.g. global or specific, short-term or long-term).

Divisions within the family of frameworks in this chapter are located around issues of how meaningful it is to talk in terms of skills or processes as mental operations when they are only observed through different tasks requiring thinking and the role of subject knowledge in thinking. Bailin identifies two kinds of approaches to critical thinking: the descriptive (psychological) approach that focuses on skills, processes and procedures and the normative (philosophical) approach that focuses on critical practices (Bailin, 1998). Whilst the frameworks included in this family span psychological and philosophical approaches to understanding thinking, authors (with the exception of de Bono) take a philosophical stance on critical thinking, viewing it as a normative endeavour located within public traditions of enquiry; so it is the quality of the thinking and not the processes employed that distinguish it from uncritical thinking.

Time sequence of the productive-thinking frameworks

Altshuller's TRIZ Theory of Inventive Problem Solving (1956)

There are four main steps: problem definition; problem-solving tool selection; generating solutions; evaluating solutions. A specific problem is an instance of a generic problem, which is solved when the appropriate generic solution is returned to a specific solution.

Allen, Feezel and Kauffie's taxonomy of critical abilities related to the evaluation of verbal arguments (1967)

Twelve abilities are involved in the recognition, analysis and evaluation of arguments. Truth claims depend on testimony and reasons. People should not be misled by rhetoric or the misuse of language.

De Bono's lateral and parallel thinking tools (1976 / 85)

The tools are designed to broaden the natural flow of thinking and redirect it away from well-worn and predictable channels. The programmes provide a framework which can be used deliberately in everyday life and in the classroom to enable innovative thinking and cross-situational problem-solving.

Halpern's reviews of critical thinking skills and dispositions (1984)

Halpern's skill categories are: memory; thought and language; deductive reasoning; argument analysis; hypothesis testing; likelihood and uncertainty; decision-making; problem-solving; and creative thinking. She also lists six relevant dispositions.

Baron's model of the good thinker (1985)

The most important components of the model are the three conscious search processes: for goals; for possibilities; and for evidence. Good thinking and the dispositions underlying it are to some extent teachable. Glatthorn and Baron (1991) later identify nine common types of thinking.

Ennis' taxonomy of critical thinking dispositions and abilities (1987)

For Ennis the basic areas of critical thinking are clarity, basis, inference and interaction. In 1998 he lists 12 relevant dispositions and 15 abilities.

Lipman's modes of thinking and four main varieties of cognitive skill (1991/95)

Judgment and reasoning can be strengthened through critical, creative and caring thinking (*caring* added in 1995). In education the four major varieties of higher-order thinking relate to: enquiry; reasoning (preserving truth); information-organising; and translation (preserving meaning).

Paul's model of critical thinking (1993)

The model has four parts: elements of reasoning; standards of critical thinking; intellectual abilities; and intellectual traits. The first three parts focus on what is essential to critical thinking and the fourth on what it is to be a critical thinker.

Jewell's reasoning taxonomy for gifted children (1996)

Jewell's taxonomy has three fields: objectives of reasoning; reasoning strategies; and reasoning dispositions. The disposition to adopt thinking about thinking (metacognition) as a habit is very important.

Petty's six-phase model of the creative process (1997)

Each of the phases (inspiration, clarification, evaluation, distillation, incubation and perspiration) is linked with desirable accompanying mindsets. All phases are essential, but not always sequential. Uncreative people tend to consider few ideas and work with a fixed mindset.

Bailin's intellectual resources for critical thinking (1999b)

Bailin emphasises critical thinking as the induction into cultural, critical practices and traditions of enquiry; and advocates the infusion of critical thinking into the curriculum. She offers a framework rather than a taxonomy, which identifies the required intellectual resources and habits of mind.

Description and evaluation of productive-thinking frameworks

Altshuller's TRIZ (Teoriya Resheniya Izibreatatelskikh Zadach) Theory of Inventive Problem-Solving

Description and intended use

TRIZ is a systematic, creativity and innovation process devised as an aid to practical problem-solving, especially in engineering. It owes much to the work of Genrich Altshuller whose study of patents led him in 1946 to devise an Algorithm for Inventive Problem Solving in the Soviet Union. This algorithm, known as ARIZ, from the Russian, is a part of TRIZ. The first published paper about TRIZ appeared in Russian in 1956 (Altshuller and Shapiro, 1956). It is estimated that, by 2002, some 1,500 person-years had gone into the development of TRIZ. The aim is to encapsulate principles of good inventive practice and set them in a generic problem-solving frame-work (for more details see Altshuller, 1996; 1999; 2000; Salamatov, 1999; Mann, 2002). TRIZ may now be described as a theory of how technology develops, a process and a series of tools to aid thinking to solve practical problems. TRIZ is intended to complement and add structure to our natural creativity rather than replace it. It is claimed to be the most exhaustive creativity aid ever assembled. More recently, it has been adapted to suit non-material problems, such as those that arise in management.

TRIZ helps the would-be problem-solver define a specific problem, see it as a particular kind of problem, identify a potential solution in general terms and translate this into a specific solution. This sequence is illustrated in figure 4.1. Note that TRIZ aims to point thinking in directions that are likely to be productive. It does not provide an algorithm that guarantees a solution: the solver must cross the space S in figure 4.1. In effect, TRIZ is a collection of tools to aid thinking. Although TRIZ has major unique features, develop-ment seems to be eclectic and thinking aids from a variety of sources are incorporated.

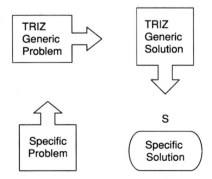

Fig. 4.1. Classifying a specific problem as an instance of a TRIZ generic problem, using TRIZ tools to identify a generic solution then translating it into a specific solution.

Problem Definition: in which the would-be solver comes to an understanding of the problem

1. The Problem Explorer provides ways of understanding the problem. These include: a benefits analysis; a problem-hierarchy explorer (the original problem, the broader problem, the narrower problem); a 'nine-windows' tool for exploring resources and constraints (in terms of past, present and future; within the system, the system itself, and around the system); and an identification of 'sore' points.
2. The Function and Attribute Analysis (FAA) identifies in detail what the solution is expected to do and what its attributes will be. For instance, these can be set out in noun-verb-noun diagrams, rather like concept maps.
3. S-curve analysis locates the problem on a general development curve (S-shaped). For instance, if the current situation lies near the beginning of the curve, solutions are likely to involve improvements to the system. If it lies at the mature (top) end of the S-curve, an entirely new system may be needed as opportunities for further improvements may be few.
4. The Ideal Final Result (IFR) describes the characteristics of the ideal solution to the problem.

Selecting a Problem-Solving Tool

Advice is given on the order in which to try the thinking tools. The order is not intended to be rigid and different authors may suggest different ways of working. It is also possible to construct short versions so that courses from two days to six months duration are offered. It is recognised that short courses are not adequate to do justice to TRIZ and should be seen as taster courses.

Generating solutions: using the tools

1. Technical Contradictions refers to the technical problems identified (e.g. high strength but low weight). The solver uses a matrix to identify which of 40 'Inventive Principles' (strategies) seem to have the potential to suggest a resolution of the contradiction. This use of these 40 generic strategies is said to account for the

success of hundreds of thousands of patents. For instance, Principle 1– *Segmentation*, suggests: A. divide a system into separate parts or sections; B. make a system easy to put together or take apart; C. increase the amount of segmentation. All 40 principles are possible ways of improving the functionality of a product by solving relevant problems.

2. Physical Contradictions refers to the physical problems identified (e.g. the object must be both hot and cold). Again, a grid provides Inventive Principles that may suggest solutions.

3. S-Field Analysis involves codifying the problem into a general form. This general form is used to identify those Inventive Principles that may be useful (as these are also expressed in a general form). In addition, additional charts suggest solutions to difficulties raised by the analysis, such as insufficient/excessive relationships.

4. Evolutionary Trends describes patterns of development that have been found to be more or less general amongst solutions to practical problems. These may suggest ways in which a product might be changed (e.g. many boundaries to few boundaries to no boundaries; commodity to product to service to experience to transformation).

5. Resources are what is in or around the system. In identifying these, it draws attention to their existence and directs thought to their potential.

6. Knowledge/Effects refers to the existence of know-what and know-how that has the potential to solve the problem. There are three resources for identifying these: a) a database of functional effects; b) a database of ways of altering attributes; and c) knowledge resources to be found on-line, through a search of patent databases.

7. ARIZ is a problem-solving algorithm originally devised by Altshuller. It involves: defining the specific problem; technical and physical contradictions; the IFR; the x-component (some magical product that eliminates the contradictions); analysing resources; and selecting and applying the Inventive Principles. ARIZ preceded TRIZ but could be used as a compact or reduced version of it.

8. Trimming is the process of reducing the parts of a solution. Having been given an existing solution or devised one, trimming is used to reduce its elements and make those left work to maximum effect.

9. IFR refers to the Ideal Final Result, described above. Having identified it in the Problem Exploration, it may point the way to solutions that are better than at present. It also serves to narrow the search space to what is manageable and potentially productive.

10. Psychological Inertia (PI) may impede changes in thought. Four ways of breaking out of PI are offered: the nine-windows tool; Smart Little People; a Size–Time–Interface–Cost Tool; and Why–What's Stopping Analysis. The first of these draws thinking away from the present and the system to the past, future, subsystem and supersystem. The second reconstructs the problem in terms of Little People and uses their behaviour as an analogy to suggest other ways of doing things. The third takes the size and time both to infinity and to zero and asks what happens. The last asks 'Why do I want to solve this problem?' And 'What's stopping me solving this problem?'

11. Subversion analysis considers matters of reliability.

Solution evaluation

Ways of analysing various qualitative and quantitative aspects of the solution are described.

Evaluation

First and foremost, TRIZ is a practical project, with an empirical basis in Altshuller's throughgoing analytic study of successful patents. While it includes a theory of how technology develops through resolving contradictions and is capable of predicting trends, it is primarily a structured set of techniques for use in designing products. Some of the techniques are psychological in nature, as they are a means of avoiding mental inertia by adopting a different strategy or perspective.

TRIZ is distinctive because it uses the study of historical information to indicate evolutionary trends and to predict the likely nature of solutions. It is also especially worthy of note because it is a generic problem-solving framework which seeks to draw on, relate and apply knowledge from different disciplines (e.g. biology, chemistry, engineering and physics). It is not unusual for important inventions to draw on knowledge from outside the particular industry within which they are applied, and sometimes from several sciences.

The idea that one can learn how to extract a core of a problem and then generalise it is a powerful one. It means that reasoning can take place at a higher level of abstraction than if the focus of attention is on the specifics of a situated problem. The use of a structured set of tools and well-proven procedures means that effort is not wasted in the divergent generation of useless ideas through brainstorming or free association. Similarly, by thinking about a problem in generic terms, focusing on an ideal final result at the early stage of problem definition and then using TRIZ tools, mental effort can be directed towards generating solutions instead of arguing about what constitutes an appropriate strategic plan.

Altshuller's approach is a challenge to popular conceptions of creativity, in that he suggests that in most cases good design is simply a matter of using a known solution in a novel way. Instead of relying on trial-and-error methods, creativity can be enhanced through the systematic study of general patterns and trends in previous design solutions. If he is right, there are enormous implications for the way in which design is taught, not only in science and technology, but across the curriculum.

TRIZ is an ongoing project, although mature enough to be useful. There is a TRIZ Journal, a range of books (e.g. published by CREAX), websites and software. TRIZ offers a structured way of working in the practical problem-solving field and elsewhere. In 1974 Altshuller prepared TRIZ courses for high school students (the material subsequently translated in Altshuller, 1999). Salamatov (1999) claims that TRIZ can be mastered readily by anyone, but in our judgment it takes time and perseverance and in its original form requires a foundation in science and technology.

Summary: Altshuller

Purpose and structure	Some key features	Relevance for teachers and learning
Main purpose(s): • to provide a systematic approach to practical problem-solving • has some application in management	**Terminology:** • few specially-defined terms • uses vocabulary of main application area: technology	**Intended audience:** • designers of instruction and assessment • teachers • researchers
Domains addressed: • cognitive	**Presentation:** • instruction manuals and websites for enthusiasts • software is available to aid users	**Contexts:** • education • work
Broad categories covered: • strategic management of thinking • productive thinking • building understanding • information-gathering	**Theory base:** • evolutionary biology • natural science • systemic theory • psychology of problem-solving	**Pedagogical stance:** • prescriptive: teacher/text-directed • intended for creative application when understood
Classification by: • temporal order of use of skills	**Values:** • skills widely accessible with training	**Practical illustrations for teachers:** • many examples provided

Allen, Feezel and Kauffie's taxonomy of concepts and critical abilities related to the evaluation of verbal arguments

Description and intended use

This classification system was created by a team of educators at the University of Wisconsin with the intention of promoting critical thinking (Allen, Feezel and Kauffie, 1967). It builds on Toulmin's analysis of the field-invariant nature of the structure of argument, i.e. truth claim, supported by warrants of various kinds which relate to relevant data (Toulmin, 1958). The authors claim that their taxonomy is systematic, coherent and empirically adequate. It is meant to encompass all arguments to be found in everyday discourse and to have mutually exclusive categories. It is claimed to be a taxonomy of the thinking skills (or critical abilities) involved in constructing and analysing arguments, and is entirely cognitive in nature. Critical abilities are defined as the application of principles and standards to newly encountered situations. There are 12 critical abilities and these are listed below, with details of the concepts involved added in. It can be seen that there are up to three levels of detail within each item and that the abilities differ substantially in complexity and difficulty.

1. Distinguishing between sentences functioning as statements and sentences functioning as performatives (i.e. not calling for affirmation or denial).
2. Distinguishing arguments (which include a claim and a justification for it) from other forms of verbal discourse (such as narration and exposition).
3. Recognising the components which are related in statements (classes, individuals and attributes).
4. Recognising types of claim in arguments (attributive, membership, indicative, responsibility and comparative).
5. Recognising testimony (source statement) offered in justification.
6. Appraising testimony in terms of internal and external criteria.
7. Recognising reasons offered as justification; classifying reasons by argumentative function (data or warrant); detecting arguments in which relational statements are suppressed.
8. Recognising various patterns of reasoning; supplying appropriate warrants to relate data to claim; appraising reasons according to relevant rules of inference. The patterns listed are: sign reasoning; individual to member; member to individual; alternate; parallel case; cause–effect, effect–cause and comparative.
9. Recognising the degree of acceptability of a claim as determined by the various elements in an argument.

10. Analysing the functions of statements in complexes of interrelated arguments.
11. Detecting irrelevance in argument (in the form of dissuasions and diversions). Dissuasions are: persuasive prefaces; glittering generalisations; name calling; technical terms; and circularity. Diversions are: attacking the person or appealing to the populace, appealing to pity, to authority, to force, to ignorance, to large numbers, to humour and ridicule or to speculation.
12. Detecting misuses of language in argument (ambiguity and equivocation).

The authors also present their material in flowchart form, to show that, apart from the overall sequential process of argument recognition, analysis and evaluation, some critical processes can take place in parallel or not at all, depending on the nature of the argument as well as individual interest or preference (e.g. identifying patterns of reasoning and evaluating the authority of an external source). The flowchart suggests a sequential order of processes in argument evaluation in which some stages are prerequisites for later stages, but experience suggests that the order is not always invariant (for example, not all arguments are part of an argument chain).

The Wisconsin team certainly intended their model to be used in schools as well as at college level, for example through Klausmeier's approach to Individually Guided Education (Klausmeier et al., 1971).

Users of the model will need to acquire new knowledge and concepts, to build understanding of processes (e.g. classifying reasons by argumentative function) and engage in productive thinking (e.g. by appraising the acceptability of claims). Insofar as the model is to be applied to one's own verbal arguments as well as to those of other people, it is clear that its use will also involve reflective thinking.

Evaluation

Although it is clearly formulated and coherent, Allen, Feezel and Kauffie's scheme does not have a consistent classificatory principle (such as semantic qualities of argument components) running throughout. As it does not identify a set of elements to be classified which share key characteristics, it is a model rather than a taxonomy.

However, there is a general progression in terms of cognitive demand from recognising a statement to recognising misuses of language in argument.

This is a distinctive model in that it brings together in an economical form a set of concepts and abilities which can be used in many content areas. It is closely related to Toulmin's views about argument, which have stimulated much enquiry in the field of informal logic and have also been applied in the field of artificial intelligence. It is compatible with the wider critical thinking frameworks of Ennis (1987) and Paul (1987), as well as with King and Kitchener's (1994) ideas about reflective judgment based on reasonable enquiry.

The scope of the model is rather narrow, covering only a subset of the 15 critical thinking abilities identified by Ennis (1998). It is not intended to apply to deductive syllogistic reasoning, but to everyday argument, which usually relies on assumptions and serves pragmatic rather than strictly logical communicative purposes. The first ten categories are about argument, taken to mean a process whereby a fact or facts convey another fact or whether assertion(s) support a truth claim. The last two categories are about argumentation or the use of rhetorical and linguistic devices, most of which come from scholastic tradition going back to Aristotle.

Inasmuch as argument is viewed as a process of reasoning based on commonly shared meanings, the Allen–Feezel–Kauffie model can be accepted as providing a comprehensive set of main categories. This acceptance depends on taking the argument patterns listed to include reasoning by analogy and from models. However, the model deals in broad categories and does not seek to provide a full set of subcategories of types of testimony or of criteria for evaluating testimony. Nor is it clear that the subcategories of irrelevance and language misuse are comprehensive. Ennis (1998) and Halpern (1997) provide further detail in these areas. We await a full philosophical analysis of spin.

This model clarifies in some detail the concepts and vocabulary needed to build and analyse arguments. Teachers may find it useful in lesson planning and in reviewing and appraising lessons to see whether their aims have been achieved. The skills involved are relevant in both oral discussion and written form, especially where students have to critically reflect on their practice or write essays. Outside formal education the model is potentially useful for all who seek to promote reasoned discussion and evidence-based decision-making. However, this potential is unlikely to be realised unless more examples of how it could be used in specific domains are developed.

Other writers have also promoted the idea of explicitly teaching reasoning skills. For example, Toulmin developed a framework to teach reasoning skills to young adults through the process of producing and evaluating arguments (Toulmin et al., 1984) and more recently, van Gelder has produced and begun to evaluate a software tool for the construction and analysis of arguments which uses a similar model (van Gelder, 2000 and 2001). Interest in teaching argument analysis in the UK enjoys periodic resurgence, as in the current AS Level in Critical Thinking and Hull University's Improving the Quality of Argument project (Andrews, Costello and Clarke, 1993) which used Philosophy for Children approaches and saw the teaching of argument skills as 'synonymous with the development of thinking skills' (p. 39).

The constructive use and analysis of verbal argument is probably one of the most undervalued and poorly developed set of skills in the world today. As Whyte (2003, p. 10) points out, 'the gap left by the education system' leaves people 'unable to resist the bogus reasoning of those who want something from them, such as votes or money or devotion'. If this is true, there is an urgent need for policy-makers and teachers to reframe their ideas about teaching and learning, putting a much higher value on the development of reasoning, not just for an intellectual elite, but for everybody. There is no point trying to raise educational standards if education does not give pride of place to these essential prerequisites for reputable research and balanced judgment.

Summary: Allen, Feezel and Kauffie

Purpose and structure	Some key features	Relevance for teachers and learning
Main purpose(s): • to promote critical thinking	**Terminology:** • clear • necessarily uses some technical terms	**Intended audience:** • teachers

Domains addressed:	Presentation:	Contexts:
• cognitive	• available only on microfiche • original has text plus flowchart	• education • work • citizenship • recreation
Broad categories covered:	**Theory base:**	**Pedagogical stance:**
• reflective thinking • productive thinking • building understanding • information-gathering	• Toulmin's work on informal argument	• not elaborated
Classification by:	**Values:**	**Practical illustrations for teachers:**
• broadly sequential processes leading to judgment	• belief in reason • pragmatism	• enough to explain core concepts

De Bono's lateral and parallel thinking tools

Description and intended use

Edward de Bono is well known for his work on lateral thinking through the CoRT (Cognitive Research Trust) programme and his Six Thinking Hats approach to parallel thinking. His emphasis is on problem-solving techniques which promote generative, or productive thinking:

Critical thinking, scholarly thinking and generative thinking all have their place. I don't mind in what order of importance they are placed. I am only concerned that education should take notice of generative thinking. Generative thinking is messy, imperfect, impure and perhaps difficult to teach. But it is important and we should try to teach it. (de Bono, 1976, p. 16)

He suggests that improved thinking is more likely to result from better perception than improved critical thinking:

In practical life very few errors in thinking are logical errors . . . The errors are not so much errors as inadequacies of perception . . . perceptions are not complicated – they don't need working out – it is simply a matter of being aware of them. And that is one of the functions of thinking: to direct attention across the perceptual field. (de Bono, 1976, pp. 62 and 72)

De Bono argues that we tend to follow conventional patterns of thought unless we are encouraged to think about things in different ways by suspending instant judgment or by requiring the thinker to direct attention to all the relevant and interesting points in the situation. This 'lateral' thinking is a cognate of creative thinking and the antidote to the 'vertical' thinking that, according to de Bono, has epitomised the Western philosophical and scientific tradition since Socrates, Plato and Aristotle.

In order to direct or focus attention de Bono claims that a framework is needed which we can use deliberately in everyday life as well as in the classroom. His programmes consist of 'thinking tools', the use of which enable cross-situational problem-solving in order to avoid being trapped by semantic thinking and content knowledge:

The dilemma is that it is usually possible to teach only situation-centred skills. You train a person to behave in a certain way in a certain situation. The way out of the dilemma is to create situations that are themselves transferable. We call such situations tools. (de Bono, 1976, p. 50)

The CoRT programme is a systematic scheme for teaching a range of tools identified by acronyms such as CAP (consider all possibilities). CoRT introduces 12 thinking tools (see table 4.1) and culminates in a protocol for tackling problems (PISCO - Purpose, Input, Solutions, Choice, Operation). The programme consists of 60 lessons organised into 6 blocks of 10 lessons.

Table 4.1. The CoRT thinking tools

PMI	Plus, Minus, Interesting points
CAF	Consider All Factors
C&S	Consequence and Sequence
APC	Alternatives, Possibilities, Choices
OPV	Other Points of View
AGO	Aims, Goals and Objectives
TEC	Target, Expand, Contract
FOW	Find Other Ways
ADI	Agreement, Disagreement, Irrelevance
EBS	Examine Both Sides
Yes, No, Po	Po (from hypothesis/proposal) ideas used creatively and without any judgments
FIP	First Important Priorities

In CoRT lessons the er   on developing the fluent use of the tools through practice, ar   .on is not considered to be central to developing skill in thinki   is curtailed. He outlines four levels of achievement in the acquisition of thinking skills through the use of the CoRT programme:

Level 1 General awareness of thinking as a skill. A willingness to 'think' about something, explore a subject and to listen to others. No recollection of any specific thinking tool.

Level 2 A more structured approach to thinking, including better balance, looking at the consequences of an action or choice (taking other people's views into account), and a search for alternatives. Perhaps a mention of a few of the CoRT tools.

Level 3 Focused and deliberate use of some of the CoRT tools. The organisation of thinking as a series of steps. A sense of purpose in thinking.

Level 4 Fluent and appropriate use of many CoRT tools. Definite consciousness of the metacognitive level of thinking. Observation and comment on the thinker's own thinking. (de Bono, 1983, p. 708)

In the 1980s de Bono turned his attention to parallel thinking and developed the tool of Six Thinking Hats (de Bono, 1985). Parallel thinking emphasises allowing different ways of thinking to co-exist (rather than compete and cancel each other out), so that they can lead to solutions beyond the limits set by the problem rather than rushing to a judgment. It is productive as opposed to reductive and aims to enrich and increase the complexity of a situation so that a creative solution can be designed.

This programme is organised around six kinds of thinking (see table 4.2). The idea that the thinker can put on or take off one of these hats is essential, as this reflects the emphasis on flexibility and changing ways of thinking about an issue or problem. Two key ideas underpin the design of the programme:

- reduction of the complexity and confusion that results from trying to do everything at once when thinking about a problem, by paying attention to different modes of thinking individually whilst allowing parallel streams of thought to co-exist;

Table 4.2. De Bono's six types of thinking

White Hat thinking	This covers facts, figures, information needs and gaps. 'I think we need some white hat thinking at this point' means 'Let's drop the arguments and proposals, and look at the data.'
Red Hat thinking	This covers intuition, feelings and emotions. 'Putting on my red hat, I think this is a terrible proposal.' The thinker has full permission to put forward his or her feelings on the subject without any need to justify them.
Black Hat thinking	This is the hat of judgment and caution. It is a most valuable hat and not in any sense inferior or negative. The black hat thinking identifies logically why a suggestion does not fit the facts, the available experience, the system in use, or the policy that is being followed.
Yellow Hat thinking	This covers positive thinking or why something will work and offer benefits. It can look forward to the results of proposed action, but can also find value in what has already happened.
Green Hat thinking	This is the hat of creativity, alternatives, proposals, what is interesting, provocations and changes.
Blue Hat thinking	This is the overview or process control hat which looks not at the subject itself but at the 'thinking' about the subject or a metacognitive perspective. 'Putting on my blue hat, I feel we should do some more green hat thinking at this point.'

- provision of the opportunity to role-play different modes of thinking, so that you avoid the premature closing down of options because only habitual modes of thinking are employed.

Six Thinking Hats is used extensively in industry and management training in order to reduce conflict in meetings and to stimulate innovation. There is overlap between the Interaction stage of the CoRT programme (CoRT 3) and Six Thinking Hats and both reflect de Bono's frustration with analytical thinking that proceeds through argument and dialectic.

Emotions play an important part in de Bono's model of thinking as they affect perception and decision-making by influencing what is recognised. He suggests that feelings probably change the chemical basis of the brain so that when we are influenced by emotions it is actually a different brain that is doing the thinking (de Bono, 1987, p. 109). However, while in CoRT 5 and White Hat thinking, the emphasis is on intellectual detachment, in Red Hat thinking intuition and feelings are unconstrained by reason. Indeed, for de Bono, a key purpose of thinking is to arrange the world so that our emotions can be applied in a valuable manner (de Bono, 1983, p. 704). He also believes that humour, by encouraging an unconventional, quixotic view of life, can also tell us something about perception that we have traditionally neglected in favour of logic.

Evaluation

In many ways de Bono was a pioneer, especially by finding real-world applications for some of the ideas developed by psychologists such as Bartlett (1958) and Wertheimer (1959). His emphasis on the way perception is influenced by previous experience and on pattern-making and pattern seeking is similar to that of Margolis (1987). At the same time his systemic view of thinking resembles earlier conceptions, such as the work of von Bertalanffy (1950).

Although not presented as a comprehensive theoretical frame-work, it has been shown by Mann (2001) that the Six Thinking Hats model is fully compatible with the problem-solving cycle and tools used in the TRIZ Theory of Inventive Problem Solving (Altshuller, 1996). Different kinds of thinking are required for different processes at each of the four stages of problem-solving: *define, select, solve, evaluate*. For example, White Hat thinking is needed when describing the functioning of an existing system and Green Hat thinking is required when seeking to translate generic-solution triggers into specific solutions. What is unclear is whether the use of these broad labels can improve the quality of outcomes from users of a sophisticated set of tools such as TRIZ, where the terminology is already highly specific.

De Bono presented in his early work an individualistic approach to generative thinking in which belonging to a tradition or a community is barely a relevant concept in a post-modern world. However, his Six Thinking Hats programme is now often used by problem-solving groups and his reservations about debate and discussion as a means of enhancing the quality of thinking are somewhat at odds with his own track record of setting up various think tanks in which he has personally played a prominent role.

There is a tension in de Bono's writing about thought as both an automatic and a conscious process. He describes thought as a flow of activation across a passive 'surface' rather than any active construction of meaning by a 'self'. De Bono's thinking tools are designed to broaden this natural flow and direct it away from predictable channels so that new 'flowscapes' consisting of patterns of concepts can be established. Key to this process is the removal of the ego investment in being a 'good' thinker, so that learners can look objectively at their thinking; he uses the analogy of a tennis player who might look objectively at his backhand in a match he is playing. Yet this analogy and the whole conception of Blue Hat (metacognitive) thinking depends on conscious reflexivity. Similarly, in another analogy, de Bono refers to the relationship between IQ and thinking as similar to that between a car and the performance of its (conscious!) driver:

Thinking is the operating skill with which intelligence acts upon experience.
(de Bono, 1976, p. 33)

De Bono is more interested in the usefulness of developing ideas than proving the reliability or efficacy of his approach. His thinking tools were explicitly designed with practical relevance and ease of communication as key attributes. His early books with their message of escape from conventional patterns of thinking made him a popular figure in the youth culture of the late 60s and early 70s. His use of acronyms as in CoRT and visual symbols as in Six Thinking Hats are certainly positive features and his programmes are now used throughout the world in the worlds of education and business. For de Bono, their widespread use is their validation. 'They must make sense because they work. That is the ultimate test of reality' (de Bono, 1987, p. 13).

There is sparse research evidence to show that generalised improvements in thinking performance can be attributed to training in the use of CoRT or Thinking Hats tools. An early evaluation of CoRT reported significant benefits for Special Educational Needs (SEN) pupils, who took an interest in and shone in the thinking lessons. De Bono suggested that this may be because SEN pupils are not dependent on knowledge, but on processing information (de Bono, 1976, p. 213). However, in a more recent study with Australian aboriginal children (Ritchie and Edwards, 1996), little evidence of generalisation was found other than in the area of creative thinking.

Summary: de Bono

Purpose and structure	Some key features	Relevance for teachers and learning
Main purpose(s): • to promote lateral and parallel thinking to stimulate originality and innovation	**Terminology:** • acronyms and symbols promote accessibility and use across contexts	**Intended audience:** • the general reader • teachers • trainers
Domains addressed: • cognitive • affective	**Presentation:** • individual tools organised into programmes • use of a range of media	**Contexts:** • education • work • citizenship • recreation
Broad categories covered: • self-regulation • productive thinking • building understanding • information-gathering	**Theory base:** • cognitive neuroscience • connectionism • pragmatism	**Pedagogical stance:** • tools and programmes for independent use and designed to be as 'teacher proof' as possible • averse to discussion and debate, as causes disputes and premature judgment

Classification by:	Values:	Practical illustrations for teachers:
• type of thinking	• originality • novelty • individuality • opposed to dialectical reasoning	• provides exemplars of use of the tools and suggestions for a range of applications • extensive support through website, additional training materials, courses and seminars

Halpern's reviews of critical thinking skills and dispositions

Description and intended use

Much of the material presented here first appeared in Halpern's influential book on critical thinking (Halpern, 1984), and was later developed into 'a taxonomy of critical thinking skills' (Halpern, 1994, p. 31). The taxonomy was intended to provide a basis for the national assessment of critical thinking skills in adults in the USA. At a government-sponsored workshop held in 1992, Halpern referred to the thinking skills needed to compete in a global economy and in the exercise of citizenship (1994, p. 29), but chose to focus on what is often referred to as 'higher-order thinking', i.e. thinking that is reflective, sensitive to context and monitored. She used the following category headings:

- verbal reasoning skills
- argument analysis skills
- skills in thinking as hypothesis testing
- using likelihood and uncertainty
- decision-making and problem-solving skills.

The 1992 workshop was set up in response to the following U.S. national objective:

The proportion of college graduates who demonstrate an advanced ability to think critically, communicate effectively, and solve problems will increase substantially. (National Education Goals Panel, 1991, p. 237)

However, the workshop participants failed to agree on a single theoretical framework on which to base the proposed national assessment and the idea was eventually abandoned. Halpern subsequently revised her lists, and presented them, not as a taxonomy, but as a set of chapter reviews in her book, *Critical Thinking Across the Curriculum* (Halpern, 1997). This book, which closely follows the chapter structure of her 1984 volume on critical thinking, includes material on memory skills and on creative thinking as well as on the types of thinking included in her 1992 taxonomy.

Halpern (1997) employs the following working definition of critical thinking as 'the use of cognitive skills or strategies that increase the probability of a desirable outcome. . . thinking that is purposeful, reasoned, and goal-directed. . . and effective for the particular context and type of thinking task' (1997, p. 4). This definition is so broad that it covers almost all thinking except basic arithmetical calculation and other automatised procedures. Halpern justifies her inclusion of memory skills by claiming that 'All thinking skills are inextricably tied to the ability to remember' (p. 19).

All the thinking skills described by Halpern in separate chapters of her book are listed in table 4.4, together with some category descriptors from Halpern (1994). What is omitted are more detailed descriptions and examples of use, all of which were written for a general readership and for 'any course where critical thinking is valued' (p. vii). Table 4.3 illustrates the level of detail provided throughout, using a single example, taken from Halpern's review of decision-making skills (p. 217).

Table 4.3. An example of one of the critical thinking skills specified by Halpern

Skill	Description	Example of use
Avoiding the entrapment bias	Entrapment occurs when a course of action requires additional investments beyond those already made.	Shana decides to stick with her boyfriend who treats her badly because she has already invested several years in the relationship.

Table 4.4. Halpern's categorisation of critical thinking skills

Memory skills
skills that are needed when learning, during retention and at retrieval
  a. monitoring your attention
  b. developing an awareness of the influence of stereotypes and other beliefs on what we remember
  c. making abstract information meaningful as an aid to comprehension and recall
  d. using advance organisers to anticipate new information
  e. organising information so that it can be recalled more easily
  f. generating retrieval cues at both acquisition and retrieval
  g. monitoring how well you are learning
  h. using external memory aids
  i. employing keywords and images, rhymes, places, and first letters, as internal memory aids
  j. applying the cognitive interview techniques (Geiselman and Fisher, 1985)
  k. developing an awareness of biases in memory

Thought and language skills
skills that are needed to comprehend and defend against the persuasive techniques that are embedded in everyday language
  a. recognising and defending against the use of emotional and misleading language
  b. detecting misuse of definitions and reification
  c. understanding the use of framing with leading questions and negation to bias the reader
  d. using analogies appropriately
  e. employing questioning and paraphrase as a skill for the comprehension of text and oral language
  f. producing and using a graphic representation of information provided in prose form

Deductive reasoning skills
skills used to determine if a conclusion is valid – i.e. it must be true if the premises are true

a. discriminating between inductive and deductive reasoning
b. identifying premises and conclusions
c. reasoning with 'if-then' statements
d. using linear ordering principles
e. avoiding the fallacies of denying the antecedent and confirming the consequent
f. using tree diagrams with branches and nodes to represent information

Argument analysis skills
skills that are needed to judge how well reasons and evidence support a conclusion, including considering counter-evidence, stated and unstated assumptions, and the overall strength of the argument
a. identifying premises (reasons), counter-arguments and conclusions
b. making strong arguments that show good thinking and communication skills
c. judging the credibility of an information source and judging the difference between expertise in factual matters and in value matters
d. understanding the difference between opinion, reasoned judgment, and fact
e. recognising and avoiding common fallacies, such as straw person, appeals to ignorance, slippery slope, false dichotomy, guilt by association, and arguments against the person
f. identifying psychological effects on reasoning
g. remembering to consider what could be missing from an argument

Skills in thinking as hypothesis testing
the skills used in scientific reasoning – the accumulation of observations, formulation of beliefs or hypotheses, and then using the information collected to decide if it confirms or disconfirms the hypotheses
a. recognising the need for and using operational definitions
b. understanding the need to isolate and control variables in order to make strong causal claims
c. checking for adequate sample size and possible bias in sampling when a generalisation is made
d. being able to describe the relationship between any two variables as positive, negative, or unrelated
e. understanding the limits of correlational reasoning

Table 4.4. (*cont.*)

Likelihood and uncertainty critical thinking skills
the correct use of objective and subjective estimates of probability
  a. recognising regression to the mean
  b. understanding and avoiding conjunction errors
  c. utilising base rates to make predictions
  d. understanding the limits of extrapolation
  e. adjusting risk assessments to account for the cumulative nature of probabilistic events
  f. thinking intelligently about unknown risks

Decision-making skills
the skills involved in the generation and selection of alternatives and in judging among them
  a. framing a decision in several ways to consider different sorts of alternatives
  b. generating alternatives
  c. evaluating the consequences of various alternatives
  d. recognising the bias in hindsight analysis
  e. using a decision-making worksheet
  f. avoiding the entrapment bias
  g. seeking disconfirming evidence
  h. awareness of the effects of memory on decisions

Problem-solving skills
skills needed to identify and define a problem, state the goal and generate and evaluate solution paths
  a. restating the problem and the goal to consider different sorts of solution
  b. recognising the critical role of persistence
  c. using a quality representation of a problem (e.g. graphs, trees, matrices, and models)
  d. understanding world-view constraints
  e. selecting the best strategy for the type of problem
  f. actively seeking analogies

Skills for creative thinking
  a. redefine the problem and goal (in several different ways)
  b. find analogies (across different domains of knowledge)

c. list relevant terms
d. brainstorm (without censoring or evaluation)
e. generate and use lists of ways a solution can vary
f. list attributes
g. list the positive, negative and interesting attributes of various solutions
h. visualise from other perspectives

As Halpern's over-riding purpose is to have her readers *use* critical thinking skills, she provides a general-purpose framework to guide the thought process. This amounts to asking people to adopt a metacognitive approach in order to become more knowledgeable about their own thinking and to be better able to regulate it. The framework consists of four questions:

1. What is the goal?
2. What is known?
3. Which thinking skills will get you to your goal?
4. Have you reached your goal?

Recognising that it takes time and conscious effort to develop the attitude and skills of a critical thinker (to the point where the approach becomes habitual), Halpern recommends that teachers provide many opportunities to use critical thinking and that teachers and learners alike value the development of the following six critical thinking dispositions:

- *willingness to plan*
- *flexibility (open-mindedness)*
- *persistence*
- *willingness to self-correct*
- *being mindful (metacognitive monitoring)*
- *consensus-seeking.*

Evaluation

Halpern does not claim to have provided comprehensive lists of critical thinking skills. It is possible to identify many gaps in her lists, some in relation to other work in the same area (e.g. Allen, Feezel and Kauffie's more detailed treatment of argument analysis skills), and even in relation to other lists provided by Halpern herself in the same chapter (e.g. 'seeking converging validity to increase your confidence in a decision' and 'considering the relative "badness" of different sorts of errors', Halpern, 1997, p. 158).

When considered in relation to Marzano's classificatory framework, Halpern's reviews address the cognitive and metacognitive systems. In particular there is a close correspondence between some of Halpern's main categories and Marzano's *knowledge utilisation* categories. When compared with Bloom's taxonomy, Halpern's reviews cover all aspects of the cognitive domain with the exception of *application*. This is not because the use of procedures is excluded from the skill areas she covers, but because of her emphasis on *critical* thinking, which, unlike most routine application, is essentially metacognitive in nature. There is one sense, however, in which she is extremely interested in *application*, not as separate category, but for its importance in all skill areas. Indeed, her main focus is on the conscious application of a 'plan–do–review' or 'plan–decide–act–monitor–evaluate' cycle to all thinking skills and orchestrated uses of skills.

Halpern deals almost incidentally with the affective aspects of thinking, as can be seen from the cognitive emphasis in her treatment of creative thinking and from her rather limited list of critical thinking dispositions (compared with those proposed by Costa, Ennis, Paul or Perkins). She takes conative aspects more seriously, as can be seen from her use of the terms 'willingness' and 'persistence'.

More than any author whose work we have reviewed, Halpern has endeavoured to translate theory and research from cognitive psychology into a form where it can be useful in everyday life. There is up-to-date teaching material to accompany the main text (Halpern, 2002). She has also drawn on relevant sources outside psychology, citing, for example the work of Polya (1945) on problem-solving, Norris and Ennis (1989) on the assessment of arguments and de Bono (1976) on creative thinking.

Halpern is a strong believer in the application of rational methods in problem-solving, including the use of controlled experiments. She points to the need for people to learn how to learn and to be critically

selective in responding to the barrage of information (including adver-
tisements and political rhetoric) around them (Halpern, 1997, pp. 1–3).
She argues that teaching and assessing critical thinking will improve the quality of teaching and learning at college level and will
increase social capital and economic competitiveness (Halpern, 1994,
pp. 25–27). These are pragmatic arguments, in support of which she
cites a number of studies to illustrate the transferability of critical
thinking skills.

Overall, Halpern provides a detailed, but not comprehensive account of thinking skills within the cognitive domain. She asks
the reader to apply a superordinate organising principle, metacognition, in order to develop an effective critical thinking approach.
This is virtually equivalent to defining critical thinking as 'mindful
thinking'.

Summary: Halpern

Purpose and structure	Some key features	Relevance for teachers and learning
Main purpose(s): • to encourage the use of critical thinking in practical problem-solving and decision-making as citizens	**Terminology:** • clear and accessible	**Intended audience:** • teachers • older secondary school and college students • adult learners
Domains addressed: • cognitive • conative • affective	**Presentation:** • use of practical everyday examples to illustrate points	**Contexts:** • education • work • citizenship • everyday life

Broad categories covered:	Theory base:	Pedagogical stance:
• self-engagement • strategic management of thinking • reflective thinking • productive thinking • building understanding • information-gathering	• learning theory from cognitive psychology • Polya on problem-solving	• use of practical examples to emphasise relevance and practice of critical thinking in a range of contexts to facilitate transfer
Classification by: • skill area	**Values:** • importance of rational thought in everyday problem-solving to overcome prejudice and superstition	**Practical illustrations for teachers:** • teaching materials available to accompany the main texts on critical thinking

Baron's model of the good thinker

Description and intended use

Baron's key interest lies in how psychology can be used to improve thinking through education. He takes the view that a major problem with our thinking and decision-making, is that much of it suffers from 'intellectual laziness' (Baron, 1985, p. 108) brought on by a lack of actively open-minded thinking. His work explores the origins and processes of irrationality and poor thinking, and aims to find ways of correcting both.

Baron argues that intelligence and rational thinking are closely related in that rationality is a function of the dispositional components of intelligence. He presents rational decision-making as being dependent upon the rational formation of beliefs about consequences. He believes that the skills involved in rational thinking are teachable, although not without reference to the thinker's beliefs and goals.

Baron uses the idea of a search–inference framework to argue that thinking begins with doubt and involves a search directed at removing the doubt. In the course of this process, which involves the consideration of *goals*, *possibilities* and *evidence*, inferences are made, in which each possibility is strengthened or weakened on the basis of evidence. Glatthorn and Baron (1991) outline the model as follows (p. 63):

1. Thinking begins with a state of doubt about what to do or believe.
2. We usually have a goal in mind when the doubt arises, but we may search for new goals, subgoals, or a reformulation of the original goal.
3. We search for possibilities.
4. We search for evidence relative to the possibilities.
5. We use the evidence to revise the strengths of the possibilities.
6. We decide that the goal is reached and conclude the search.

Glatthorn and Baron go on to identify the characteristics of the 'good thinker' in contrast to those of the 'poor thinker'. A good thinker:

- welcomes problematic situations and is tolerant of ambiguity
- is self-critical, searches for alternate possibilities and goals; seeks evidence on both sides
- is reflective and deliberative; searches extensively when appropriate
- believes in the value of rationality and that thinking can be effective
- is deliberative in discovering goals
- revises goals when necessary
- is open to multiple possibilities and considers alternatives
- is deliberative in analysing possibilities
- uses evidence that challenges favoured possibilities
- consciously searches for evidence against possibilities that are initially strong, or in favour of those that are weak.

Baron concentrates upon *how* information is processed in thinking, in terms of searching for goals, possibilities and evidence to evaluate possibilities. It is important to note that these processes do not go on in any fixed or hierarchical order, but occur in a flow of dynamic interaction. The search processes are relevant in all types of thinking, which we summarise below, using Glatthorn and Baron's terminology as far as possible:

- *diagnosis* – trying to find the source of a problem
- *hypothesis testing* – forming and testing theories
- *reflection* – controlled searching for general principles
- *insight* – where only the search for possibilities is controlled

- *artistic creation* – searching for and evaluating possibilities and goals
- *prediction* – searching for principles and analogies to explain imagined consequences
- *decision-making* – choosing between plans on the basis of imagined consequences
- *behavioural learning* – learning about the effects of one's conduct in certain situations
- *learning from observation* – including language learning and culturally-transmitted knowledge, where the search for evidence is not controllable.

Evaluation

Although Baron's model is broad in scope, he admits that it is not a comprehensive account of thought, as it deals only with thinking as a consciously-controlled purposive activity. It does not deal with the psychological conceptions of attention, memory and intellectual abilities. For Baron, intelligence is a set of characteristics consisting of capacities and dispositions. Capacities are ability parameters that affect success at tasks and may be affected by prior practice but which are not under control at the time a task is done. Dispositions, on the other hand, are seen as being parameters which affect success in tasks but which are subject to learner and teacher control under instruction. Rationality is taken to be an important subset of dispositions, and involves following the rules of a sound prescriptive model of decision-making or belief formation.

Baron's three search processes (for goals, possibilities and evidence) appear to be relatively distinct, apart from the sometimes seamless psychological transition between possibility and goal. They may be accepted as general and comprehensive inasmuch as they characterise goal-directed conscious enquiry. However, Glatthorn and Baron's lists of dispositions and types of thinking show a considerable amount of overlap and are certainly not comprehensive. When compared with other critical thinking theorists, there are some serious gaps in their enumeration of the qualities of a good thinker. Empathy, humility, respect for other points of view, clarity and integrity are signally absent. It is also surprising that *building understanding, justification, seeking consensus*, and *formal problem-solving* are not included in the list of 'common' types of thinking.

It is not clear why Glatthorn and Baron drew up a list of different types of thinking, other than to illustrate aspects of everyday life in which good thinking is important and to suggest that some kind of balance is required in the quantity as well as the quality of thinking that is going on. However, the list of the general characteristics of the good thinker is of limited value in determining what counts as the rational pursuit of goals in a particular situation. It is almost a truism that irrational, impulsive, rigid, restricted, self-satisfied and biased thinking are to be avoided.

Glatthorn and Baron's linking of information-processing, mental capacities and dispositions may be helpful in providing insight into some of the dynamics between cognitive, affective and psycho-motor domains of thinking, but their analysis remains at a very general level and they are highly suspicious of intuition, which they place in opposition to rationality. Their treatment of observation as an unproblematic passive process is also highly questionable.

Baron provides clear definitions and examples from diverse domains, including real-life problems. His model is easy for teachers and learners to understand, but the most valuable part of it is the simplest: the idea of thinking and learning as enquiry.

Summary: Baron

Purpose and structure	Some key features	Relevance for teachers and learning
Main purpose(s): • understanding and correcting irrationality and poor thinking	**Terminology:** • clear • non-technical	**Intended audience:** • teachers • social scientists • students
Domains addressed: • cognitive • (affective) • conative	**Presentation:** • logical • concrete examples given	**Contexts:** • education • psychology • work • citizenship

Broad categories covered:	Theory base:	Pedagogical stance:
• self-engagement • reflective thinking • productive thinking • building understanding • information-gathering	• Dewey • Simon's concept of bounded rationality • role of strategies in intelligent behaviour • psychological research on bias in judgment	• teach thinking in each subject, using teacher explanation and enquiry-based learning with an emphasis on problem finding • provide time for and value reflection
Classification by:	Values:	Practical illustrations for teachers:
• type of search • quality of thought and behaviour	• rationalistic • individualistic • pragmatic	• some examples provided of how the model might be used

Ennis' taxonomy of critical thinking dispositions and abilities

Description and intended use

Ennis' views have developed over time (he has been publishing in this area since 1962) and there have been significant changes in his thinking, particularly in the area of critical thinking dispositions (e.g. 1996). However, his basic definition has remained almost constant, worded as follows: 'Critical thinking is reasonable and reflective thinking that is focused on deciding what to believe or do' (1985, p. 45). His intention is to provide a rationale for the teaching of critical thinking and a taxonomy of 'goals for critical thinking' (1985, p. 46) or an 'outline of a conception of critical thinking' (1998, p. 17). He claims that the significant features of this taxonomy are as follows:

- it focuses on belief and action.
- it contains statements in terms of things that people actually do or should do.
- it includes criteria to help evaluate results.
- it includes both dispositions and abilities.
- it is organised in such a way that it can form the basis for a thinking-across-the-curriculum programme as well as a separate critical thinking course at the college level.

Although Ennis includes creative thinking in this definition, he considers that critical thinking is not equivalent to higher-order thinking, since critical thinking also involves dispositions. He proposes a set of six criteria for judging a set of critical thinking dispositions: *simplicity; comprehensiveness; value; comprehensibility; conformity of its language to our everyday meanings*; and *the fitting of subordinates (if any) under superordinates*. He rejects a further criterion, mutual exclusivity, on the basis of comprehensibility (1996). He claims that in order to ensure that categories in a critical thinking taxonomy do not overlap, it becomes necessary to redefine words with such precision that they can no longer be easily understood.

The 1998 version of his taxonomy, which is summarised below, consists of three main dispositions (with sub-categories) and 15 abilities presented as a list (some with sub-categories) to provide a 'content outline' for a critical thinking curriculum. The original 1987 version contained a longer and more complex list of abilities and sub-categories. Ennis does not claim that either list is exhaustive.

Dispositions
Critical thinkers:

1. *Care that their beliefs are true, and that their decisions be justified; that is care to 'get it right' to the extent possible, or at least care to do the best they can.* This includes the interrelated dispositions to do the following:
   a Seek alternatives (hypotheses, explanations, conclusions, plans, sources) and be open to them;
   b Endorse a position to the extent that, but only to the extent that, it is justified by the information available;
   c Be well informed; and
   d Seriously consider points of view other than their own.
2. *Represent a position honestly and clearly* (theirs as well as others'). This includes the dispositions to do the following:
   a Be *clear* about the intended meaning of what is said, written, or otherwise communicated, *seeking as much precision as the situation requires*;
   b Determine and maintain focus on the conclusion or question;
   c Seek and offer *reasons*;

   d Take into account the total situation; and

   e Be reflectively *aware of their own basic beliefs.*

3. *Care about the dignity and worth of every person.* This includes the dispositions to:

   a *Discover and listen to others' views and reasons;*

   b *Take into account others' feelings and level of understanding,* avoiding intimidating or confusing others with their critical thinking prowess; and

   c *Be concerned about other's welfare.*

Abilities

Ideal critical thinkers have the ability to:

Clarify

1. identify the focus: the issue, question, or conclusion
2. analyse arguments
3. ask and answer questions of clarification and/or challenge
4. define terms and judge definitions and deal with equivocation

Judge the basis for a decision

1. judge the credibility of a source
2. observe and judge observation reports

Infer

1. identify unstated assumptions
2. deduce and judge deductions
3. induce and judge inductions
   a to generalisations, and
   b to explanatory conclusions
4. make and judge value judgments

Make suppositions and integrate abilities

1. consider and reason without letting the disagreement or doubt interfere with their thinking (suppositional thinking);
2. integrate the other abilities and dispositions in making and defending a decision

Use auxiliary critical thinking abilities

1. proceed in an orderly manner appropriate to the situation, for example,
   a follow up problem-solving steps
   b monitor their own thinking
   c employ a reasonable critical thinking checklist
2. be sensitive to the feelings, level of knowledge, and degree of sophistication of others
3. employ appropriate rhetorical strategies in discussion and presentation.

Evaluation

Ennis defines the basic areas of critical thinking as 'clarity, basis, inference and interaction', which he has then broken down into the list of abilities. He acknowledges the importance of the content domain in which critical thinking is applied. He acknowledges that his taxonomy does not incorporate suggestions for 'level, sequence and repetition in greater depth, emphasis or infusion in subject matter area, which might be either exclusive or overlapping'. He claims that the first two dispositions are 'essential' for critical thinking and that the third, sensitivity to others, is 'correlative' and desirable rather than 'constitutive' (Ennis, 1996, p. 171). The 'taxonomy' is therefore a list of dispositions and abilities relevant to critical thinking. Ennis does not include reflection as a major heading, despite its explicit role in his definition of critical thinking.

The underpinning values of Ennis' work are those of rationality and logical thinking, with little attention paid to the impact of feelings on thinking. For this reason he has been challenged by Martin (1992) about the 'dangerous distance' required for critical thinking. Elsewhere, Ennis defends critical thinking against cultural bias (1998), whilst accepting that culture and context have serious implications for such an approach. He has also vigorously defended the concept of critical thinking dispositions as extending across subject boundaries.

Ennis aimed to produce a taxonomy which enables critical thinking to be used practically. He says that his taxonomy is 'simple and comprehensible' (1996, p. 173) and considers that it can be implemented successfully in different ways, though he acknowledges that it needs further research to validate detailed aspects. As it stands, it should be particularly useful for analysing curriculum units in critical thinking or auditing subject-specific critical thinking programmes. However, the number and relevance of the broad categories and their sub-categories to particular fields may make it somewhat daunting to apply.

Although Ennis' list of critical thinking abilities may also be helpful in the field of assessment, the assessment of critical thinking per se is problematic. Ennis analyses different approaches to assessing critical thinking, rejecting multiple-choice assessment for all but self-assessment and research. He also questions performance-based assessment on grounds of cost, focus and context (the more realistic the performance the more complex the problem). Context-based assessments require information gathered over time and across a range of situations (Blatz, 1992).

Summary: Ennis

Purpose and structure	Some key features	Relevance for teachers and learning
Main purpose(s): • to provide a rationale for critical thinking • to set out a taxonomy of objectives for critical thinking	**Terminology:** • sparing use of technical terms	**Intended audience:** • designers of instruction and assessment • teachers • college students
Domains addressed: • cognitive • conative	**Presentation:** • through a series of articles and books • clearly set out, but some may find it rather difficult to apply in a particular field	**Contexts:** • education • citizenship

Broad categories covered:	Theory base:	Pedagogical stance:
• self-regulation • reflective thinking • productive thinking • building understanding	• rationalist	• critical thinking needs to be taught but also needs to be applied to specific content domains.
Classification by:	Values:	Practical illustrations for teachers:
• types of disposition • mental competencies required when deciding what to believe or do	• belief in reason and logical thinking • humanistic values	• only a few, but sufficient to communicate key ideas

Lipman's three modes of thinking and four main varieties of cognitive skill

Description and intended use

While a philosophy lecturer, Matthew Lipman was struck by the fact that even highly qualified undergraduates were not good thinkers; so he designed *Philosophy for Children* to facilitate the creation of 'communities of enquiry' in classrooms. Although more concerned to create an appropriate pedagogy through this programme, he does offer a theoretical framework and, in several places, ways of classifying thinking (albeit illustrative rather than comprehensive). The significant features of this framework are (a) a tripartite model of thinking in which *critical, creative* and *caring* thinking are equally important and interdependent (Lipman, 2004) and (b) his account of four varieties of cognitive skill: *enquiry, reasoning, concept formation* and *translation*.

Lipman defines cognitive skills as 'the ability to make cognitive moves and performances *well*' (Lipman, 1991, p. 76). Building on Bloom (1956), he distinguishes between lower-order and higher-order cognitive skills in terms of complexity, scope, the intelligible organisation of a complex field, the 'recognition of causal or logical compulsions and 'qualitative intensity' (Lipman, 1991, p. 94). He sees value in a curricular sequence whereby an initial emphasis on comparing, distinguishing and connecting leads to classification, seriation, analogical reasoning and immediate inference; and finally to *higher-order thinking*, involving syllogistic reasoning and the use of criteria.

Lipman portrays higher-order thinking as involving both *critical* and *creative* thinking, which are guided by the ideas of truth and meaning respectively. Critical and creative thinking are interdependent, as are criteria and values, reason and emotion. They both aim at judgment, but critical thinking is 'sensitive to context' and self-correcting, while creative thinking is 'governed by context' and 'self-transcending' (Lipman, 1991, p. 25). *Critical thinking* resembles Bloom's *analysis*; *creative thinking* Bloom's *synthesis*; and *judgment* Bloom's *evaluation*.

A significant shift in Lipman's thinking is evident in his 1995 paper 'Caring as Thinking' (Lipman, 1995). Here he presents a tripartite account of higher-order thinking, tracing its lineage to the ancient Greek regulative ideals of the True (critical thinking), the Beautiful (creative thinking) and the Good (caring thinking). In this account, feelings and emotions play a much more important role than previously, since, in matters of importance, caring thinking enacts values and is equated with judgment. The three dimensions or modes of thinking, with their corresponding emphases on technique, invention and commitment, are said to be present in varying degrees in all higher-order thinking. Drawing on Dewey and Peirce, Lipman elaborates this model arguing that an enquiry-driven society requires critical, creative and caring thinking. These help build the individual's character structure of *reasonableness* and the social structure of *democracy*. For each type of thinking he identifies value–principles (criteria), which are set out in figure 4.2.

Lipman claims that the most relevant skill areas for educational purposes are: *enquiry, reasoning, information-organising* and *translation* (Lipman, 1991, p. 45):

Inquiry is a self-corrective practice in which a subject matter is investigated with the aim of discovering or inventing ways of dealing with what is problematic. The products of inquiry are judgments.

Reasoning is the process of ordering and coordinating what has been found out through the inquiry. It involves finding valid ways of extending and organising what has been discovered or invented while retaining its truth.

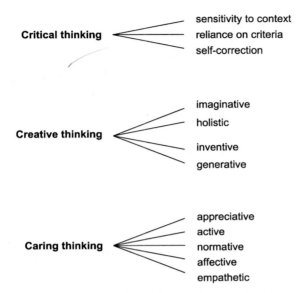

Fig. 4.2. Major modes of thinking (with criteria).

Concept formation involves organising information into relational clusters and then analysing and clarifying them so as to expedite their employment in understanding and judging. Conceptual thinking involves the relating of concepts to one another so as to form principles, criteria, arguments, explanations, and so on.

Translation involves carrying meanings over from one language or symbolic scheme or sense modality to another and yet retaining them intact. Interpretation becomes necessary when the translated meanings fail to make adequate sense in the new context in which they have been placed.

Lipman identifies a list of 13 dispositions which are fostered by the meaningfully orchestrated use of cognitive skills in a community of enquiry setting. These are:

- to wonder
- to be critical
- to respect others
- to be inventive
- to seek alternatives
- to be inquisitive

- to care for the tools of enquiry
- to cooperate intellectually
- to be committed to self-corrective method
- to feel a need for principles, ideals, reasons, and explanations
- to be imaginative
- to be appreciative
- to be consistent.

Could link with dialogic talk

Three kinds of relationship that a curriculum must incorporate are: 'symbolic relationships (e.g. linguistic, logical, and mathematical relationships); referential relationships (i.e. those between symbolic terms or systems and the world they refer to); and existential relationships (i.e. connections between things in the world': see Lipman, 2003, p. 61).

Arguing that a taxonomy of judgment 'would be invaluable for curriculum development in the cognitive aspects of education' (2003, p. 61), Lipman offers us instead the following list of procedures which he claims students need to practise:

- prejudice reduction
- classification
- evaluation
- criterion identification
- sensitisation to context
- analogical reasoning
- self-correction
- sensitisation to consequences
- adjusting means and ends
- adjusting parts and wholes.

Review for portfolios.

Lipman blames 'the Piagetian empire in education' for promoting the widespread belief that young children are 'not capable of monitoring their own thought, of giving reasons for their opinions, or of putting logical operations into practice' (Lipman, 2003, p. 40). He claims that teachers have misinterpreted Bloom's taxonomy as a theory of developmental stages, so that it might not be until late secondary school or even college before they 'arrive at the adult level, the pinnacle of the entire process, the evaluational stage'. He argues strongly for a non-hierarchical approach to excellence in thinking, claiming that even in the preschool years children are potentially young philosophers.

He considers *Philosophy for Children* to be an approach that goes beyond critical thinking in its emphasis on the purpose as well as the process of thinking:

When I first became interested in this field, I thought that children could do no better than 'Critical Thinking' – that is, having their thinking trained to make it more rigorous, consistent and coherent. But critical thinking contains no concept formation, no formal logic, and no study of the works of traditional philosophy, all of which I have endeavoured to supply in Philosophy for Children. Critical Thinking does not lead children back into philosophy, and yet it is my contention that children will not settle for anything less. Nor should they have to. Critical Thinking seeks to make the child's mind more precise; philosophy deepens it and makes it grow. (Lipman, 2004)

The programme consists of a series of sequential narratives designed to introduce children and young people to key philosophical ideas and concepts. The narratives provide the stimulus for children's questions, which then form the agenda for the lesson as they are discussed. As his work has developed, Lipman has become more interested in the affective as well as the cognitive aspects of thinking and he stresses the role of relationships in fostering dispositions that sustain enquiry.

[in the community of inquiry] the teacher's main role is that of a cultivator of judgment who transcends rather than rejects right–wrong answers in the sense of caring more for the process of inquiry itself than the answer that might be right or wrong at a given time. It is the behaviour of such a teacher . . . that is especially cherished . . . it has an integrity they are quick to appreciate. (Lipman, 1991, p. 219)

Evaluation

The model of critical, creative and caring thinking has an intuitive appeal, since it does not separate the emotional from the rational. In this way it resonates with Gardner's ideas of intrapersonal and interpersonal intelligence and with the 'emotional intelligence' of Salovey and Mayer (1990). Lipman's 'caring thinking' also encompasses a wide range of dispositions which resemble those proposed by other critical thinking theorists.

Critical thinking and creative thinking are for Lipman both forms of enquiry, while caring thinking facilitates it. Reasoning, concept formation and translation are clearly involved in all three kinds of thinking, but Lipman does not explore these relationships in any detail, either conceptually or pedagogically.

For Lipman the goal and product of thinking is good judgment, and judgments are of meanings. He values thinking and learning as the active search for meaning, but goes further, arguing that identifying relationships and forming judgments (Lipman, 1991, p. 62) is an essential aspect of schooling in order to develop meaning and understanding. Education, he argues, is a mode of enquiry, so philosophy as a mode of enquiry into that enquiry should form an essential component in the intellectual growth of young people. The aim of education for Lipman is to foster reasonableness in personal character and democracy in social character. For Lipman reasonableness encompasses the search for meaning, intellectual rigour, the disposition to be open to argument and a concern to form judgments that sustain democracy.

Lipman refers to a number of philosophers and psychologists who emphasise the role of language and social interaction in the formation of an individual's intellect and character as influences on his thinking (Lipman, 2004). Dewey and Vygotsky were key figures in the formation of Lipman's approach. From Dewey he takes the emphasis on the need for experience to be mediated effectively if learning is to take place; the importance of working in a community of enquiry; and the idea of teaching and learning as a democratic process.

Educators who see learning as a socially interactive process will accept Lipman's claim that reasoning based on logic only becomes alive when through dialogue people interpret ideas in different ways on the basis of different assumptions and beliefs. A case can also be made, however, that understanding and reasoning can be enhanced by access to existing bodies of knowledge and by personal reflection as well as through interpersonal dialogue.

Sternberg and Bhana (1986) expressed concern about the methodological quality of 20 evaluation studies of *Philosophy for Children*, but Trickey and Topping (2004) were able to locate 10 controlled studies which yielded eight effect sizes. The mean effect size of 0.43 reflects moderate gains (close to the average for any educational intervention) on (in most cases) reading or reasoning tests. Other qualitative evaluations (Andrews et al., 1993; Baumfield, 2004) indicate that the community of enquiry approach appears to be successful in securing wider participation and sustained interaction in classroom dialogue, with a shift in focus from teacher-led to learner-centred education.

If Lipman is correct that effective pedagogy for all learners depends on experiential learning through participation in enquiry as well as from the philosophical study of reasoning, concept-formation and judgment, there are profound implications for education.

Summary: Lipman

Purpose and structure	Some key features	Relevance for teachers and learning
Main purpose(s): • to make learning meaningful • to encourage active enquiry • to promote democracy • to encourage good judgment	Terminology: • clear • simple	Intended audience: • teachers of school children from K-12, but his methods are also used with adults
Domains addressed: • cognitive • conative • affective	Presentation: • enthusiastic, personally-committed writing • use of narrative to convey philosophical ideas	Contexts: • education • citizenship
Broad categories covered: • self-engagement and self-regulation • reflective thinking • productive thinking • building understanding	Theory base: • Dewey • Vygotsky • Bloom	Pedagogical stance: • learner-centred enquiry-based learning using dialogue and discussion • democratic teaching, with the teacher as facilitator not instructor

Classification by:	Values:	Practical illustrations for teachers:
• lower or higher-order thinking • modes of thinking • types of disposition	• reasonableness • democracy • education as the communal pursuit of the classical virtues of truth, beauty and goodness	• resources available in a series of separate narrative-based age-related resources and teacher handbooks

Paul's model of critical thinking

Description and intended use

Richard Paul's model of critical thinking has evolved over a number of years and remains a work in progress. His definition of critical thinking gives an insight into his underpinning philosophy of education and contains a valuable distinction between two kinds of critical thinking.

Critical thinking is disciplined self-directed thinking which exemplifies the perfections of thinking appropriate to a particular mode or domain of thinking. It comes in two forms. If the thinking is disciplined to serve the interests of a particular individual or group, to the exclusion of other relevant persons and groups, I call it *sophistic* or *weak sense* critical thinking. If the thinking is disciplined to take into account the interests of diverse people or groups, I call it *fair-minded* or *strong sense* critical thinking. (Paul, 1993, p. 33).

Paul's 1993 model has four parts: *elements of reasoning* (sometimes referred to as 'elements of thought'); *standards of critical thinking*; *intellectual abilities*; and *intellectual traits*. The first three categories focus on what is essential to critical thinking, while the last dimension focuses on what it is to be a critical thinker.

Elements of reasoning

This is what Paul refers to as the 'parts' of thinking or *the fundamental structures of human thought*. He maintains that these eight elements are always present in human thinking and that the ability to recognise these elements of reasoning is essential to critical thinking. Paul and

Elder (2001, p. 53) summarise this interrelated set of elements in the following statement:

Whenever you are reasoning, you are trying to accomplish some purpose, within a point of view, using concepts or ideas. You are focused on some question, issue or problem, using information to come to conclusions, based on assumptions, all of which has implications.

Standards of critical thinking

The 12 standards in Paul's model are an attempt to identify what constitutes the *quality* component of critical thinking. Unlike the *elements of reasoning* which Paul claims to be universal, the following list of standards seeks to encompass those that are the most fundamental:

- clarity
- precision
- specificity
- accuracy
- relevance
- consistency

- logic
- depth
- completeness
- significance
- adequacy (for purpose)
- fairness.

In order to learn to reason well, it is necessary to gain mastery of both the *elements of reasoning* and the *standards of critical thinking*.

Intellectual abilities

According to Paul, an ability is composed of a process, plus an object, plus a standard. Someone can have the *ability* to drive (process) a truck (object) safely (standard). Nosich (2000) proposes that an *intellectual ability* would be the ability, for instance, to identify (process) a conclusion (object) accurately (standard). In Paul's model, *abilities* (higher-order thinking skills) rest on a prior understanding of the elements and standards of critical thinking.

Although the lists of macro- and micro-cognitive strategies do not appear in Paul's most recent 1993 model of critical thinking, they are shown in table 4.5, since they are rich in detail compared with those of other authors. They are intended as an aid for redesigning lessons, to ensure that critical thinking is required.

166 Frameworks for Thinking

Table 4.5. Cognitive strategies (formerly 'elements of critical thinking')

Macro-abilities	Micro-abilities
• Refining generalisations and avoiding over-simplifications	• Comparing and contrasting ideals with actual practice
• Comparing analogous situations: transferring insights to new contexts	• Thinking precisely about thinking: using critical vocabulary
• Developing one's perspective: creating or exploring beliefs, arguments or theories	• Noting significant similarities and differences
• Clarifying issues, conclusions, or beliefs	• Examining or evaluating assumptions
• Clarifying and analysing the meanings of words or phrases	• Distinguishing relevant from irrelevant facts
• Developing criteria for evaluation: clarifying values and standards	• Making plausible inferences, predictions or interpretations
• Evaluating the credibility of sources of information	• Giving reasons and evaluating evidence and alleged facts
• Questioning deeply: raising or pursuing root or significant questions	• Recognising contradictions
• Analysing or evaluating arguments, interpretations, beliefs, or theories	• Exploring implications and consequences
• Generating or assessing solutions	
• Analysing or evaluating actions or policies	
• Reading critically: clarifying or critiquing texts	
• Listening critically: the art of silent dialogue	
• Making interdisciplinary connections	
• Practising Socratic discussion: clarifying and questioning beliefs, theories, or perspectives	
• Reasoning dialogically: comparing perspectives, interpretations, or theories	
• Reasoning dialectically: comparing perspectives, interpretations, or theories	

Intellectual traits

The final dimension of Paul's model focuses on what it is to *be* a critical thinker. He has identified a number of affective traits that he considers to be essential to 'strong sense' critical thinking (Elder and Paul, 1998, p. 34):

- intellectual humility
- intellectual courage
- intellectual empathy
- intellectual integrity
- intellectual perseverance
- faith in reason
- fairmindedness.

These are not things a person does, but describe fundamental dispositions. These 'traits of a disciplined mind' are what Paul calls the affective and moral dimensions of critical thinking. Paul (1991) claims that there are many ways in which teachers can foster these traits of mind. To do this successfully, he advocates a re-conceptualisation of the nature of teaching and learning in every context of school life, involving a move from a didactic approach to one based on a critical theory of education. Paul presents the traits of the disciplined mind as ideals to strive towards. He outlines six stages of critical thinking, moving from the unreflective thinker to the master thinker. According to Paul, master thinkers will only emerge when society begins to value and reward these qualities of thinking. Given the extent of deep social conditioning, he believes it unlikely that anyone currently meets his definition of master thinker.

Evaluation

Paul's model of critical thinking takes account of cognitive, affective and conative components. He is aware of the importance of being sensitive to the circumstances in which thinking occurs. His lists of abilities and traits do not have any significant omissions when compared with those of Ennis (1998) or Perkins, Jay and Tishman (1993). Although Paul does not use the term 'metacognition', his account of intellectual integrity does recognise it implicitly through his emphasis on reflection and self-awareness.

Nosich (2000) believes that it is because Paul's model of critical thinking is concept-based (as opposed to having rules, procedures or steps to follow), that it is effective in curriculum development. The model is extremely flexible, applicable to any subject matter and to any level of thinking. Nosich uses Paul's concept of evidence to illustrate his point. Asking a student to 'identify the evidence a conclusion is based upon' is a critical thinking step. The ability to do it well is a higher-order thinking skill, but is limited, in that there are many other things students should be able to do with evidence, such as realise that more evidence is required or balance the weight of conflicting evidence. Paul's solution is to make the concept of evidence an essential part of all thinking processes. Nosich (2000) believes that the ability to think in terms of the concept of evidence allows one to think about evidence in a range of settings, at different levels of expertise and to gain further insight into the concept of evidence itself.

Paul is one of a number of philosophers whom Thayer-Bacon criticises for their 'Euro-western cultural bias' (1998, p. 125) and a belief in rational thought as the dominant mode of thinking within a critical thinking framework. It is evident from Paul's definition of critical thinking and his other work, including the development of a taxonomy of Socratic questioning, that he sits firmly in the rationalist camp. For Paul, the spirit of critical thinking is to have the confidence in one's ability to use reason appropriately to solve problems and answer questions. He acknowledges that there have been criticisms of critical thinking for being too Western in its orientation, not dealing with creativity, ignoring the role of emotion in thought and failing to address feminist or sociological insights. However, he claims that previous attempts to widen the scope of critical thinking to accommodate these concerns meant sacrificing some of the rigour found in formal and informal logic courses.

Paul's major contribution to the area of critical thinking is his idea of 'weak' versus 'strong sense' critical thinking. The latter is what Paul refers to as the ability to discover and contest one's own egocentric and socio-centric habits of thought. Paul (1991, p. 77) claims that his nine traits of thought, which are moral commitments and intellectual virtues, transfer thinking from 'a selfish, narrow-minded foundation to a broad open-minded foundation'.

The clear language and writing style make Paul's work accessible without sacrificing conceptual clarity. It is unlikely that his writing would prove a barrier to anyone with an interest in critical thinking. Those already committed to teaching critical thinking will find Paul's work helpful and possibly inspirational, given its emphasis on 'strong sense' thinking.

While Paul offers some teaching strategies to support the development of pupils' thinking, his aim is not to tinker with classroom practice by proposing thinking skills programmes. His goal is a reworking of education where students construct knowledge through the application of their own reasoning rather than through transmission of information by the teacher. This calls for a re-evaluation of what is judged important in both education and more broadly valued in society.

Summary: Paul

Purpose and structure	Some key features	Relevance for teachers and learning
Main purpose(s): • to provide a model of critical thinking • to justify the importance of critical thinking in education	**Terminology:** • clear and straightforward language	**Intended audience:** • teachers • students
Domains addressed: • cognitive • affective • conative	**Presentation:** • through a series of articles and books	**Contexts:** • education • citizenship
Broad categories covered: • reflective thinking • productive thinking • building understanding • information-gathering	**Theory base:** • philosophical	**Pedagogical stance:** • critical thinking needs to underpin education and be the basis for enquiry

Classification by:	Values:	Practical illustrations for teachers:
• elements of reasoning • standards of critical thinking • intellectual abilities and intellectual traits	• belief in reason and rationality	• some teaching strategies outlined

Jewell's reasoning taxonomy for gifted children

Description and intended use

In a web-posted conference paper, Jewell (1996) outlines a reasoning taxonomy for gifted education. This is presented, largely from a philosophical perspective, in response to a perceived need to understand how gifted students think and reason. Jewell sees his taxonomy being applied to text-based and other classroom activities which have been designed to provide a foundation for advanced reasoning (to determine what the activities are trying to achieve and how best to match them to student needs).

Jewell considers the nature v. nurture debate and argues that giftedness manifests as learned behaviour. Following Lipman, he identifies the types of behaviour which may be characteristic of giftedness as:

- creative thinking
- logical / rational / critical thinking
- caring thinking (interpersonal skills and moral behaviour).

The paper focuses on critical thinking, but Jewell argues that creative, critical and caring thinking are not mutually exclusive and should be regarded as complementary aspects of human behaviour. He accepts Ennis' definition of critical thinking as 'reasonable and reflective thinking focused on deciding what to believe or do' (Ennis, 1985, p. 45). It has the characteristics of being purposeful, ordering information in order to produce a result and providing reasons for adopting a belief or course of action.

Jewell's taxonomy or 'overview of reasoning objectives, strategies and habits available to the advanced thinker' (Jewell, 1996) is summarised in table 4.6.

Table 4.6. Jewell's reasoning taxonomy for gifted children

Section A - *the objectives of reasoning*
To discover how things work in order:
1. to plan
2. to problem-solve
3. to decide
4. to recommend
5. to communicate

Section B - *reasoning strategies*
1. Community of Inquiry (presented by Jewell as a five-point code)
2. Model construction
3. Argument construction
4. Considering the evidence
5. Moral reasoning

Section C - *reasoning dispositions/attitudes/habits*
Adopting metacognition as a habit, which involves:
1. questioning own position
2. seeking and offering justification for views
3. constructing or adopting alternative models
4. monitoring own assumptions and thinking habits
5. changing one's mind for good reasons
6. empathising with the beliefs, values and thinking processes of other people

The exceptionally competent reasoner is seen as a self-directed, self-disciplined, self-monitoring, and self-corrective thinker. Jewell identifies the components of thinking as: *reasoning; purposeful thinking; ordering information; producing results; and adopting a belief or course of action.* He claims that such a list helps teachers to foster reasoning strategies.

Jewell argues that to enable gifted students to develop a disposition for reasoning and mental self-management, a qualitatively different curriculum is required. A school-wide environment should value open-mindedness, objective thinking, impartiality, intellectual integrity and independent judgment.

Evaluation

This reasoning taxonomy is also described by Jewell as an overview, and it is not a taxonomy in the strict sense of being organised at each level by a single principle. It is therefore more appropriate to call it an overview, framework or model.

If compared, for example, to Sternberg's (2001) theory of giftedness as developing expertise, which explores the relationship between abilities and expertise, Jewell's model is limited in scope. However, he deliberately limits his focus to the reasoning involved in critical thinking, and has succeeded in providing a simple framework in which there are no major omissions. While Jewell does not break down reasoning into detailed categories in terms of logical structure, he does identify the main functions of reasoning. Although he is not fully consistent in his use of terminology within each section of the taxonomy, a comparison of his model with that of Ennis (1987) reveals a concise coverage of the field of critical thinking and the omission of only a few dispositions, such as seeking to be well-informed, precise and relevant.

The structure of the framework is a logical one, in that using strategies to achieve the purposes of reasoning helps students develop the dispositions or habits of mind which in turn facilitate the ongoing process of enquiry. The inclusion of purposes is a useful feature, which is taken for granted in many of the taxonomies we have evaluated.

Although it is presented as a taxonomy for gifted children, there is no reason why its use should be limited to that field. It is essentially an overview of the nature and purposes of reasoning, an activity in which people engage both as individuals and in groups.

Jewell's view of giftedness accords with the increasing acceptance that talents are not automatically transformed into high performances, but are dependent on specific environmental factors (Howe et al., 1998).

Enquiry and understanding are presented as the superordinate goals of reasoning. Jewell's phrase 'to discover how things work' can be interpreted as covering human behaviour and social interaction, but rather unfortunately suggests a mechanistic model which does not sit well with the view that good reasoning depends on the three Cs of critical, creative and caring thinking. This view is grounded in Lipman's work (Lipman, 1995) and is consistent with Renzulli's definition of giftedness in terms of high intelligence, creativity and task commitment (Renzulli, 1975; 1986). Jewell's emphasis on reasoning strategies and reasoning dispositions accords with mainstream theoretical and research orientations in the fields of critical thinking and gifted education. For example, Neber and Schommer-Aikins' study of self-regulated learning in highly gifted students (2002) indicates the importance of exploration and discovery activities to determine motivational and epistemological prerequisites for self-regulatory strategies.

This taxonomy of reasoning is intended to help teachers understand the claims made for texts and classroom practices intended to advance thinking skills. The first question to be asked is whether the claims relate to reasoning: if not, the framework does not apply. We have no information as to whether educationists have found practical uses for the taxonomy, but its economy and clear descriptions and explanations are commendable.

Summary: Jewell

Purpose and structure	Some key features	Relevance for teachers and learning
Main purpose(s): • to help teachers understand a how gifted students think and reason b claims made for published materials	**Terminology:** • clear • simple • not fully consistent	**Intended audience:** • teachers • designers of instruction
Domains addressed: • cognitive • affective • conative	**Presentation:** • understandable by teachers and learners • economical	**Contexts:** • education • citizenship
Broad categories covered: • self-engagement • reflective thinking • productive thinking	**Theory base:** • Ennis • Lipman	**Pedagogical stance:** • Lipman's Community of Enquiry

Classification by:	Values:	Practical illustrations for teachers:
• types of knowledge • types of cognitive skill • dispositional qualities	• seeking and giving reasons • humanism • independence of thought	• very few

Petty's six-phase model of the creative process

Description and intended use

Petty uses the term 'creative' in a broad sense to refer to invention, design, problem-solving and entrepreneurial initiatives, as well as to the creative arts and household decision-making. According to him (Petty, 1997), the creative process has six phases: inspiration; clarification; evaluation; distillation; incubation; and perspiration. These are experienced in no fixed order and usually several times during a particular piece of creative work. To be successful (avoiding blocks and being flexibly responsive), different mental attitudes ('mindsets') are said to be needed at each phase, as illustrated in table 4.7. In that table 'Perspiration' is placed next to 'Evaluation' to bring out the interplay which Petty claims often takes place between them.

Although he writes largely for educators, Petty's audience includes people in the business sector, where the need to encourage creative thinking is widely recognised. His purpose is more practical than theoretical, but he does seek to portray the creative process as complex and variable, yet disciplined, requiring above all flexibility in making appropriate choices at different phases of problem finding and problem-solving. While he acknowledges that there are individual personality factors which affect 'mindsets', he believes that teachers can help bring about massive improvements in learners' creative processes and products. To this end he offers a range of strategies and tools to help learners appreciate the value of different mindsets and to understand the need to switch between them.

Evaluation

Petty provides a balanced view of creativity in that he sees that it involves achieving synergy between apparently polar opposites:

Table 4.7. Petty's six phases with desirable accompanying mindsets

Phase	Description	Mindsets
Inspiration	you research and generate many ideas	spontaneous, experimental, intuitive and risk-taking
Clarification	you focus on your goals	strategic, unhurried and logical, not afraid to question
Distillation	you decide which of your ideas to work on	positive and intrepid about ideas: strategic about choices
Incubation	you leave the work alone	unhurried, trusting that a way forward will emerge, forgetful
Perspiration	you work determinedly on your best ideas	uncritical, enthusiastic and responsive to shortcomings
Evaluation	you review your work and learn from it	self-critical, analytic, positive and willing to learn

divergent and convergent thinking; playfulness and goal-directedness; freedom and constraints; unconscious and conscious thought. His model provides an implicit definition of creativity in that all phases and their linked 'mindsets' are seen as essential, while uncreative people tend to consider few ideas and work with a fixed mindset and without a clear sense of purpose.

It is not difficult to defend the claim that creative work necessarily involves varying amounts of planning, monitoring and evaluating in addition to inspiration (or insight). Perhaps the most controversial claim made by Petty is that creative work should always include an incubation phase. While this may be desirable, it is hardly a necessary pre-condition for creative thought.

The six phases are not intended to be mutually exclusive and some may include others. For example, 'distillation' and 'evaluation' clearly overlap and Petty acknowledges that 'perspiration' usually involves further 'inspiration', 'distillation' and 'clarification'. Similarly, there is considerable overlap in the descriptors used by Petty to characterise mindsets (e.g. 'positive', 'strategic', 'unhurried'). This reflects the fact that creativity is a complex and holistic process which cannot be defined with any precision using everyday language. As Rhodes (1961) argued, creativity goes beyond person, process and product. Domain is also important, as is 'press', the interaction between people and environment (Rhodes, 1961).

The links posited by Petty between phases and desirable accompanying mindsets have a common-sense appeal but little empirical support other than anecdotal evidence. Petty claims that many learners adopt the 'wrong' mindsets and can correct bad habits through practice with various techniques (including several originated by de Bono). This is an important but largely unsubstantiated claim.

Petty does not compare his formulation to those of others, but there is a clear affinity between his model and those of Williams (1970) and Herrmann (1989). All three authors value flexibility, see effective thinking as a whole-brain activity and link modes of thinking with mental attitudes. They also believe that it is possible to develop and strengthen what Williams calls 'affective behaviours' and Petty 'mindsets', but are now more often referred to as dispositions or 'habits of mind'.

The examples provided by Petty to assist with the crucial 'inspiration' phase seem to emphasise individual rather than collaborative thinking, but he correctly points to research evidence which shows that brainstorming is often ineffective. Social and cultural aspects of creativity are, however, generally underplayed, especially when compared with the work of Csikszentmihali (1990), Herrmann (1996) and Craft (2000).

By providing a practical framework which teachers can easily explain to learners, Petty has performed a very useful service. His model has cross-curricular relevance and can easily be applied in fields as diverse as drama and computerised brainstorming. It succeeds in its aim of popularising the idea of 'little c' creativity (Craft, 2000) as a form of productive thinking and action which is 'one of life's greatest challenges and one of its greatest rewards' (Petty, 1998, p. 278).

Summary: Petty

Purpose and structure	Some key features	Relevance for teachers and learning
Main purpose(s): • to encourage practitioners to understand and foster creativity as a 'how-to' skill	**Terminology:** • very clear and jargon-free	**Intended audience:** • students • teachers • trainers
Domains addressed: • cognitive • affective • conative	**Presentation:** • full of examples, both graphic and textual • practical strategies offered under sub-headings	**Contexts:** • education • work • citizenship • recreation
Broad categories covered: • self-regulation • reflective thinking • productive thinking • building understanding • information-gathering	**Theory base:** • cognitivist • Maslow's hierarchy of human needs	**Pedagogical stance:** • learning as active meaning-making • guided discovery • practice and repeated success are important
Classification by: • psychological process	**Values:** • humanistic: people need to explore and express meanings and to make things • self-direction and self-improvement	**Practical illustrations for teachers:** • worked out in some detail

Bailin's intellectual resources for critical thinking

Description and intended use

Bailin is interested in philosophical enquiries into critical thinking, creativity and aesthetic education and she considers critical and creative thinking to be overlapping concepts. Her work is aimed at establishing clarity regarding the concept of critical thinking and suggesting proposals for an appropriate pedagogy. She has concentrated on demonstrating a framework for critical thinking rather than a systematic taxonomy. Bailin does not offer lists of characteristics, as this would be inconsistent with her essential position that critical thinking is a highly contextualised, normative endeavour, but she does identify necessary intellectual resources. Whilst she is concerned with the pedagogical implications of her work and has provided guidelines for policy makers (Bailin, Case, Coombs and Daniels, 1993), she has not produced any teaching materials, although her colleagues (Case and Daniels, 2000) have edited a collection of materials for use in schools.

She argues that if critical and creative thinking are to be developed, then, 'educators need a defensible conception of critical thinking and a perspicuous account of the characteristics or qualities necessary for being a critical thinker' (Bailin, Case, Coombs and Daniels, 1999b). Her stated purpose is to provide a robust conceptual basis for critical and creative thinking; one which demonstrates the flaws in approaches to critical thinking that favour a pedagogy based on identifying and teaching specific skills.

Bailin defines competence in critical thinking as having the required intellectual resources to accomplish certain tasks adequately along with the habits of mind to apply them appropriately. The intellectual resources she identifies are:

- background knowledge
- knowledge of critical thinking standards (these are described as 'cultural artefacts')
- possession of critical concepts
- knowledge of strategies/heuristics useful in thinking critically
- certain habits of mind.

She provides a representative list of these habits of mind, which she says have been drawn from a number of sources:

- respect for reason and truth
- respect for high-quality products and performances

- an enquiring attitude
- open-mindedness
- fair-mindedness
- independent-mindedness
- respect for others in group enquiry and deliberation
- respect for legitimate intellectual authority
- an intellectual work-ethic

    (Bailin et al., 1999b)

As such, her approach conceptualises critical thinking as involving the cognitive, affective and conative domains. She locates her work alongside that of Ennis, Paul and Lipman, but also claims some distinctive aspects based on her emphasis on the role of intellectual resources and the need for infusion of critical thinking into the curriculum.

In her work, Bailin sets out what she considers to be the limitations and misconceptions inherent in the cognitive, psychological and philosophical approaches to critical thinking which use the language of skills and processes. For Bailin the ambiguity and abstraction of terms such as 'skill' and 'mental process' are the main source of difficulty in establishing a sound basis for critical thinking in education (Bailin, Case, Coombs and Daniels, 1999a). When 'skill' is understood as proficiency, being a skilled thinker is relatively unproblematic, but the positing of general skills in thinking presents difficulties because it suggests a separation from the intellectual resources employed in critical practice (Bailin, 1998). It also has unfortunate consequences for pedagogy as it suggests that critical thinking can be improved by simply practising the skills. Bailin also objects to the idea that critical thinking consists of mental processes, on the grounds that this view of thinking fails to accommodate reasoned judgment which is the essential characteristic of critical thinking (Bailin, 1998) and cannot be made routine (Bailin et al., 1999a). Processes serve no useful purpose in pedagogy as they are an example of: 'unwarranted reification – reading back from outcomes to mysterious antecedent processes' (Bailin et al., 1999a). Whilst it may be the case that critical thinking situations may have common features, speaking in terms of processes is of no value.

Critical thinking as the utilisation of general procedures fares no better in the critique of Bailin and her colleagues on the grounds that it understates the significance of contextual factors and begs the question of the quality of the outcomes of their application. The critical thinker is someone who can make judgments with reference to criteria and standards that distinguish thoughtful evaluations from sloppy ones, fruitful classification systems from trivial ones, and so on. Whilst she does include knowledge of strategies or heuristics in her list of intellectual resources, Bailin also stresses that they should be those deemed to be useful in thinking critically and suggests that most procedures or heuristics are likely to be either so vague as to be pointless or so specific as to have little generalisability.

Bailin claims that an approach to critical thinking focused on intellectual resources rather than on skills reframes the issue of generalisability. The question is not, then, whether a certain supposed mental ability transfers to a variety of contexts but rather, what constellation of resources is required in particular contexts in response to particular challenges? (Bailin, 1998). Critical thinking is coterminous with increased competence in the mastery of the standards for judging what to do in a particular context.

Essentially, critical thinking for Bailin is the induction into the public tradition of enquiry, so educators should focus on the induction of students into complex critical practices developed within 'our culture' for disciplining thinking and increasing its fruitfulness (Bailin et al., 1999b). Critical thinking is emancipatory in the sense that it enables students to deploy a carefully articulated set of intellectual resources, enter into critical discussions and so make reasoned judgments. Although initiation into cultural critical practices begins long before children attend school, Bailin sets out the implications for pedagogy:

What is essential is that appropriate habits of mind and appropriate use of intellectual resources are exemplified for students, and that they are given guided practice in critical thinking in appropriately rich contexts. (Bailin et al., 1999b)

She outlines three components of a critical thinking pedagogy:

- engaging students in dealing with tasks that call for reasoned judgment or assessment
- helping them to develop intellectual resources for dealing with these tasks
- providing an environment in which critical thinking is valued and students are encouraged to engage in critical discussion.

Bailin is, as we have seen, opposed to the teaching of critical thinking skills or processes and sees only limited value in developing strategies and heuristics. However, she also warns against assuming that the highly contextualised nature of critical thinking means that it will automatically be developed through immersion in a subject. There is a need for an explicit pedagogy for critical thinking, particularly given the nature of subjects as conceived within the typical school curriculum, which are not necessarily synonymous with the traditions of enquiry that support the development of critical practices.

Evaluation

Bailin locates her work in the field of critical and creative thinking and seeks to show where existing approaches have strengths and limitations. She follows other writers in distinguishing between knowledge, concepts, strategies and dispositions (habits of mind). Her easily understandable framework can be usefully compared to the more detailed work of Paul (Paul, 1993). What is distinctive about Bailin's contribution is the emphasis she places on critical thinking as induction into cultural, critical practices and traditions of enquiry. She takes account of the cognitive, affective and conative aspects of critical thinking and provides detailed accounts of the first two but does not develop the idea of how to engage learners in critical thinking in any depth. There is a suggestion that critical thinking is a cultural phenomenon that can engage learners from their early years, so it is a question of their becoming more conscious and effective in its use. Bailin's analysis of the current situation regarding critical thinking (at least in the USA and Canada) is coherent and persuasive and she offers some suggestions for establishing appropriate pedagogy for critical thinking.

In Bailin's writing it is sometimes difficult to distinguish between the components of critical thinking and what others might simply describe as a liberal education. This is particularly evident in the list of intellectual resources, which can be seen as extremely general and hard to operationalise. Bailin is not, however, alone in exhibiting this tendency and it would seem to be the case that those writers who position themselves at the philosophical, normative end of the critical thinking spectrum avoid what they see to be the pitfalls of a skills-based approach by losing the specificity of what the teacher should instil or develop in learners. When Bailin does offer more focused advice and recommendations, the distinction between intellectual resources and what other writers would call skills or mental abilities begins to be eroded.

Bailin's framework/model relies on concepts such as strategies and dispositions which can be reified just as much as those which she criticises so strongly (thinking skills, processes and procedures). It is therefore unlikely to resolve what is often a sterile philosophical debate regarding the existence of generalisable critical thinking skills. However, teachers may find her framework helpful when thinking about how to provide experiences and guidance that can promote critical thinking and as a stimulus for their own pedagogical enquiry.

Bailin's writing is clear and accessible but does assume prior knowledge of approaches to critical thinking. Unfortunately, the practical examples she herself offers (such as the lesson on logging in British Columbia in Bailin et al., 1999b) fall somewhat short of the vision outlined elsewhere in her writing.

Summary: Bailin

Purpose and structure	Some key features	Relevance for teachers and learning
Main purpose(s): • to provide greater conceptual clarity so that educators can make informed choices and develop an appropriate pedagogy for critical thinking	**Terminology:** • assumes prior knowledge of existing approaches to critical thinking	**Intended audience:** • educators • policy makers

Domains addressed:	Presentation:	Contexts:
• cognitive • affective • conative	• clear and accessible writing	• education
Broad categories covered:	Theory base:	Pedagogical stance:
• self-regulation • reflective thinking • productive thinking	• refers explicitly to Paul, Ennis and Lipman and echoes Dewey in her emphasis on enquiry and habits of mind	• emancipatory role of teacher who should model critical thinking and provide a range of rich contexts in which learners can exercise judgment • does not agree with the teaching of isolated skills or general heuristics
Classification by:	Values:	Practical illustrations for teachers:
• type of intellectual resource	• induction through education into the public tradition of enquiry and cultural critical practices	• limited examples in Bailin's work, but colleagues have produced a companion volume with classroom strategies

Some issues for further investigation

- To what extent do the approaches privilege particular forms of thinking, particularly logical reasoning, to the detriment of other traditions?
- What is the place of scholarship and tradition in critical and productive thinking?
- Can these theorists be placed on a continuum from individualism to social responsibility?
- Can (and should) programmes for critical and productive thinking be divorced from culturally specific, normative views of what constitutes 'good thinking'?

- Do the differences between some of the approaches outweigh any similarities, the contrast between de Bono and Lipman or Bailin for example, and so challenge the parameters of this family?
- What are the similarities and differences between a psychological and a philosophical treatment of critical thinking (Halpern and Paul, for example)?
- Does any treatment of creative thinking include important features which are not found elsewhere?
- How do conceptualisations of *tools* differ from conceptualisations of *abilities*?
- What does *reflection* add to good thinking?
- What moral judgments are implied by the lists of dispositions provided by different authors?
- Which of these frameworks is the most analytic and which the most intuitive – and why?
- How far have we progressed in developing appropriate, rigorous assessments of critical and productive thinking?
- How do you explain the wide take-up of certain frameworks and not others?

5

Frameworks dealing with cognitive structure and/or development

Introduction

This family group consists of a set of frameworks that are less easily contained within a single defining category. All but two (Belenky, and King and Kitchener) were developed by psychologists, but they differ considerably in aims and epistemological assumptions. Some were developed by interpreting interviews and questionnaires, while others reflect the content of psychometric test batteries, especially intelligence tests. Some deal with thinking across the lifespan, while others are specifically concerned with how adults think. Finally, the frameworks differ to the extent that they emphasise genetic or environmental influences. What ties them together, however, is that they are predominantly concerned with the nature of cognition; its structure and development.

The influence of psychological theories about thinking and learning extends across disciplines and can be recognised in the fields of instructional design and productive thinking which are covered in Chapters 3 and 4. Here we draw attention to some major figures in academic psychology, some of whom (like Piaget and Gardner) have had a major impact on educational theory and practice. Others have had relatively little impact, perhaps because they have pursued ideas for their own sake rather than being constrained by political correctness or fashion.

One subgroup of authors (Carroll, Guilford and Gardner) focus on identifying what constitutes 'intelligence'. Carroll and Guilford employ factor analytic techniques to identify underlying components of intelligence tests, but come up with very different results. Carroll's examination of large numbers of datasets supports the central beliefs of 'g' theorists (Carroll, 2003); in contrast, Guilford identifies as many as 180 subcategories. Gardner shares Guilford's belief in a multifactorial conception of intelligence, but eschews the psychometric approach, contending that there are many forms of intelligence that conventional tests fail to examine.

A second set of frameworks (Piaget, Perry, King and Kitchener, Koplowitz) is concerned with the development of thinking through increasingly more complex phases or stages. While employing rather different definitions, frameworks and methodologies, they draw upon the disciplines of both psychology and philosophy in examining 'personal epistemological development and epistemological beliefs: how individuals come to know, the theories and beliefs they hold about knowing, and the manner in which such epistemological premises are a part of and an influence on the cognitive processes of thinking and reasoning' (Hofer and Pintrich, 1997, p. 88).

The father of this approach was Piaget, whose theory of 'genetic epistemology' was a powerful counter to the contemporary stranglehold of behaviourism (Hofer and Pintrich, 1997). Piaget's stage approach to development was an inspiration for theorists working in many domains of human functioning. Koplowitz's theory has a strong Piagetian basis but extends consideration of cognitive development into adulthood. However, Perry's theorising, based upon two longitudinal studies of epistemological development in college students, also had a major impact in the US. Perry's focus on male college students was followed up by Belenky's examination of women's ways of knowing (Belenky et al., 1986) and Baxter Magolda's examination of the beliefs of both men and women (Baxter Magolda, 1987; 1992). King and Kitchener's stage model of reflective judgment is also underpinned by epistemological concerns and reflects the influence of both Piaget and Perry (King and Kitchener, 1994).

Demetriou, a neo-Piagetian, draws upon psychometrics, information processing, stage, and sociocultural approaches in formulating a complex model of the developing mind. As we note in our evaluation of his model, he draws upon a diverse range of theorists, both from this and other families: Piaget, Carroll, Gardner, Sternberg, and Marzano.

Pintrich's framework is concerned with cognition, conation and affect, yet the over-arching emphasis is upon the operation of a cognitive process, self-regulation, within these domains. While he provides a series of phases, rather than stages, of self-regulation, Pintrich emphasises that these are not necessarily passed through in a linear sequence and phases may operate simultaneously.

We end our survey of frameworks with a composite presentation and evaluation of recent work on the structure, function and development of executive function. This is a key area of psychological research and holds the promise of bringing together different traditions in psychology: experimental; neuropsychological; differential; developmental; social; and even transpersonal. It also seeks to provide an empirical evidence base to inform philosophical accounts of consciousness and the self.

At times, appropriate allocation of frameworks to this family was problematic. While it was comparatively easy to rule out those that were designed for the purposes of instructional design or critical thinking, there was more debate and uncertainty about which should be regarded as 'all-embracing' frameworks. Locating Sternberg's theory was particularly difficult. His triarchic model of intelligence is clearly a model of cognitive structure, yet his model of abilities as developing expertise is much broader and has an applied as well as a theoretical purpose.

Time sequence of theoretical frameworks of cognitive structure and/or development

Piaget's stage model of cognitive development (1950)

There are three main stages in intellectual development: sensorimotor; representational; and formal. In middle childhood, thinking becomes logical rather than intuitive. Not all adults reach the formal operations stage and think in terms of abstract rules and systems.

Guilford's Structure of Intellect model (1956)

This is a three-dimensional model in which five cognitive operations work with four types of content to produce six types of product. The operations are: cognition; memory; divergent thinking; convergent thinking; and evaluation.

Perry's developmental scheme (1968)

The scheme consists of nine positions which liberal arts college students take up as they progress in intellectual and ethical development. They move from the modifying of 'either–or' dualism to the realising of relativism and then to the evolving of commitments.

Gardner's theory of multiple intelligences (1983)

Gardner identifies eight kinds of intellectual ability: verbal/linguistic; logical/mathematical; musical; visual/spatial; bodily/kinaesthetic; interpersonal; intrapersonal; and naturalist.

Koplowitz's theory of adult cognitive development (1984)

Koplowitz builds on Piaget's stage theory, but adds two postmodern stages beyond the formal operations stage – post-logical and unitary thinking. The stages reflect changes in how people understand causation, logic, relationships, problems, abstractions and boundaries.

Belenky's 'Women's Ways of Knowing' developmental model (1986)

Women in adult education tended to progress from: silence (a reaction to authority); to received knowledge; to subjective knowledge; to procedural knowledge (including separate and connected knowing); and finally to constructed knowledge.

Carroll's three-stratum theory of cognitive abilities (1993)

This theory has a well-founded empirical basis for thinking of cognitive tasks as making demands on narrow and/or broad abilities as well as on general intelligence.

Demetriou's integrated developmental model of the mind (1993)

For Demetriou, mind and personality interact at all levels of self-oriented and environment-oriented systems. There are long-term and working self systems, representational and regulatory. Progress through Piaget's stages can be seen in categorical, quantitative, causal, spatial, verbal, social and drawing 'modules'.

King and Kitchener's model of reflective judgment (1994)

This is a seven-stage model of progression in adolescent and adult reasoning. Assumptions about knowledge and strategies for solving ill-structured problems can move from pre-reflective through quasi-reflective to reflective stages.

Pintrich's general framework for self-regulated learning (2000)

Pintrich identifies four phases of self-regulation. Cognition, motivation/affect, behaviour and context can be regulated by: (1) forethought, planning and activation; (2) monitoring; (3) control; and (4) reaction and reflection.

Theories of executive function

The main components of executive function are: attention control; task analysis; strategic planning; monitoring progress and taking appropriate action; and maintaining mental flexibility in support of goal-directed or problem-solving behaviour. These processes take place in working memory.

Description and evaluation of theoretical frameworks of cognitive structure and/or development

Piaget's stage model of cognitive development

Description and intended use

For many, Piaget is *the* cognitive developmental psychologist of the twentieth century. Drawing upon biology, sociology and philosophy, his psychological theorising and methodologies revolutionised a field that was dominated by the contrasting perspectives of environmentalism and biological determinism. His 'clinical method' involving naturalistic observations of, and interviews with, children engaged in various intellectual tasks, originating in the 1920s, but not well known in the English speaking world until the 1950s, highlighted the value of seeing and understanding the world from the child's perspective.

At the heart of his theory of cognitive development was the notion that the child passed through a set of ordered, qualitatively different stages. Intellectually, the child was not seen as a young adult, but rather, as one employing very different cognitive structures and processes. The stage theory was first expressed in a series of lectures presented to French scholars during the Second World War (Brainerd, 2003, p. 257) and subsequently in a series of publications, most notably, *The Psychology of Intelligence*, published in 1950.

According to Piaget, development unfolds through a series of stages, characterising an invariant developmental sequence. The child must progress through each of the stages in exactly the same order and no stage can be missed out. The stages are associated with characteristic age periods although considerable individual differences can be observed.

During the **sensorimotor stage** (0–2 years) the individual is seen to pass through a stage of profound egocentrism whereby the child is unable to separate itself from its environment. As development in this period is so great, this period is divided into six substages from the newborn with built-in schemas and reflexes, to the comparatively sophisticated two-year old. During this period, the infant uses its motor and sensory skills to explore and gain understanding of its world and thus physical experiences are the basis for the development of knowledge. Their senses are largely unrelated to the actions that they perform on objects. Thus, when objects are out of the young infant's field of vision or reach, they are considered to no longer exist. When an infant begins to search for objects outside of the field of vision (at about 8 months), he or she is said to have acquired object permanence.

During the **pre-operational stage** (2 to 7 years) the child is still dominated by external appearances. During this stage the child begins to use symbols and language. Piaget considered the ability to grasp the logic of relations and classes as underpinning intelligence and argued that children at this stage tend to focus upon one aspect of an object or a situation at a time. Through a number of ingenious experiments, Piaget concluded that children, at this stage, experience difficulty in solving problems involving class-inclusion, conservation and transitive reasoning. At this age children continue to display egocentrism, experiencing difficulty in recognising that their own thoughts and perceptions may differ from those of others.

At the **concrete operational stage** (7 to 11 years), the child is no longer so easily deceived by perceptually dominant appearance. It is now possible for the child to carry out mental operations such as conservation, classification, seriation, and transitive reasoning. At this stage, egocentricity begins to decline, and children are able to de-centre, that is, examine more than one dimension of a problem, and understand the notion of reversibility and identity. However, Piaget believed that at this stage children cannot apply such thinking to consideration of hypothetical events. Such mental operations still require physical manipulation of concrete objects – hence the notion of 'concrete' operations.

From about 11 years, the child becomes increasingly capable of **formal operational thought**. This is characterised by the ability to think logically about abstract, hypothetical or imaginary concepts and situations. The formal thinker no longer requires concrete aids as ideas and reasoning can be carried out by means of internal representations. The approach to problem-solving is now more ordered and system-atic. It is now possible to think of possibilities and potentialities that have not been hitherto encountered.

Piaget argued that cognitive change (growth) becomes necessary when present cognitive structures are incapable of reconciling conflict between existing understandings and current experience. Develop-ment is achieved through the processes of assimilation, disequilibra-tion and accommodation. Assimilation involves the interpretation of events in terms of existing cognitive structures, whereas accommoda-tion describes the process by which existing representations (sche-mata) are modified to encompass new experiences that cannot be assimilated (a phenomenon known as equilibration). Cognitive re-structuring involving the development of more sophisticated schemata is the natural outcome. Some have likened this process to the oper-ation of a filing system in which assimilation involves filing material into existing categories, and adaptation involving modification of the existing system because new material does not fit these.

Evaluation

Piaget's work 'remains the single most comprehensive theory of intellectual development. . . No theory even comes close' (Sternberg, 2002b, p. 483). Piaget's ideas were subsequently harnessed along cognitive psychology's information-processing paradigm resulting in the neo-Piagetian theories of writers such as Pascual-Leone (1970), Fischer (1980), Case (1985) and Demetriou (1998a). His work ultimately 'caused a revolution in developmental theory with . . . such concepts as activity, adaptation, self-regulation, construction, and cognitive structures occurring in a universal sequence of qualitatively different developmental stages' (Weinert and Weinert, 1998, p. 17).

Piaget's ideas have also had a major impact upon educational practice, particularly in primary (elementary) education. Although more concerned with epistemology, the nature and development of thought, than with prescribing educational practice, his ideas revolutionalised ideas about pedagogy. The notion of the child as a lone scientist exploring his or her world, and developing intellectually by means of disequilibration, underpinned the child-centred educational philosophies of the 1960s and 70s and still has strong resonance today. The key principle was that the children should not be seen as passive recipients of external knowledge but, rather, as active constructors of their own knowledge. The teacher's role was to provide a context whereby the child was challenged to engage with activities requiring adaptation that are appropriate to their developmental level. According to Pascual-Leone (Cardellini and Pascual-Leone, 2004), teachers should function like sports coaches. They should provide appropriate tasks, strategic advice, endeavour to motivate, yet recognise that ultimately everyone has to learn from their own existing repertoire. For this reason, Pascual-Leone advocates minimising any emphasis upon errors and, instead, advocates the highlighting of positive achievements geared to increasing productive and creative thinking.

The importance of ensuring challenge suited to the child's present capacities resulted in the notion of readiness, whereby tasks beyond the child's level were deemed to be inappropriate. Unfortunately, some academics and practitioners understood these ideas in an overly rigid fashion and, on occasions, this resulted in the important role of the teacher being underplayed and undervalued. A further misunderstanding of the theory led to a belief on the part of some that students, particularly those in primary and elementary schools should not be stretched by demanding material, as this might result in harmful 'pressure' (Damon, 1995, p. 204). The subsequent popularity of Vygotskian theory, in part, reflected recognition that teachers had a more direct role in instruction; although the differences, particularly in relation to the social nature of learning, between Piaget and Vygotsky are not as great as sometimes claimed (cf. Smith, 1996).

Piaget's theory has been highly influential in the development of thinking skills intervention programmes (e.g. Cognitive Acceleration in Science Education (CASE) and mathematics education (CAME); Bright Start (Haywood, Brooks and Burns, 1992)); and in the derivative generation of other taxonomies, models or stages of thinking that were applied to the teaching of academic subjects, for example, in the arts (Gouge and Yates, 2002), and mathematics (Griffin and Case, 1997).

There have been many theoretical and methodological criticisms of Piaget's theories:

1. Although studies, repeating Piaget's methodology, have largely supported his findings, other investigations, adopting different approaches, have demonstrated that children are capable of performing many cognitive tasks and operations at an earlier age than Piaget outlined. It is now widely accepted that Piaget underestimated the importance of the social meaning and context of his experiments, and the importance of children's linguistic facility in understanding and responding to his questions. As a result, many children failed to demonstrate their true capability in the experiments.
2. Much of Piaget's work centred upon scientific, logico-mathematical thinking. Other modes of thought, such as those encompassed by the arts, were comparatively neglected.
3. Studies have indicated that individuals operate at different levels in different domains, thus challenging Piaget's notion that

developmental stages had overarching structures that operated across multiple domains (Bidell and Fischer, 1992).

4. There appears to be so much overlap (decalage) between stages, it may be more appropriate to consider development as a continuous, rather than a stepwise, process.

5. Piaget's ideas neglected to take into sufficient consideration, important social processes on development (although this is now disputed by Piagetian scholars such as Smith, 1996).

6. Piagetian-inspired constructivist pedagogy has been widely attacked by politicians and the popular press.

Summary: Piaget

Purpose and structure	Some key features	Relevance for teachers and learning
Main purpose(s): • to increase understanding of the ways by which children develop knowledge	**Terminology:** • many complex terms are introduced that have now entered the educational lexicon	**Intended audience:** • Piaget's theory was not designed for pedagogical purposes, but has had a significant impact upon educational practice
Domains addressed: • cognitive	**Presentation:** • material in primary sources is often complex and difficult to grasp, but many simplified outlines have been written	**Contexts:** • early years, primary and secondary school education
Broad categories covered: • reflective thinking • productive thinking • building understanding • information-gathering	**Theory base:** • Piaget's genetic epistemology integrates ideas from biology, psychology and philosophy	**Pedagogical stance:** • teachers should provide learning contexts that maximise opportunities for disequilibration and cognitive restructuring

Classification by:	Values:	Practical illustrations for teachers:
• developmental level	• a mission as a	• many have been
• structural complexity	major theorist	produced by Piagetian
• quality of	• formal logical	scholars, but a significant
thought/action	thinking	proportion of these are now
		considered to be misleading
		or inappropriate

Guilford's Structure of Intellect model

Description and intended use

Guilford's Structure of Intellect (SI) model is a theory which aims to explain the nature of intelligence (Guilford, 1956; 1967; 1977; 1982; 1983; Guilford and Hoepfner, 1971). The purpose of the theory is to provide 'a firm, comprehensive and systematic foundation' and 'empirically based' concept of intelligence (Guilford, 1967, p. vii). It is based on experimental application of multivariate factor analysis of extensive studies of performance on psychometric tests. The resulting model (figure 5.1) is represented as a three-dimensional cuboid ($5 \times 4 \times 6$) with three main dimensions: operations, content and product complexity. The SI model is therefore a way of explaining thinking processes with these dimensions as key interrelated concepts. Subsequently, Guilford increased the possible number of subcategories to 150 (Guilford, 1982) and to 180 (Guilford, 1983).

The first dimension of 'operations' represents main intellectual functions, namely:

1. Cognition: recognising, understanding or comprehending information
2. Memory: stored information
3. Divergent production: generating a variety or quantity of alternative information
4. Convergent production: generating information through analysis and reason
5. Evaluation: comparing the information generated with established criteria.

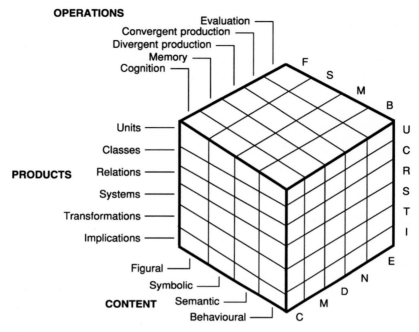

Fig. 5.1. Guilford's Structure of Intellect model.

The second concept is 'content' or broad classes of information. These are identified as:

1. Figural: concrete information in images, using the senses of sight, touch, and hearing
2. Symbolic: with information represented by signs, letters, numbers or words which have no intrinsic value in and of themselves
3. Semantic: where meaning is contained in words such as verbal communication and thinking, or in pictures
4. Behavioural: nonverbal information about people's attitudes, needs, moods, wishes and perceptions.

Products, or the form or characteristics of processed information make up the third concept:

1. Units: the separated items of information
2. Classes: items grouped by common characteristics
3. Relations: the connections between items based on the characteristics that can change

4. Systems: interrelated parts and/or structured items of information
5. Transformations: changes in the existing information or its function
6. Implications: predictions, expected outcomes, or the particular consequences of the information.

Guilford is well-known for his work on creativity, where divergent production is the key concept (Guilford, 1950; 1986). In his view, creative people are sensitive to problems, fluent in their thinking and expression, and flexible (i.e. spontaneous and adaptable) in coming up with novel solutions.

The distinction between convergent and divergent production is just one of the features of the Structure of Intellect model which led Guilford (1980) to propose that it also provides a unifying theoretical basis for explaining individual differences in cognitive style as well as intelligence. He suggested that field independence may correspond with a broad set of 'transformation' abilities and that many cognitive style models are based on preferences for different types of content, process or product (e.g. visual content, the process of evaluation, products which are abstract).

Evaluation

SI theory is intended to be a general theory of human intelligence, capable of describing different kinds of skilled thinking as well as more basic cognitive processes. It is, for example, a high-level skill to evaluate (E) non-verbal information (B) about people's attitudes to war and make reasonable predictions (I). Guilford's cuboid model successfully conveys the idea that any or all of the operations, contents and products can work together in the course of thinking. His three dimensions are hard to challenge, since they refer to mental processes, forms of representation and structural properties of the elements and outcomes of thought. However, as Guilford himself notes, SI theory takes little account of the social nature of cognition (1967, p. 434).

Guilford researched and developed a wide variety of psychometric tests to measure the specific abilities predicted by the model. These tests provide operational definitions of these abilities. Factor analysis has been used to determine which tests appear to measure the same or different abilities and the literature contains both confirmatory evidence and criticism of the methods used by Guilford (see, for example, Horn and Knapp, 1973; Kail and Pellegrino, 1985; Bachelor, Michael and Kim, 1992; Sternberg and Grigorenko, 2000/2001).

There are clear theoretical links with Piaget (Guilford, 1967, p. 23) and with Bloom's taxonomy (Guilford, 1967, p. 67). Guilford's *operations* dimension lacks only Bloom's 'apply' category. Sternberg and Grigorenko (2000/2001) state that Guilford was an early exponent of a broad definition of intelligence and, thus, he is owed a debt by later theorists such as Sternberg and Gardner who have argued for other conceptions than 'g'.

A key facet of Guilford's approach is his interest in creativity (Guilford, 1950). The 'divergent production' operation encompasses different combinations of process, product and content, and later theorists have built on these ideas (e.g. Torrance, 1966, McCrae, Arenberg and Costa, 1987 and Runco, 1992). However, Sternberg and Grigorenko (2000/2001) point out that more recent theories of creativity (including Sternberg's own) differ from Guilford's largely cognitive focus by also incorporating affective and motivational elements. They suggest that tests that include only cognitive variables will not strongly predict creative performance.

In relation to education, an important aspect of Guilford's theory is that it considers intelligence as modifiable and that through accurate diagnosis and remediation, an individual's performance in any of the areas of thinking can be improved. In addition, it can help educators to determine which skills are emphasised in any educational programme or system and which are neglected (Groth-Marnat, 1997). However, the very large number of different components of intelligence that can be derived renders practical examination and utilisation very complex.

Guilford's SI model has been widely applied in employment recruitment through personnel selection and placement, as well as in education (e.g. the SOI programmes developed by Meeker, 1969). Sternberg and Bhana (1986) acknowledge that most children completing SOI programmes perform better on the post-test than on the pre-test, but suggest that this may be because of the similarity between SOI items and test items.

Concluding their review of his work, Sternberg and Grigorenko (2000/2001) acknowledge that 'the interpersonal and intrapersonal factors of Gardner's theory and the creative and practical facets of Sternberg's theory both were adumbrated by Guilford's behavioral dimension' (Sternberg and Grigorenko, 2000/2001, p. 314). They also praise his scientific approach to theorising which permits rigorous testing and the possibility of disconfirmation.

Summary: Guilford

Purpose and structure	Some key features	Relevance for teachers and learning
Main purpose(s): • to explain the nature of intelligence	**Terminology:** • terminology is clear, but combinations of terms in the model are harder to understand	**Intended audience:** • academics • educationists • personnel officers
Domains addressed: • cognitive • affective (some aspects through 'behavioural' content)	**Presentation:** • through academic publications in books and journals • the cuboid model brings logical structure to a highly complex field	**Contexts:** • education • vocational selection
Broad categories covered: • productive thinking • building understanding • information-gathering • perception	**Theory base:** • psychometrics and psychology • links are made to the work of Piaget and Bloom	**Pedagogical stance:** • practice and feedback are important, to overcome confusion and help develop transposable skills • diagnosing difficulties can lead to successful remediation

Classification by:	Values:	Practical illustrations
• three key dimensions: content, product and operations	• intelligence is multifaceted and modifiable	for teachers: • none

Perry's developmental scheme

Description and intended use

As director of the Bureau of Study Counsel at Harvard College from 1947, Perry decided to study 'the variety of ways in which the students responded to the relativism which permeates the intellectual and social atmosphere of a pluralistic university' (Perry, 1970, p. 4). Accordingly he devised in 1954 a measure called *A Checklist of Educational Views* (CLEV) which embodied the essential ideas of the scheme (dualism, multiple frames, relativism and commitment). The initial purpose was to enable undergraduate students to think about their own thinking and value systems and so to make progress.

All students participating in the study completed the CLEV and then volunteered to be interviewed towards the end of each year. The developmental scheme was fully worked out after analysis of 98 tape-recorded one-hour interviews, including complete four-year records for 17 students. Perry first published his scheme in a project report (Perry, 1968). The sample was later extended by another 366 interviews, including complete four-year records for 67 students. Only two of the 84 complete records were for women students. Trained judges reached high levels of agreement in assigning the interview transcripts to one of nine positions on the Chart of Development.

The following outline of the Chart of Development is taken from Perry, 1970, pp. 10–11:

> *Position 1 (strict dualism):* the student sees the world in polar terms of we-right-good v. other-wrong-bad. Right Answers for everything exist in the Absolute, known to Authority whose role is to mediate (teach) them. Knowledge and goodness are perceived as quantitative accretions of discrete rightnesses to be collected by hard work and obedience (paradigm: a spelling test).
>
> *Position 2 (dualism with multiplicity perceived):* the student perceives diversity of opinion, and uncertainty, and accounts for them as unwarranted

confusion in poorly qualified Authorities or as mere exercises set by Authority 'so we can learn to find The Answer for ourselves'.

Position 3 (early multiplicity): the student accepts diversity and uncertainty as legitimate but still temporary in areas where Authority 'hasn't found The Answer yet'. He/she supposes Authority grades him/her in these areas on 'good expression' but remains puzzled as to standards.

Position 4 (late multiplicity): (a) the student perceives legitimate uncertainty (and therefore diversity of opinion) to be extensive and raises it to the status of an unstructured epistemological realm of its own in which 'anyone has a right to his own opinion,' a realm which he sets over against Authority's realm where right–wrong still prevails, or (b) the student discovers qualitative contextual relativistic reasoning as a special case of 'what They want' within Authority's realm.

Position 5 (relational knowing): the student perceives all knowledge and values (including Authority's) as contextual and relativistic and subordinates dualistic right–wrong functions to the status of a special case, in context.

Position 6 (anticipation of commitment): the student apprehends the necessity of orienting himself/herself in a relativistic world through some form of personal Commitment (as distinct from unquestioned or unconsidered commitment to simple belief in certainty).

Position 7 (initial commitment): the student makes an initial Commitment in some area.

Position 8 (multiple commitments): the student experiences the implications of Commitment, and explores the subjective and stylistic issues of responsibility.

Position 9 (resolve): the student experiences the affirmation of identity among multiple responsibilities and realizes Commitment as an ongoing, unfolding activity through which he/she expresses his/her life style.

Perry found that most students, although having different starting positions, went through the developmental stages in the same order. However, some got stuck for a year or more, some became alienated and escaped, and some retreated to Positions 2 or 3, still believing in absolute, divine or Platonic truth.

The principles and values underlying the scheme are clearly stated, and Perry provides a glossary of key terms. The dimension along which students were expected to progress was a purposive move away from authoritarianism (Adorno et al., 1950) towards a synthesis of contextual pragmatism and existential commitment (Polanyi, 1958). For some this involved rejecting a literal interpretation of the Bible, but ending up with a renewed and more tolerant religious faith. The ideal is portrayed as the achievement of a courageous and creative balance between dialectically opposed intellectual and ethical influences, 20 of which are specified. Perry acknowledges a debt to Piaget and sees his scheme as in some ways going beyond Piaget's framework by adding a 'period of responsibility' in which there are 'structural changes in a person's assumptions about the origins of knowledge and value' (Perry, 1970, p. 229). The process is seen as a cyclical one in which people are driven by an 'aesthetic yearning to apprehend a certain kind of truth: the truth of the limits of man's certainty' (p. 63).

Evaluation

Perry presents his scheme as a means of classifying ways of thinking and valuing, not as a set of skills. Nevertheless, the performances required of students are expected to be skilful and Perry clearly believed that higher-level intellectual and ethical positions were 'better' than lower ones.

The developmental scheme was drawn up in the specific context of two high-status American liberal arts colleges 'where the teaching of the procedures of relativistic thought is to a large extent deliberate' (1970, p. 232). The students took modular courses and almost half of the examination questions set in Government, History, English Literature and Foreign Literatures required consideration of two or more frames of reference. Perry was aware of the dangers of generalising beyond this particular social, gendered and historical context, but nevertheless believed that it would prove possible to do so. However, Zhang (1999) found that the Perry stages of cognitive development (as measured by her own questionnaire) showed little progression from year to year in her US sample and were reversed in one Beijing sample, demonstrating that cognitive–developmental patterns are influenced by different cultural and education systems.

The Perry scheme has in fact proved useful in other contexts, for example in the teaching of technology and chemistry (Finster, 1989 and 1991). Belenky and others (1986), working with female non-traditional adult learners, developed a stage model which has much in common with Perry's scheme, while King and Kitchener (1994) developed a similar stage theory of reflective judgment which was intended for use in schools and colleges as well as with non-college students.

Perry's scheme has the advantage of having clear definitions and providing a set of categories which, in his pioneering study, proved sufficiently comprehensive for the reliable classification of students' oral accounts of their thinking and learning behaviour and of the values which inform them. Perry's students were steered towards the kind of reflection required by completing a CLEV questionnaire, and later work showed that an essay or questionnaire can be used instead of a lengthy interview (Moore, 1988 and 1989).

While Perry believed that his scheme describes personal growth much more than responses to environmental pressures, he did acknowledge that individuals often adopt different positions in relation to academic, extracurricular, interpersonal, vocational and religious 'sectors' and even from one course to another. In his study, the move towards commitment tended to coincide with the realisation by students that after college they would have to earn a living, preferably in contexts in which intellectual, gentlemanly qualities were valued. The structure of the scheme is bound to reflect such pressures, as well as the assessment practices and expectations of college staff at the time. It was in the post-war years that many academics themselves abandoned religious beliefs for other philosophical or political lifestyles.

Perry acknowledges a philosophical debt to Dewey (1958) and Polanyi (1958), among others. However his scheme is compatible with an unusually broad range of Western philosophical and psychological positions, from Piaget to postmodernism and equally with Goffman's (1959) sociological analysis of the self in interaction and performance.

Perry places great stress on courage and responsibility, as well as on the creative achievement of synthesis and balance in one's life. When he speaks of stylistic balance between dialectical poles such as choice v. external influence; involvement v. detachment and self-centred v. other-centred, he expresses faith in 'ultimately aesthetic' standards (1970, p. 234). These values are explicitly stated and he sees 'Escape' or 'Retreat' as 'a failure of growth or maturity' (p. 199). As his scheme is concerned with the development of the whole person, thought, feeling and will all play a part.

The scheme was developed on the basis of phenomenological research, thereby grounding theory in lived experience. However, Perry did not approach his task without prior assumptions. He undertook the student interviews because he believed that thinking about thinking is a uniquely human capacity and would reveal generalisations at a high level of abstraction. What was revealed was a fundamental distinction between reflective and non-reflective approaches. The borderline is between dualistic and relativistic thinking and the step to Position 5 is taken only through reflective detachment. This borderline can be equated with Bloom's distinction between lower and higher-order thinking and with the threshold of 'critical thinking'. Moving from 'relational knowing' to 'commitment' is analogous to the strengthening of the Perkins, Jay and Tishman's key dispositions or Costa's 'habits of mind'.

We can be confident about the basic structure of Perry's scheme, even though it may need modification to accommodate other ideas such as Belenky's 'connected knowing' and reversal theory (Smith and Apter, 1975; Apter, 2001). No evidence has been adduced to support the idea that the scheme charts a biologically-determined progression possible only at 16 plus. It is more helpfully seen as a model for explaining the personal and social construction of academically valued meanings, and is clearly compatible with Lipman's conception of the development of critical and creative thinking through communities of enquiry.

Perry's influence has been substantial. Among the many theorists who acknowledge a debt to him are Belenky, Kegan, King and Kitchener and Kolb. Mezirow's ideas about transformative learning and critical reflection are in many respects indistinguishable from Perry's (Mezirow, 1978; 1998). Perry has also inspired large numbers of practitioners, many of whom recognise from their own experience what the students in Perry's book have to say (despite much of it being at a fairly abstract level).

It is above all the resonance that can be found between Perry's ideas and those in other frameworks that make it attractive. For example, Biggs and Collis' SOLO taxonomy maps very easily onto Perry's scheme, with the SOLO 'extended abstract' level corresponding to Perry's 'commitment' positions 7–9.

The Perry scheme has many potential uses in education and training: in planning, instruction and assessment. Perry himself listed selection, grouping, curriculum design, teaching method and guidance as areas in which the scheme could profitably be used. He saw it as encouraging openness, visibility and participatory inclusiveness in the practice of educators, recommending that, in the words of one student, 'Every student should have an interview each year like this' (1970, p. 240).

On the other hand it is far from clear that the ability to deal with ill-structured problems should be the be-all and end-all of higher education, let alone lifelong learning. There are many kinds of learning where skilful performance can be impeded by too much analytic thought, including a great deal of decision-making in the business world where intuitive thinking is often highly effective (Allinson, Chell and Hayes, 2000). Also there are many fields in which there are right and wrong ways of doing things, where procedures have to be followed, albeit with some flexibility and understanding. Perry's scheme has the merit of encouraging independent learning through the appropriate questioning of authority, but would be misused if it led to the devaluing of all non-reflective procedural and routinised learning.

Summary: Perry

Purpose and structure	Some key features	Relevance for teachers and learning
Main purpose(s): • to understand and facilitate intellectual and moral growth in a pluralistic society	**Terminology:** • clear definitions provided where needed	**Intended audience:** • teachers • college students
Domains addressed: • cognitive • conative • affective	**Presentation:** • accessible and persuasive • good use of case vignettes	**Contexts:** • education • citizenship

Broad categories covered:	Theory base:	Pedagogical stance:
• self-engagement • reflective thinking • productive thinking • building understanding	• Dewey (pragmatism) • existentialism • Piaget	• open, participatory, constructive, holistic
Classification by: • stages in coming to understand the nature of knowledge and belief	**Values:** • humanistic • liberal, democratic • ultimately aesthetic	**Practical illustrations for teachers:** • many examples of student views and perceptions

Gardner's theory of multiple intelligences

Description and intended use

Gardner first proposed his theory of multiple intelligences (MI theory) in his 1983 book, *Frames of Mind*. The theory was a challenge to the 'classical view of intelligence' (Gardner, 1983; 1993, p. 5) that perceived it as a unitary capacity, genetically determined and which could be measured simply by an IQ test. Instead, he began to think of the mind 'as a series of relatively separate faculties, with only loose and non-predictable relations with one another' (p. 32).

Gardner made the following observations while working with children and with brain-damaged adults:

- people have a wide range of capabilities
- a person's strength in one area of performance does not predict any comparable strengths in other areas
- likewise, weakness in one area does not predict either success or failure on most other cognitive tasks
- some children seem to be good at many things, others at very few
- in most cases strengths are distributed in a skewed fashion.

Then, with funding for a five-year project, he systematically read studies in the biological, social and cultural sciences about the nature and realisation of human potential. This resulted in *Frames of Mind*, in which he initially proposed seven intelligences. These represent different ways of thinking and are connected with different areas of experience. As the concept of an intelligence is built around the idea of a core operation or set of operations, it is reasonable to consider it as a set of thinking skills.

Gardner (1999, pp. 35–49) applied eight inclusion and exclusion criteria to determine what should count as an intelligence. These were:

1. the potential of isolation by brain damage.
2. an evolutionary history and evolutionary plausibility
3. an identifiable core operation or set of operations
4. susceptibility to encoding in a symbol system
5. a distinct development history, along with a definable set of expert 'end-state' performances
6. the existence of idiot savants, prodigies, and other exceptional people
7. support from experimental psychological tasks
8. support from psychometric findings (e.g. scores on interpersonal reasoning tasks are relatively uncorrelated with IQ scores).

Gardner thinks of an intelligence as 'a biopsychological potential to process information that can be activated in a cultural setting to solve problems or create products that are of value in a culture' (Gardner, 1999, p. 33). Whether or not an intelligence is activated depends on 'the values of a particular culture, the opportunities available in that culture, and the personal decision made by individuals and/or their families, schoolteachers, and others' (p. 34). By way of illustration, Gardner makes reference to the high spatial abilities of the Puluwat people of the Caroline Islands, that assist them to navigate their canoes in the sea; and the important personal intelligences required to thrive in Japanese society.

There is no leader or executive among the multiple intelligences to enable people to function effectively. However, each intelligence comprises constituent units or 'sub-intelligences' which are useful for certain educational or training purposes. In practice, these often work together.

Since the publication of *Frames of Mind*, other intelligences have been considered for inclusion in the list, such as naturalist intelligence, existential intelligence, spiritual intelligence, and moral intelligence. In 1999, Gardner added naturalist intelligence to the original list of seven, but expressed strong views against the inclusion of moral intelligence. To date, there are eight confirmed intelligences:

1. Linguistic intelligence – involves sensitivity to spoken and written language, the ability to learn language, and the capacity to use language to accomplish certain goals.
2. Logical–mathematical intelligence – involves the capacity to analyse problems logically, carry out mathematical operations, and investigate issues scientifically.
3. Musical intelligence – entails skills in the performance, composition, and appreciation of musical patterns.
4. Bodily–kinaesthetic intelligence – entails the potential of using one's whole body or parts of the body to solve problems or fashion products.
5. Spatial intelligence – features the potential to recognise and manipulate the patterns of wide space as well as the pattern of more confined areas.
6. Interpersonal intelligence – denotes a person's capacity to understand the intentions, motivations, and desires of other people, and consequently, to work effectively with others.
7. Intrapersonal intelligence – involves the capacity to understand oneself, to have an effective working model of oneself, including one's own desires, fears, and capacities, and to use such information effectively in regulating one's own life.
8. Naturalist intelligence – demonstrates core capacities to recognise and classify living creatures, to distinguish among members of a species, to recognise the existence of other, neighbouring species, and to chart out the relations, formally or informally, among the several species.

Gardner (2004) has suggested that sufficient evidence may accrue to justify existential intelligence (the capacity to be aroused and engaged in circumstances which are essential to human life, and the ability to ask profound questions about the meaning of life and death). Yet, to date, the case for this possible addition has not been fully made.

Gardner makes two essential claims about multiple intelligences: (1) the theory is an account of human cognition in its fullness;

(2) people have a unique blend of intelligences which 'arise from the combination of a person's genetic heritage and life conditions in a given culture and era' (Gardner, 1999, p. 45). As human beings, we can mobilise and connect these intelligences according to our own inclinations and cultural preferences, and we can also choose to ignore our uniqueness, strive to minimise it or revel in it. Gardner stresses that all intelligences can be used in constructive or destructive ways.

Evaluation

Gardner's theory often arouses strong feelings – for and against. For some (Sternberg, 2003d), the theory deals with domains rather than processes. Academics, particularly psychometricians and experimentalists, have criticised Gardner's unwillingness to seek empirical validation of his intelligences: 'his theories derive rather more strongly from his own intuitions and reasoning than from a comprehensive and full grounding in empirical research' (Smith, 2002, p. 10), and, to date, there have been no published empirical tests of the theory as a whole (Sternberg, 2004). While eschewing psychometrics, Gardner has endeavoured to draw upon evidence from the biological and neurosciences to support his ideas, although this has yet to convince his detractors. Nor does it appear that others have successfully done this on his behalf (Klein, 2003).

While Gardner is but one of many who have challenged the primacy of 'g', his ideas have probably had most impact on lay conceptions. Like Sternberg (1997), he accepts that 'g' exists as a phenomenon, but sees this as a function of the type of measures that are routinely employed to measure intelligence. While his theory has helped us see beyond g, other leading psychometricians have for many years worked with complex and multidimensional models and several of Gardner's intelligences overlap almost perfectly with ability constructs in psychometric models such as those presented by Carroll (1993, p. 641) and Messick (1992). However, while verbal, spatial and numerical abilities are generally thought to be positively correlated with each other, Gardner argues that they are largely independent intelligences.

Debates about his conceptualisation of multiple intelligences have centred around three key questions (Smith, 2002):

1. Are the criteria Gardner employs adequate?
2. Does Gardner's conceptualisation of intelligence hold together?
3. Is there sufficient empirical evidence to support his conceptualisation?

White (1997, cited by Smith) questions the individual criteria of the multiple intelligence theory. He asks whether all intelligences are symbolically encoded, how are the criteria to be applied; and, more fundamentally, why are these particular criteria relevant? He points out that there is a lack of answers in Gardner's writing.

These questions tend to be raised by researchers and scholars who have traditionally viewed intelligence as, effectively, that which is measured by intelligence tests. They can still point to a substantial tradition of research that uses correlations between different abilities to identify a general intelligence factor. However, it is not clear that Gardner's intelligences are accurate, and he has admitted that his list of intelligences was not necessarily logical nor one borne out of scientific necessity (1999, p. 48). Klein (2003, pp. 51–52) argues that for the distinctive claims of the theory to be valid it is necessary to show that:

- the mind consists of eight modules specific to the intelligences proposed
- each needs to demonstrate coherence (convergent validity)
- each is largely independent of the others (divergent validity).

According to Klein's analysis, there is insufficient evidence to justify such claims.

Others, such as Messick and Scarr (Gardner et al., 1996) have criticised Gardner's claim that intelligences are autonomous, and have pointed to the lack of a central executive to hold the intelligences together. Gardner counters these criticisms, by saying that to understand that intelligences are autonomous we need 'intelligence-fair' measurement, using materials and media most relevant to each intelligence. He also suggests that intrapersonal intelligence may fulfil a central coordinating role.

While many have questioned the absence of empirical support for the theory, it is unquestionable that it has met with approbation from significant numbers of educators. The theory has been: 'adopted and implemented for use in schools on six continents, from grade levels spanning kindergarten through college, and for an enormous diversity of student populations: "typical", special needs, gifted, juvenile delinquents, and adult learners' (Kornhaber, 2004, p. 67). One adaptation of the theory deserves mention because the study combined the advantages of a design experiment and a randomised controlled trial as well as combining the ideas of two of the world's best-known psychologists. Williams et al. (2002) report on the Practical Intelligence for School (PIFS) intervention in which, within each of Gardner's seven domains, emphasis was given to analytical, creative and practical ways of using and developing intelligence (according to Sternberg's triarchic theory). Large effect sizes on outcome measures of practical intelligence (but much less impressive academic gains) were found in one area where class sizes were small and where 90% of the PIFS lessons were delivered. However, in another area, despite receiving weekly support, teachers became more selective in their use of the programme in the second year, with the result that the differences in outcome between experimental and control groups were negligible.

The popularity of Gardner's theory appears, in part, to reflect the fact that it provides a formal structure for pre-existing beliefs, tacit knowledge and values (Kornhaber and Krechevsky, 1995; Smith, 2002). The suggestion that children learn in multiple ways and that education should be concerned with the 'whole' child does not, for many, require a reordering of existing professional belief systems. However, as Klein (2003) suggests, many current progressive educational practices do not require MI theory as justification. Furthermore, it should be recognised that in the US, as in most other cultures, the various intelligences do not have equal status; neither does the theory sit easily within a competitive society (Eisner, 2004).

Gardner's theory draws attention to the differentiation of individual learning needs and learning styles and leads us to question the inequality of educational opportunity offered by the conventional curriculum and practice (Dare, 2001). It encourages teachers to opt for depth over breadth. Noble (2004) describes how, with support, 16 teachers successfully used a matrix which combined the revised Bloom taxonomy with Gardner's multiple intelligences in order to formulate their own differentiated curriculum objectives.

Changes have been reported in the literature in curriculum design, adoption of multiple intelligence theory into pedagogy, provision of facilities/access and alternative assessment procedures in order to nurture learners' abilities, develop their full potential, and maximise their access to education and success. For instance, there are developments in the United States towards individual learner-centred curricula, intelligence-based pedagogy and teaching materials, and wider opportunities for assessment other than standardised tests, such as the use of portfolio projects, exhibition, and presentation (Kezar, 2001).

Criticisms of the application of the theory of multiple intelligences have been noted, as Gardner's (1983; 1993) text provided little guidance for educational practice. However, there now exists a growing wealth of publications designed for this purpose (e.g. Kornhaber, Fierros and Veenema, 2004) and several accounts by school districts have described attempts to apply the theory (Campbell and Campbell, 1999; Hoerr, 2000). Nevertheless, there is a dearth of systematic and rigorous evaluations of programmes based upon the theory although one 'careful evaluation of a well-conceived program' (Sternberg, 2004, p. 428) showed no significant gains in student achievement of self-concept (Callahan, Tomlinson and Plucker, 1997).

While Gardner's theory emphasises cultural variation in those intelligences that are most valued, this can lead to difficulty when attempts are made to promote intelligences that are perceived as less important. Thus, Costanzo and Paxton (1999) report some initial resistance from ESOL students who expected a more traditional mode of teaching and learning.

Summary: Gardner

Purpose and structure	Some key features	Relevance for teachers and learning
Main purpose(s): • to provide a full account of human cognition • to broaden educational experience, enabling more to succeed	**Terminology:** • clear definitions • technical terms explained in simpler language	**Intended audience:** • academics • educationists • others interested in learning

Domains addressed:	Presentation:	Contexts:
• cognitive • affective • psychomotor	• in addition to primary sources, many other accounts are available	• education • work • citizenship • recreation
Broad categories covered: • self-engagement • reflective thinking • productive thinking • building understanding • information-gathering • perception	**Theory base:** • psychometrics • neuropsychology • evolutionary psychology	**Pedagogical stance:** • provide for multiple ways of learning • learner-centred, recognising individual differences • seeks to raise teacher expectations
Classification by: • areas of experience	**Values:** • equal opportunities • cultural sensitivity	**Practical illustrations for teachers:** • enough to encourage teachers to generate many more

Koplowitz's theory of adult cognitive development

Description and intended use

The theoretical foundations of Koplowitz's theory are Piagetian (Koplowitz, 1984). The first two stages of his theory correspond to Piaget's 'concrete operations' and 'formal operations'. The remaining stages are two post-formal stages that go beyond Piaget's stage theory. At the third stage, post-logical or system thinking, the individual understands that there are often simultaneous causes that cannot be separated. Koplowitz then offers a fourth stage, unitary operational thought, where the way we perceive the external world is only one of many possible constructs; and causality which had been thought of as linear is now seen as pervading all the universe, connecting all events with each other. This connectivity of all things is holistic, going beyond rational linear thinking and can best be conveyed through context, metaphors, paradoxes, experience and even mysticism (Koplowitz, 1990). Koplowitz believes that, although very few people are capable of sustaining a unitary consciousness, many can achieve momentary unitary perspectives of situations.

As implicitly shown in table 5.1, Koplowitz sees his theory as applying to problem-solving in personal and social contexts. He illustrates the potential use of the theory (Koplowitz, 1987) by describing a troubled organisation and explaining how individuals at different developmental stages analyse a problem. He maintains that the theory has three main uses:

1. it helps determine the cognitive development level that an adult is operating at and whether an intervention strategy is required
2. it provides an insight into where and how it is appropriate to teach critical thinking and the limitations of critical thinking
3. it is inspirational, in that encourages us to be passionate about thinking and improving thinking. Logic is not seen as an abstract standard by which thinking can be measured but rather as a characteristic of one stage of human development.

Koplowitz suggests that there is a need to teach not only logical thinking but also post-logical thinking. In such teaching three balances must be maintained. First, there needs to be a balance between thought and action. While it is important to search for evidence and not be impulsive, it is also important to know when to stop thinking and take action. Second, while it is important to be unbiased in use of evidence, it is also important to trust in one's own hunches and intuitive processes. Third, although adults need to think abstractly, they also need to think concretely and emotionally (although Koplowitz does acknowledge that it might take years of Gestalt therapy to arrive at the ability to move from 'confrontation is rude' to 'I get embarrassed when confronted').

Evaluation

For Koplowitz the most important aspect of his theory is its inspirational quality. He is concerned with encouraging people to be passionate about thinking and improving thinking.

Although he states the foundation of his theory is Piagetian, his post-logical stage and unitary stage transcend Piagetian theory. Koplowitz's post-logical thinking is closely aligned with systemic thinking which, for some authors (Demetriou, 1990; Kallio, 1995; and Kohlberg, 1990) would be identical to Piaget's 'consolidated

Table 5.1. Koplowitz's stages in adult cognitive development

	Pre-logical	Logical	Post-logical	Unitary
Cause	one-step	linear	cyclical	all-pervading; cause and effect as manifestations of one dynamic
Logic	emotion over logic; process not separated from content	logical	logic in context	one communication tool out of many
Relation among variables	unrelated	independent	interdependent	constructed
Blame/problem location	others	where problem starts	in the system	problems as opportunities/boundary constructed
Intervention site	others	where the problem is	where there is leverage	where appropriate
Ability to deal with the abstract	concrete	abstract	relationships	spiritual; non-material
Boundaries	closed	closed	open	constructed

formal operations'. A recurring theme in the literature that criticises Piaget's formal operation stage for overemphasising the power of pure logic in problem-solving seeks to differentiate post-formal thinking in that it places greater emphasis on problem finding than problem-solving. Marchand (2001) maintains that, given the inconclusiveness of the research carried out so far, it is not possible to determine the true nature of what post-formal thought is.

Koplowitz believes that individuals operating at his highest stage, the unitary approach, no longer work out their answers but rather have a direct or observational access to them, and therefore there is no 'unitary thought'. This unitary approach receives scant treatment in the literature outside of spiritual disciplines and modern physics.

A thorough search of the literature would indicate that Koplowitz's work has not influenced educational practice. In the early 1990s Koplowitz moved out of academia and into management consultancy. Since then, he has not elaborated on his theory and, outside of transpersonal psychology, it has received little attention. Where Koplowitz has exemplified his stages of thought, he has done so through showing how they manifest themselves in daily life at work. He describes the stages, but offers no explanation as to how you can move individuals through his stages of thought.

Summary: Koplowitz

Purpose and structure	Some key features	Relevance for teachers and learning
Main purpose(s): • to promote an inspirational concept of post-logical thinking • to provide a tool for consultants to use in assessment and intervention	**Terminology:** • clear, with unfamiliar terms well-defined	**Intended audience:** • designers of instruction and assessment • teachers • researchers

Domains addressed:	Presentation:	Contexts:
• cognitive	• enthusiastic writing, with persuasive use of 'Aunt Maud' parable	• education • work • citizenship • recreation
Broad categories covered:	**Theory base:**	**Pedagogical stance:**
• self-engagement • reflective thinking • productive thinking • building understanding • information-gathering	• Piagetian • systems theory • constructivist theories of knowledge • Buddhist	• guru
Classification by:	**Values:**	**Practical illustrations for teachers:**
• stages of development	• pragmatism • spiritual elitism	• few

Belenky's 'Women's Ways of Knowing' developmental model

Description and intended use

In *Women's Ways of Knowing* Belenky and her co-authors presented a qualitative study of epistemological development in women (Belenky et al., 1986). They set out to explore women's experiences and problems as learners and knowers through in-depth interviews with 135 female participants. Their informants were rural and urban American women of different ages, class, ethnic backgrounds, and educational histories.

The study is an attempt to identify aspects of intelligence and thinking that may be more common and highly developed in women. Belenky and others contrast their approach with those in previous studies of women's intellectual competencies that sought to minimise intellectual differences between the sexes. The team acknowledge the importance of Perry's scheme (1968) in stimulating their interest in modes of knowing and share his phenomenological approach, based on open and leisurely interviews that establish rapport with the interviewees.

When Belenky et al. mapped their data onto Perry's scheme, they found that women's thinking did not fit neatly into his categories. Building on his scheme, they grouped women's ways of knowing into the five categories outlined below:

Silence – a position in which women experience themselves as mindless and voiceless and subject to whims of external authority;

Received Knowledge – a perspective from which women conceive of themselves as capable of receiving, even reproducing, knowledge from the all-knowing external authorities but not capable of creating knowledge on their own;

Subjective Knowledge – a perspective from which truth and knowledge are conceived of as personal, private, and subjectively known or intuited;

Procedural Knowledge – a position in which women are invested in learning and applying objective procedures for obtaining and communicating knowledge;

Constructed Knowledge – a position in which women view all knowledge as contextual, experience themselves as creators of knowledge, and value both subjective and objective strategies for knowing.

On a priori grounds Belenky et al. 'suspected that in women one mode often predominates' (p. 16), namely that women tend to be:

process-oriented	rather than	goal-oriented
intuitive	rather than	rational
personal	rather than	impersonal

and to value:

discovery	rather than	didacticism
related	rather than	discrete approaches to
being with others	rather than	life/learning
breadth	rather than	being alone or on own
support	rather than	concentration
responsibility and	rather than	challenge
caring for others		self-concern
inner	rather than	
listening	rather than	outer control and validation
		speaking

They believe that male-dominated conventional educational practice often treats women's ways of knowing as deficient, so that some 'women come to believe that they cannot think and learn as well as men' (p. 16). Belenky et al. argue that challenging women's thinking does not necessarily lead to cognitive growth, as most women in their study found the experience of being doubted debilitating rather than energising. The metaphor for women's intellectual development that Belenky and others most emphasise is that of 'gaining a voice'.

Evaluation

Belenky and others argue for a change in education practices that allow women to experience what they call 'connected' teaching. They call for a move away from a model of teaching that is adversarial and authoritarian (male?) to one where teachers trust students' thinking and encourage them to expand upon it (female?). It is hard to disagree with the argument that a supportive and trusting climate is needed if students are to expose their beliefs to critical scutiny in the interests of personal and interpersonal growth, but it is more difficult to find evidence that women are especially disadvantaged in the present education system in western countries.

Belenky's ideas resonate with Knowles' work on andragogy and Freire's on education as a means of raising consciousness. Her argument for pedagogical change, like those of others who favour more person-centred approaches, can be ideologically supported for both genders.

Belenky and her colleagues acknowledge that the question of why or when women shift in their perspectives is not addressed well by their data, since they used only a cross-sectional design. They also acknowledge (and Fishback and Polson (1998) have subsequently confirmed) that similar categories apply just as well to men's thinking. In their case studies, describing how people move from one perspective to another, no consistent influences seem to operate. Instead, each person studied had a story about what prompted a change in the way they 'knew', but nothing that provides remarkable insights for educators.

Neverthess, the central thesis that females differ from males in their 'ways of knowing' has subsequently received persuasive support from Baron-Cohen's research on empathising as a biologically-influenced female strength and 'systemising' as a male strength (Baron-Cohen, 2003). Further support comes from Herrmann (1996), who reported a clear gender difference in interpersonal/empathetic as opposed to analytic problem-solving preferences and self-ratings. Belenky's *connected way of knowing* can be equated with Baron-Cohen's *empathy,* which 'triggers you to care how the other person feels and what they think' (2003, pp. 26–27). Her *separate way of knowing* resembles the way in which a detached *systemiser* tries to understand and control a finite, rule-governed system by systematically analysing 'input-operation-output relationships' (Baron-Cohen, 2003, p. 63).

Belenky's belief that there is a need to reconcile both subjective and objective strategies for knowing suggests that both females and males are capable of integrating different ways of knowing. In this volume we argue for just this kind of integration (e.g. between reason and emotion; analysis and intuition; critical and 'caring' thinking) when critiquing other frameworks for thinking where a balance has not been achieved.

Summary: Belenky

Purpose and structure	Some key features	Relevance for teachers and learning
Main purpose(s): • to make teaching less adversarial and authoritarian • to contrast female with male approaches and values	**Terminology:** • non-technical	**Intended audience:** • teachers of non-traditional learners as well as those in universities
Domains addressed: • cognitive • affective	**Presentation:** • uses illustrative case studies	**Contexts:** • education • work • citizenship • recreation
Broad categories covered: • self-engagement • reflective thinking • productive thinking • building understanding • information-gathering	**Theory base:** • Perry's Developmental Scheme • feminism	**Pedagogical stance:** • learner-empowerment through co-operative learning • learners construct knowledge

Classification by:	Values:	Practical illustrations for teachers:
• hypothesised developmental progression	• women 'gaining a voice' • anti-authoritarian • humanistic	• evidence from interviews

Carroll's three-stratum theory of cognitive abilities

Description and intended use

This theory is the outcome of factor analyses of some 460 data sets. Carroll (1993) found evidence for a 'substantial number of different cognitive abilities' (p. 712) that differ in generality. The purpose of the study was to order the field of cognitive abilities and guide psychological research and thinking in that domain. Carroll's factor analyses allowed him to identify three strata of abilities: *general* (applying to all cognitive tasks); *broad* (relating to about 10, moderately specialised abilities); and *narrow* (numerous abilities, specialised in specific ways). This hierarchical model does not, however, imply a tree-structure in which higher factors branch individually into clusters of subordinates. A narrow ability may have loadings on more than one factor at a higher level.

Any relevance of the theory for thinking skill taxonomies rests on the extent to which a cognitive ability can be seen as a certain, purposive facility in thinking that is also open to instruction. Since Carroll defines cognitive ability as the conscious processing of mental information that enables a more or less successful performance on a defined task (paraphrasing the original on pp. 8–10), it admits a certain, purposive facility in thinking. Elsewhere, Carroll writes, 'No simple answer can be given to the question of whether cognitive abilities are malleable or improvable through specific types of experiences and interventions. Undoubtedly, some abilities are more malleable than others' (p. 686). He sees general and broad abilities as relatively long-lasting and persistent attributes but allows that narrow abilities may be open to instruction. This stratum of abilities, then, could have relevance for thinking skills taxonomies. Carroll does, however, say that the general ability (g) stratum is the best predictor of 'school success' (p. 687) but this could reflect an absence of attempts to improve narrow abilities rather than a difficulty in doing so. Insofar as his data sets allowed, Carroll also looked for differences in factor structures across cultural, ethnic and racial groups and across gender and found little evidence of systematic variation.

The following list indicates what is in each level (but is highly selective at Stratum 3, where our selective focus is productive reasoning):

Stratum 1: **General intelligence** *(likely to be correlated with speed of information processing and capacity of working memory)*

Stratum 2: **Broad abilities**
fluid intelligence *(concerned with the basic processes of reasoning that have a minimal dependency on learning)*
crystallised intelligence *(mental processes which depend heavily on developed abilities, especially those involving language)*
indeterminate combinations of fluid and crystallised intelligence
broad visual perception *(involved in tasks requiring the perception and visualisation of shapes and spatial relationships)*
broad auditory perception *(involved in tasks requiring the perception of sounds, including speech sounds and music)*
broad cognitive speediness *(involved in tasks that require rapid transmission and processing of information)*
general memory ability *(involved in tasks where new content or responses are held in short-term memory)*
broad retrieval ability *(involved in retrieval from long-term memory)*

Stratum 3: **Narrow abilities** (approx. 170 of these)
e.g.
sequential reasoning *(starting from stated premises, rules or conditions and engaging in one or more steps of reasoning to reach a conclusion that follows from the premises)*
induction *(discovering the rules that govern the materials or the similarities or contrasts on which rules can be based)*
quantitative reasoning *(reasoning with concepts involving mathematical relations in order to arrive at a correct conclusion: the reasoning can be either inductive or deductive or both)*
Piagetian reasoning *(at different levels of complexity and abstraction)*

visualisation *(ability to manipulate visual patterns)*

originality/creativity *(success in thinking of original verbal/ ideational responses to specified tasks)*

The examples above of narrow abilities which are relevant to productive thinking are drawn from what Carroll calls 'level factors'. These factors can exist at various levels of ability. There are also speed factors but these have not been illustrated here. In education, the prime concern is generally to establish a certain level of functioning before speed of functioning is addressed, if addressed at all. The stratum is an indication of the degree of generality but there may be intermediate strata.

Evaluation

This is not a taxonomy of thinking skills, or even of human mental abilities. However it does reflect the range of abilities and skills which have been of interest to the constructors of psychological tests and is a comprehensive attempt to order the field. The three-stratum theory makes the prediction that success in learning will very often depend to a certain extent on general intelligence and to a lesser extent on broad abilities. It also predicts that where narrow abilities are concerned, transfer is unlikely to happen spontaneously between skilled activities which make demands on unrelated abilities. These ideas have pedagogical implications and have been supported by empirical findings, for example the meta-analysis of learning skills interventions by Hattie, Biggs and Purdie (1996) which confirmed that near transfer is more readily achieved than far transfer.

The view that abilities range from general to narrow will feel intuitively sound to teachers. Carroll's 'ambitious attempt to create order among the primary abilities' (Gustafsson and Undheim, 1996, p. 193) points to a hierarchy of three levels of generality and identifies abilities in each. For a teacher, the crucial matter is the extent to which these abilities are malleable. Carroll is of the view that the narrow abilities are more likely to be susceptible to instruction than abilities at higher levels. Again, this has intuitive appeal but it has yet to be substantiated. Assuming it to be correct, teachers and researchers interested in thinking should attend to areas such as sequential reasoning, induction, Piagetian reasoning and creative thinking. Of course, these may not be equally susceptible to instruction or equally susceptible to the same instructional strategy. However, there has to be a caveat, as the practical value of the list of narrow abilities has been questioned on the grounds that they do not seem to predict particular kinds of achievement (Ree and Earles, 1991).

We offer some further comments about the relevance of Carroll's theory for teachers who are interested in thinking skills:

- the 'three-stratum theory' may be useful in thinking about thinking skills (e.g. What are the aims of a thinking skills programme? What thinking skills might be relevant? How fundamental/elemental are these skills? Are there other skills that have been overlooked? Do some skills underpin others?)
- some abilities (such as visualisation) are specific to a particular mode of representation and may not therefore be most effectively taught or assessed through different modes or even through the use of language
- the narrow abilities are founded on empirical study, but they do not map easily onto popular lists of thinking skills
- many of the narrow abilities have been studied only in laboratory settings and teachers are likely to see only about one third of them as having direct curricular or pedagogical relevance.

Summary: Carroll

Purpose and structure	Some key features	Relevance for teachers and learning
Main purpose(s): • to provide a structure to guide research and thinking	**Terminology:** • generally uses specialised vocabulary	**Intended audience:** • researchers
Domains addressed: • cognitive • psychomotor	**Presentation:** • academic weighty tome with detailed statistical analyses	**Contexts:** • academic and applied psychology

Broad categories covered:	Theory base:	Pedagogical stance:
• productive thinking	• psychometry	• none noted
• building understanding	• cognitive psychology	
• information-gathering		
Classification by:	**Values:**	**Practical illustrations**
• level of generality	• conscious processes	**for teachers:**
of the cognitive ability	in the individual	• none
• factor structure	• empiricism	

Demetriou's integrated developmental model of the mind

Description and intended use

Demetriou and his colleagues set out to validate through empirical research an integrated developmental model of the mind, first outlined in 1985 (Demetriou and Efklides, 1985) and further developed by Demetriou (1993) and Demetriou, Efklides and Platsidou (1993). In addition to a series of cross-sectional studies (reported in Demetriou and Kazi, 2001), they carried out a longitudinal study in which specially devised assessments were regularly administered over a three-year period (reported by Demetriou, Christou, Spanoudis and Platsidou, 2002). Demetriou and Kazi also developed and researched an integrated model of the mind and personality, showing that personality is closely associated with cognition and interacts with it at the levels of self-representation, executive functioning and action/reaction. Here we shall focus on Demetriou's general model of the developing mind, while acknowledging that his theorising extends to a dynamic and systemic understanding of intersubjectivity and to the influence of sociocultural contexts on life choices and activities.

Demetriou's overall aim is to build and validate an overarching theoretical model, thereby 'laying the ground for integrating the study of intelligence and cognitive functioning with the study of personality and self' (Demetriou and Kazi, 2001, p. 218). In pursuit of this primarily academic aim, Demetriou and his colleagues have devised a wide range of assessment tools, which they see as having practical applications in psycho-educational assessment. Demetriou's mapping of cognition owes much to the psychometric approach of theory-building, test construction and construct validation through

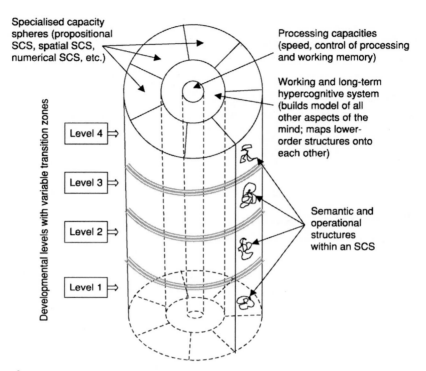

Fig. 5.2. Demetriou's general model for the architecture of the developing mind (based on Demetriou et al. 2002, p. 5).

factor analysis and structural equation modelling. He seeks to achieve a theoretical synthesis by incorporating ideas from the three traditions of experimental, differential and developmental psychology.

Demetriou builds his general model of the mind on the three concentric circles shown in figure 5.2, which represent *processing capacities, hypercognition* and seven *specialised capacity spheres* (SCSs) which mediate interaction with the external world. The processing capacities (speed of processing, attentional control of processing and working memory) are present in all thinking and have a major influence on general problem-solving (or psychometric *g*). *Hypercognition* (meaning the supervision and co-ordination of cognition) is conceived as being an interface between mind and reality, between aspects of cognition, and between processing capacities and the SCSs. Its working and long-term functions are summarised in figure 5.3. The

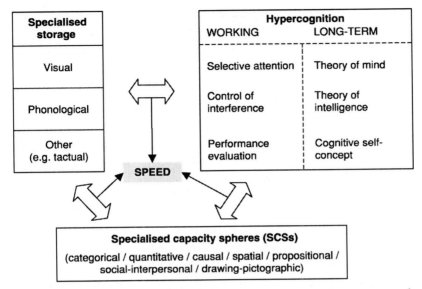

Fig. 5.3. Demetriou's model of working memory (based on Demetriou et al. 2002, p. 8).

seven domain-specific SCSs (also shown in figure 5.3) are close to the cognitive abilities identified by Carroll (1993) and Gardner (1983; 1993), as well as to Kant's 'categories of reason'. Each SCS is symbolically based and is to some degree autonomous. The seven SCSs cover the following types of thinking: categorical; quantitative; causal-experimental; spatial-imaginal; verbal-propositional; social-interpersonal; drawing-pictographic.

Development of thinking and problem-solving within each SCS is influenced through the combined influence of constitutional, socio-cultural and experiential factors, and inconsistent performance at the transition zones between levels is very common. Equally, development is very often uneven across domains. Nonetheless, there are important generic influences at work, involving processing efficiency, working memory, self-awareness and self-regulation. The four developmental stages identified in figure 5.2 are essentially those of Piaget (1950): sensorimotor, pre-operational, concrete operational and formal operational. Possible factors which influence developmental changes and mechanisms which enable them are discussed by Demetriou and Raftopoulos (1999).

For Demetriou, working memory 'refers to the processes enabling a person to hold information in an active state while integrating it with other information until the current problem is solved' (Demetriou et al., 2002, p. 7). This is a key concept, since the relevant information may come from at least three main sources, as shown in figure 5.3. It may come from the SCSs, which 'contain' rules, operations, skills concepts and beliefs; from specialised short-term storage buffers; and from the hypercognitive system.

The hypercognitive system is described as having an active self-knowing component (working hypercognition) and a self-descriptive component (long-term hypercognition). Working hypercognition (the efficiency of which depends on the processing capacities described above) is concerned with organising, monitoring and evaluating the responses and performances of the self and of others, while long-term hypercognition incorporates a model of the mind, a general model of intelligence and self-image. Working hypercognition 'is responsible for the management of the processing system' and 'carries over to the processing system, so to speak, both the person's personhood and the person's more general views about the mind' (Demetriou and Raftopoulos, 1999, pp. 328–329).

Evaluation

The quantity and quality of the research undertaken by Demetriou and his colleagues is truly impressive, and empirical support for his models has steadily accumulated. Demetriou is well aware of the limitations of factor analysis and structural equation modelling, but has used other methods, such as comparing means, and has triangulated test performance with self-reports and parental ratings. His model has more solid empirical support than any others we have encountered.

Support for Demetriou's ideas comes from a wide range of sources. His treatment of cognitive abilities has affinities with Carroll's three-stratum theory (Carroll, 1993), Sternberg's triarchic theory (Sternberg, 1985) and Gardner's multiple intelligence theory (Gardner, 1983; 1993) – although Demetriou has not yet found room for the musical and kinaesthetic domains. His model of working memory incorporates and extends that of Baddeley and Hitch (1974). Demetriou presents a richer account of metacognition and self-regulation than many authors. Like Marzano (1998) he distinguishes between cognitive, metacognitive (termed 'hypercognitive' by Demetriou) and self systems ('self-representation' for Demetriou). Demetriou's theory is the more ambitious and complex of the two, as it has parallel interacting structures for cognition and personality (for example interacting mental representations of general cognitive efficiency and general self-worth). Demetriou also adopts a more systemic approach, specifically addressing interpersonal, situational and developmental contexts.

While Demetriou provides a general account of problem-solving, he has relatively little to say about either critical or creative thinking. Neither has he explicitly illustrated how the self-regulatory functions of hypercognition might operate in the management of motivation and affect. Pintrich's general framework for self-regulated learning (Pintrich, 2000) is more detailed here, as it specifies four areas for regulation.

Although no simple set of dimensions and categories can do full justice to the complexities of human thought and action, Demetriou has succeeded in bringing together theories from diverse sources, in identifying their philosophical and psychological ancestries and in generating a substantial amount of supportive evidence. Throughout, his stance is that thinking and learning exhibit both general patterns and individual differences. Some patterns (including core features in the domains of thought) relect 'hard-wired' characteristics, while individual differences usually reflect complex systemic interactions and personal constructions of meaning.

The task facing educators is be sensitive to how others understand their own minds and personalities and to facilitate the developmental process at all levels both within and across domains. For this to happen, more is required than a rather complex model which incorporates some unfamilar theoretical constructs. It is difficult, due to its complexity, to see how practitioners will be able to use Demetriou's model to plan for and mediate teaching, learning and assessment without considerable and extended support. However, to start the ball rolling, Demetriou has outlined the basic principles of his model and its implications for instruction and assessment (Demetriou, 1998b).

Summary: Demetriou

Purpose and structure	Some key features	Relevance for teachers and learning
Main purpose(s): • to achieve a unified theory of the mind • to provide a new model of working memory • to provide empirical support for these models	**Terminology:** • assumes familiarity with cognitive psychology • Demetriou uses the term *hypercognition* instead of *metacognition*	**Intended audience:** • designers of assessment • theorists and researchers
Domains addressed: • cognitive • conative • affective	**Intended audience:** • not an easy read, as the claims are supported in detail by statistical analyses	**Contexts:** • life in general, especially during the school years
Broad categories covered: • self-engagement • reflective thinking • productive thinking • building understanding • information-gathering	**Theory base:** • Kantian philosophy • developmental psychology (especially Piaget and neo-Piagetian theories) • cognitive psychology • psychometry • 'constrained constructivism'	**Pedagogical stance:** • for transfer, teachers should encourage domain-general learning at a metacognitive level
Classification by: • structural features and functions of the mind • domain of thought • developmental level	**Values:** • empirical • open-minded about the interplay of nature, nurture and culture	**Practical illustrations for teachers:** • the importance of working memory, speed of processing and cognitive complexity are well illustrated

King and Kitchener's model of reflective judgment

Description and intended use

King and Kitchener propose a seven-stage model of reflective judgment in their book *Reflective judgment: understanding and promoting intellectual growth and critical thinking in adolescents and adults* (1994). The model is aimed at those who work in the area of critical thinking at college level, particularly in regard to its development and assessment, though the authors also indicate that it should be of value for use in schools and in other adult learning contexts. The model is based on Dewey's (1933, 1938) conception of reflective thinking and the epistemological issues resulting from attempts to resolve 'ill-structured problems'. It draws on other work, such as Fischer's (1980) skill theory and is related to the work of Perry (1970) and Baron (1985). It is summarised in table 5.2.

Evaluation

King and Kitchener (1994) distinguish reflective judgment from logical, verbal and moral reasoning. Their model is based on 15 years of theory building and empirical research into the development of reflective judgment in late adolescence and middle adulthood. It shows further development from their original study of reflective judgment (Kitchener and King, 1981). On the basis of more than 30 studies, they claim – we believe fairly – that the model is complex, inclusive and integrated, with qualitative differences that are stable across domains observable in reasoning about knowledge.

Hofer and Pintrich (1997) have pointed to structural similarities between King and Kitchener's model, Perry's account (1968, 1970) of intellectual and ethical development and the work of Belenky et al. (1986) on 'Women's Ways of Knowing'. King and Kitchener's concept of stages is heavily influenced by Piagetian and neo-Piagetian theory.

There are two related issues which King and Kitchener do not fully address. The first is the extent to which reflective judgment, as assessed by being asked to solve a set of ill-structured problems, relates to thinking and performance in other fields – personal and professional. The second issue is a concern about whether, in a series of

Table 5.2. King and Kitchener's seven-stage model

Pre-reflective thought

Stage 1   Knowing is limited to single concrete observations: what a person observes is true. Discrepancies are not noticed.

Stage 2   Two categories for knowing: right answers and wrong answers. Good authorities have knowledge; bad authorities lack knowledge. Differences can be resolved by more complete information.

Stage 3   In some areas, knowledge is certain and authorities have knowledge. In other areas, knowledge is temporarily uncertain; only personal beliefs can be known.

Quasi-reflective thought

Stage 4   The concept that knowledge is unknown in several specific cases can lead to the abstract generalisation that knowledge is uncertain. Knowledge and justification are poorly differentiated.

Stage 5   Knowledge is uncertain and must be understood within a context; thus justification is context-specific. Knowledge is limited by the perspective of the person who knows.

Stage 6   Knowledge is uncertain, but constructed by comparing evidence and opinion on different sides of an issue or across contexts.

Reflective thought

Stage 7   Knowledge is the outcome of a process of reasonable enquiry. This principle is equivalent to a general principle across domains. Knowledge is provisional.

reflective judgment interviews, respondents simply learn to provide more sophisticated answers to a specific set of increasingly familiar questions.

The model identifies a progression of seven distinct sets of judgments about knowledge and how knowledge is acquired. Each set has its own logical coherence and is called a stage, with each successive stage 'posited to represent a more complex and effective form of justification, providing more inclusive and better integrated assumptions for evaluating and defending a point of view' (King and Kitchener, 1994, 13). Individuals are said to pass through these stages in the order specified, though they may operate across a range of stages at any point in time. This still leaves questions about how individuals progress through the stages and about the relationship between maturation, education and culture.

King and Kitchener have studied the relationship between reflective judgment and moral reasoning. While they endorse the view that the college experience should provide an education in character development, they see progress through the seven stages of development in reflective judgment as furnishing necessary, but not sufficient, conditions for corresponding progress in moral reasoning.

The model of reflective judgment is a coherent, well-argued and extensively researched account of the development of epistemological reasoning, though there are some issues that remain unresolved. The authors acknowledge limitations in their sample selection, which may not make it representative of a larger population outside US midwestern high-school and college students. Also, the epistemological assumptions at stages 6 and 7 may be less prevalent in some cultures (Bidell and Fischer, 1992).

There is evidence from other sources that assumptions about knowledge do alter according to the subject context (e.g. Schoenfeld, 1992). This suggests that the confidence of the authors that students' scores on subject-based problems are almost identical to standard reflective judgment interview scores may need further investigation across disciplines.

Chapter nine of King and Kitchener's book contains explicit recommendations for teaching, using the reflective judgment model as an 'heuristic tool' to help educators to develop courses or activities to help learners to think more reflectively and make more reasoned judgments. The basis for using the model is set out in a series of assumptions, supporting activities to develop personal relevance and a detailed breakdown of each of the stages 2–7 with characteristics, instructional goals, difficult tasks, sample activities or assignments and developmental support. These are sufficiently clear and detailed to be applicable to educational practice in a range of settings. The main challenge in using the model is how to develop a clear understanding of each of the seven stages and how to recognise learners' behaviours at each stage.

Summary: King and Kitchener

Purpose and structure	Some key features	Relevance for teachers and learning
Main purpose(s): • to promote and assess reasoned reflective thinking when dealing with ill-structured problems	**Terminology:** • accessible: technical terms are clearly explained and examples are given	**Intended audience:** • teachers of high school and college students • researchers
Domains addressed: • cognitive • conative	**Presentation:** • well-written, with clear chapter summaries and good illustrative use of interview material	**Contexts:** • education • citizenship
Broad categories covered: • self-engagement • reflective thinking • productive thinking • building understanding • information-gathering	**Theory base:** • Dewey • Piaget • Kohlberg • Perry	**Pedagogical stance:** • teachers need to provide structures and languages that enhance and challenge students' capacities
Classification by: • stages in coming to understand the nature of knowledge and belief	**Values:** • liberal tolerance • it is important to work for shared understandings through the use of reason	**Practical illustrations for teachers:** • the description of characteristics, instruction goals, difficult tasks and sample activities is a helpful and practical section, aimed at teachers and other educators

Pintrich's general framework for self-regulated learning

Description and intended use

Pintrich produced his framework in an edited text (Boekaerts, Pintrich and Zeidner, 2000) devoted to issues concerning aspects of self-regulation. In his chapter, he seeks to synthesise common features of several SRL models in order to provide a means of examining learning and motivation in academic contexts. Pintrich (2000) defines self-regulated learning (SRL) as 'an active, constructive process whereby learners set goals for their learning and then attempt to monitor, regulate and control their cognition, motivation and behaviour, guided and constrained by their goals and the contextual features in the environment' (p. 453). Table 5.3, closely modelled upon that provided in the chapter, displays a framework for classifying the different phases of, and areas for, regulation.

It can be seen that Pintrich differentiates between regulation in four domains, *cognition, motivation and effect, behaviour* and *context*.

Regulation of cognition

Although cognitive skills are clearly central to thinking skills, they also play a part in the regulation of motivation and affect, behaviour and context.

Cognitive planning and activation

The framework proposes three general types of planning or activation.

1. *Target goal setting:* once task-specific goals have been identified, they can then be used to guide cognition and monitoring processes. These goals may need to be adjusted or changed during task performance as part of the monitoring, control and reflection processes.
2. *Prior content knowledge activation:* refers to when learners actively search their memory for relevant prior knowledge (both content and metacognitive) before performing the task.
3. *Metacognitive knowledge activation:* metacognitive task knowledge concerns understanding about the influence of different types and forms of task upon cognitive demands (e.g. the more information that is provided, the easier the task becomes). Knowledge of

Table 5.3. Pintrich's phases and areas for self-regulated learning

Areas for regulation

Phases	Cognition	Motivation/affect	Behaviour	Context
1. Forethought, planning and activation	Target goal setting Prior content knowledge activation Metacognitive knowledge activation	Goal orientation adoption Efficacy judgments Ease of learning judgments; perceptions of task difficulty Task value activation Interest activation	Time and effort planning Planning for self-observations of behaviour	Perceptions of task Perceptions of context
2. Monitoring	Metacognitive awareness and monitoring of cognition	Awareness and monitoring of motivation and affect	Awareness and monitoring of effort, time use, need for help Self-observation of behaviour	Monitoring and changing task and context conditions
3. Control	Selection and adaptation of cognitive strategies for learning, thinking	Selection and adaptation of strategies for managing motivation and affect	Increase/decrease effort Persist, give up Help-seeking behaviour	Change or renegotiate task Change or leave context
4. Reaction and reflection	Cognitive judgments Attributions	Affective reactions Attributions	Choice behaviour	Evaluation of task Evaluation of context

Source: (Pintrich (2000), p. 454)

strategy variables concerns those procedures that might help with cognitive processes such as memorising and reasoning. As with prior content knowledge, this activation can be automatic, can be prompted by particular features of a given task or context, or can be employed in a more controlled and conscious fashion.

Cognitive monitoring

This involves both being aware of and monitoring one's cognition, so it closely resembles what has traditionally been understood by the term 'metacognition'. Pintrich contrasts *metacognitive knowledge*, a relatively static element that one can claim either to have or to lack, with *metacognitive judgments and monitoring*, which tend to be more dynamic and relate to processes that occur as one undertakes a given task.

Pintrich highlights two important types of monitoring activity: *judgments of learning* which refer to gauging personal success at learning something and *feeling of knowing* (e.g. when one feels one knows something but cannot quite recall it – the 'tip of the tongue' phenomenon).

Cognitive control and regulation

This refers to the cognitive and metacognitive activities that individuals engage in to adapt and change their cognition. These are closely tied to monitoring and involve the selection and use of various cognitive strategies for memory, learning, reasoning, problem-solving and thinking. Specific techniques include the use of visual imagery, mnemonics, advanced organisers, and specialised methods of note taking. Located within this cell are the strategies that learners employ to help them with their learning, though, as Pintrich indicates, these can be both cognitive and metacognitive.

Cognitive reaction and reflection

These processes are concerned with personal reflection on performance and involve both evaluation and attribution. According to Zimmerman (1998), evaluating one's performance is a characteristic of superior self-regulation. Similarly, 'good' self-regulators are more likely to make attributions for performance outcomes that emphasise the influence of the learner's efforts and strategies (internal and controllable), rather than features beyond the learner's control, such as a lack of ability.

Regulation of motivation and affect

While there has been much research examining awareness and control of cognition (metacognition), there has been much less work concerning similar processes with respect to motivation.

Motivational planning and activation

Bandura's work on self-efficacy (1997) has highlighted the way an individual's beliefs about likely success in undertaking a particular task will influence the effort subsequently employed. Other factors highlighted in the motivation literature, such as the value of the task to the learner, personal interest in the task or content domain, and fear of failure, can all be made susceptible to student regulation and control in ways that can improve the quality of the learning.

Motivational monitoring

While the literature in this domain is more sparse than that for metacognitive awareness and monitoring, it is reasonable to assume that to engage effectively in the control and regulation of efficacy, value, interest and anxiety, students need first to be consciously aware of their beliefs and feelings and to monitor them. Approaches that have been employed in the scientific literature include attempts to make explicit, and subsequently change, students' maladaptive self-efficacy and attributional beliefs. Other studies have sought to reduce student anxiety by increasing coping skills or by showing how one may change aversive environmental conditions.

Motivational control and regulation

Pintrich lists several methods that students can employ to heighten their motivation. These include increasing your sense of self-efficacy (e.g. telling yourself that you can succeed in the task); promising yourself extrinsic reinforcers (e.g. going to the pub once the assignment has been completed); or attempting to heighten intrinsic motivation by restructuring the task to make it more interesting. Other strategies involve overcoming the tendency to avoid working hard because of a concern that poor performance may suggest a lack of natural ability, a phenomenon known as self-worth protection (Covington, 1992).

Motivational reaction and reflection

Drawing on attribution theory (Weiner, 1986), Pintrich suggests that individuals will try to understand the reasons for success or failure by attributing the outcome to such factors as skill, luck and effort. A belief that failure occurred through lack of natural ability is likely to undermine a student's motivation. Attribution retraining, therefore, generally tries to help the student to see learning as something that he/she can achieve and control by working hard and using effective strategies. Pintrich argues that changing attributions for life events will lead to new beliefs that will have a bearing on new tasks at the planning phase.

Regulation of behaviour

Behavioural forethought, planning and action

Pintrich recognises that planning one's behaviour in a purposive manner is essentially a cognitive function. However, he considers it reasonable to locate student attempts to plan their behaviour in an intentional fashion within the column dealing with behavioural regulation. Strategies for learners may include various time-management activities (e.g. planning an examination revision schedule or deciding when to tackle homework); and self-observation and monitoring (e.g. recording how many new French vocabulary words are learned each week, or how many pages of a new novel are read). Such information may result in further planning and action.

Behavioural monitoring and awareness

This involves relating the monitoring of behaviour and effort levels in the light of progress made. A student may, for example, plan to work at French course assignments on two evenings each week, but may find that this is insufficient and that additional time or greater effort is required.

Behavioural control and regulation

Here Pintrich refers to the learner's actual control and regulation of behaviour; for example, applying persistence and effort. It is important to know when, and from whom, to seek help. The skilled learner does not wish to become overly dependent on others, but does obtain assistance in dealing with particularly difficult problems.

Behavioural reaction and reflection

This concerns student evaluations of the effectiveness of their current behaviour (e.g. that studying in four-hour blocks is not the best use of time, or that putting off homework to the last minute often results in poor marks). Students may react by changing their time management, level of effort or, indeed, the course they are following.

Regulation of context
Contextual forethought, planning and activation

This concerns the individual's perception of task and context. Students may, for example, have different ideas about collaborative learning, the type of answer expected, or about classroom climate. Pintrich points out that perceptions may not be highly accurate, yet these may still have a major influence.

Contextual monitoring

Often students experience difficulty when moving from school to college or university because they fail to grasp fully the different requirements of adult learning, and thus do not adjust their learning strategies or general behaviour. Examining and monitoring contextual factors that may have a bearing upon achievement is therefore also important, particularly as such rules, routines and criteria are rarely made explicit.

Contextual control and regulation

Adult learning provides greater opportunities to control and regulate classroom environments, although less confident students often prefer to retain a more passive role. Outside the lecture hall or workshop, students need to take responsibility for regulating their study environment to facilitate their learning (e.g. removing distractions and having an organised study space).

Contextual reaction and reflection

This involves the student in evaluating aspects of the task or classroom environment. Evaluations may concern feelings about engaging in the activities concerned, or be more focused upon aspects of the student's learning and achievement. As with cognition and motivation, such evaluations can have an important influence upon the student's approach to new tasks (at phase 1 – forethought, planning and activation).

Evaluation

Pintrich's framework draws extensively on leading-edge psychological research about SRL, a field in which he has a substantial reputation. He successfully synthesises the work of leading theorists, notably Boekaerts and Niemivirta (2000), Butler and Winne (1995), Corno (1993), Pintrich and De Groot (1990), Pintrich, Wolters and Baxter (2000), Pressley (1986), Schunk (1994), Schunk and Zimmerman (1994), Winne (1995) and Zimmerman (2000).

As a synthesis of current theorising, his framework differs from other leading theorists such as Boekaerts (1997) whose model is divided into cognitive and motivational self-regulation; and Zimmerman (2000) whose triadic model emphasises personal self-regulation (which involves monitoring and regulating one's thoughts and feelings to aid performance), behavioural self-regulation (where one observes and modifies one's performance), and environmental self-regulation (which involves gauging and altering one's current environment). In addressing the comprehensiveness of his framework, Pintrich points out that not all academic learning falls within the four phases outlined, as there are many occasions when students learn implicitly or unintentionally, rather than in a focused, self-regulatory fashion. The phases are presented as an heuristic device to organise thinking and research on SRL. They can also be seen as an organising 'plan-do-review' principle for classifying the thinking skills involved in SRL.

It is also important to recognise that the four phases are not necessarily passed through in a linear sequence, and often phases may operate simultaneously. Indeed, Pintrich argues that recent research provides little evidence that *monitoring* (phase 2) and *control* (phase 3) are separate in people's experiences. The appropriateness of the fourth column, *context*, might seem questionable to some, as in many conceptions, self-regulation refers only to aspects of the self that are being controlled or regulated. In line with Zimmerman (2000), however, Pintrich's model is based upon a belief that one's attempts to monitor and control the environment are an important aspect of SRL. Perhaps the most valuable part of Pintrich's framework, for those with a good knowledge of the field, is his discussion of motivational factors – an area where he is a leading theorist.

Pintrich's main focus is essentially academic: theory building and empirical research. His classificatory framework is a useful introduction to self-regulation and is helpful for those who wish to examine similarities and differences between different theoretical models. Pintrich also hopes that his formulation will draw attention to areas which are currently under-researched and may require further investigation. While there are likely to be important implications for practitioners, he tends to leave the detailed articulation of these to others. For practitioners, each of the various cells in the framework table may need to be fleshed out in greater detail through reference to other publications.

Summary: Pintrich

Purpose and structure	Some key features	Relevance for teachers and learning
Main purpose(s): • to synthesise common features of several SRL models in order to provide a means of examining learning and motivation in academic contexts	**Terminology:** • some familiarity with psychological terms is assumed	**Intended audience:** • academics • educationists
Domains addressed: • cognitive • affective • conative • context	**Presentation:** • the framework is outlined in an academic book chapter • the tabular presentation is helpful	**Contexts:** • education settings • Pintrich recognises that the model reflects Western values and perspectives and may not apply in all cultures
Broad categories covered: • self-engagement	**Theory base:** • educational psychology • personal epistemology	**Pedagogical stance:**

• reflective thinking
• productive thinking
• building
  understanding
	• goal theory	• students benefit
		  from guidance on
		  learning to learn

Classification by:
• phases and areas for
  self-regulated learning
	Values:
	• choice enhances
	  motivation for
	  independent learning
		**Practical
		illustrations for
		teachers:**
		• largely left for
		  others to derive

Theories of executive function

Description and potential relevance for education

We can direct and manage some of our thought processes. Theories of executive function describe the nature and extent of this management. Arising from different perspectives, some of these theories use similar terms in different ways. Nevertheless, what they have to say is important for those who research and attempt to foster productive thinking.

Some theorists have a fairly general view of executive function as a control system that manages the ability to hold information in the mind and process it (Just and Carpenter, 1996). On this basis, it is an umbrella term for a set of domain-general control processes that organise and integrate thought (Denckla, 1996). They are distinguished from other brain functions in that they are a means of self-regulation for analysis, alteration, and management of thought (Barkley, 1996, p. 319; Lane and Nadel, 2000; Borkowski et al., 2004). In routine matters, these control processes may not be called into action but when some goal is to be achieved or problem solved, they enable an orderly approach (Welsh and Pennington, 1988; Morris, 1996; Borkowski and Burke, 1996; Rabbit, 1997; Roberts et al., 1998). They also come into action in managing processes associated with social interaction (Eslinger, 1996) and with emotions (Lane and Nadel, 2000). Pintrich (2000) includes the management of cognition, motivation/affect, behaviour and context in his comprehensive model of self-regulation.

Torgensen (1996) equates executive function with metacognition. It clearly overlaps that concept but others see the overlap as incomplete (Denckla, 1996; Demetriou and Kazi, 2001; Borkowski and Nicholson, 2004). Demetriou distinguishes executive functioning (which he calls 'working hypercognition') from representations of mind and personality built up in 'long-term hypercognition'. Jacob Bronowski (1967, 1977) provided an early model of executive function, drawing attention to the way other animals respond immediately and totally to events. In contrast, we are able to *delay* the response and, to some extent, separate emotions that the event engenders from the informational content. We can *prolong* the representation of the event in the mind (giving a sense of the past); formulate a response (in the present); and construct a scenario (for the future). This prescient model captures the essence of the functions of the control system (Barkley, 1996). Recent accounts tend to describe these as:

- to inhibit an immediate response
- to initiate mental activity directed at a specific end, maintaining or sustaining it and inhibiting distractions and impulses (including attention-diminishing emotions)
- to plan, organise, sequence, prioritise, select mental actions, apply and monitor their progress, and assess the accuracy of predictions
- to maintain a mental flexibility, stop a line of thought and initiate a change in it, in support of goal-directed or problem-solving behaviour.

The mental arena where information is maintained on-line and processed has been called *working memory* (Denckla, 1996, p. 266), a term introduced by Baddeley (e.g. 1976, 1996), and a concept possibly implied in Bronowksi's model. Working memory is a 'workspace where things can be compared and contrasted and mentally manipulated' (Lane and Nadel, 2000, pp. 144–145; Ohbayashi et al., 2003). Beyond that, the term does not mean entirely the same to everyone (Dosher, 2003). For example, for Baddeley (1976, 1996), it incorporates a central executive which manages the processing of information and certain slave systems. For Cowan (1995), on the other hand, it is the currently active part of the memory system together with the strategy and attention functions that maintain it. Whatever the theory, it may be better to think of working memory as a capacity rather than a tightly defined location (Dosher, 2003). This capacity, however, is limited. For our purpose the limited capacity of working memory is of particular interest, since neo-Piagetian stage theory is based on developmental changes in the number of distinct 'schemas' which can be 'kept in mind' (Fischer, 1980; Pascual-Leone, 1988).

Executive control processes are situation-dependent in that some people find some situations (lessons, lectures or subjects) inherently more interesting (and so easier to engage with, sustain attention in and plan for). There is also good evidence that executive control processes are ability-dependent (Miyake et al., 2001). The processes are also person-dependent in that some people may be better at some of these than at others. Those with marked deficits in executive functioning may exhibit difficulties in managing attention, following instructions, planning, time management, changing the approach, and in decontextualising thinking (Handley et al., 2004).

Failures to regulate thought can adversely affect learning. As a consequence, attempts are made to remedy such deficits (Spodak, 1999). For example, children may be taught explicit strategies for planning and working through the plan (Lyon and Krasnegor, 1996), and Graham and Harris (1996) found that students can develop strategy skills through instruction that includes modelling of the strategy by the teacher; memorisation of the steps; and collaborative and independent practice (see also, Pressley et al., 1990 for useful advice). This illustrates that executive actions (which could be thought of as thinking skills) may be taught. Working memory capacity, however, also varies from person to person. Deficits in this capacity are associated with learning disabilities (Swanson and Sáez, 2003) and weakness in the ability to reason (Handley et al., 2004). In the context of special education, pedagogical strategies intended to make thinking more productive should therefore not overburden working memory.

Executive function is significantly associated with activity in the prefrontal cortex, although that is neither the sole function of the pre-frontal cortex nor the only active area when the system operates. Posner and Raichle (1994) describe how the amount of cortical brain activity decreases with practice on a task, while the amount of sub-cortical (cerebellar) activity increases. This may reflect the 'chunking' of concepts, routines and 'schemas' which takes place as understanding and performance become automatic.

Evaluation

Theories of executive function have been criticised as invoking an homunculus, someone inside the head who controls what goes on. The problem is obvious: who controls the homunculus? The mind, however, does behave as though it has executive control over some kinds of thinking and these theories, metaphorical or otherwise, have the potential to suggest skills that may be practised and enhanced in the classroom.

Executive function has also been criticised on the grounds that it is simply re-introducing the concept of general intelligence (g) under another name. However, executive functioning is recognised as a hallmark of intelligence and it distinguishes general giftedness from more specific forms of giftedness and from other students (Sternberg, 1985, 87). Moreover, Colom et al. (2004) have shown in three studies that performance on a battery of working-memory tests can be predicted to a high level of accuracy by measures of general intelligence (g).

Working memory, the arena managed by the executive control processes, can also register emotion and integrate it with other information (Lane and Nadel, 2000). Theories of executive function may, therefore, help us understand some of the interaction between cognition and affect. They already have the potential to help us understand something of the progressive unfolding of a child's thinking abilities – 'the difference between child and adult resides in the unfolding of executive function' (Denckla, 1996, p. 264) – and they point to specific control processes that may be developed in the classroom. Gathercole (1998) and Romine and Reynolds (2004) have similarly drawn attention to the development of memory in children and how it affects their ability to think productively. Luna et al. (2004) have shown that spatial working memory continues to develop during adolescence, evening out at the age of 19. Perhaps students can be taught effective ways of using external extensions to working memory, such as pencil and paper.

On this basis, if the concept of executive function guides thought and practice in productive ways, then it has value. Some ask what is meant by terms such as *problem, strategy,* and *plan.* They feel that these are too vague to be meaningful and prefer to look at behaviours. Nevertheless, from a practical point of view, some degree of vagueness need not be an obstacle if there is enough shared meaning to make them useful. Theories of executive function are works in progress. They have the potential to guide thought and action and may give rise to strategies that help students manage their thinking better and, hence, achieve more.

Summary: Theories of executive function

Purpose and structure	Some key features	Relevance for teachers and learning
Main purpose(s): • to provide a structure to understand controlled thought	**Terminology:** • the same words do not always mean the same thing in different versions	**Intended audience:** • researchers applied psychologists
Domains addressed: • cognitive • conative • affective	**Presentation:** • academic	**Contexts:** • psychology • education • work • citizenship • recreation
Broad categories covered: • self-engagement • reflective thinking • productive thinking	**Theory base:** • cognitive psychology • neuroscience	**Pedagogical stance:** • self-controlled learning

Classification by:	Values:	Practical illustrations for teachers:
• structural features and dynamic functions of the mind	• empiricism	• not applicable

Some issues for further investigation

- Do complex, general models, such as Demetriou's, offer more helpful insights for practitioners than those with a more narrow emphasis?
- To what extent can factor-analytic approaches yield meaningful insights into the nature and structure of intelligence?
- Is it meaningful to consider cognition independently of conation and affect?
- How far do these frameworks help us understand creativity?
- To what extent have Piaget's ideas been superseded by the neo-Piagetians?
- Is a 'clinical' approach to data gathering, such as that used by Piaget, compatible with psychology's predominant emphasis upon scientific method?
- To what extent do stage models misrepresent the essential complexity of development?
- Why has Gardner's theory met with such acclaim from teachers and lay audiences?
- To what extent are these frameworks universally applicable across cultures and contexts?
- Are theories of executive function helpful in explaining and predicting social ways of knowing and learning?
- What can epistemological debates and explorations offer to educationalists operating within contexts subject to high stakes testing?
- Is the conception of 'g' relevant in the 'information age'?
- Can, and should, cognitive processes be subject to formalised individual assessment? If so, which processes should be highlighted as key?
- Which subject areas, occupations and forms of assessment make high demands on working memory?

- Can people reach the mature levels of developmental schemes such as those of Perry, Koplowitz, Belenky, and King and Kitchener through informal learning?
- Is post-modernity a developmental stage?
- What are the advantages and disadvantages of self-awareness?
- What is common sense?

6

Seven 'all-embracing' frameworks

Introduction

The frameworks included in this chapter are ambitious in scope in that they seek to provide a comprehensive account of how people think and learn in a broad range of contexts. Four of them cover the psychomotor as well as the cognitive domain and all present a 'whole-person' psychological account of thinking and learning, in that they deal with motivational influences as well as with the structure of cognition. While they tend to treat thinking and learning in terms of individual psychology, in four frameworks (those of Romiszowski, Wallace and Adams, Jonassen and Tessmer, and Hauenstein) the domain of social learning is also considered.

Another common feature of these frameworks is that they all use metacognition and self-regulation (or closely-related ideas) as explanatory constructs, whether the authors are psychologists or educators. Rather than simply listing skills or skill areas, the authors of these frameworks are concerned with the deliberate use of skills in problem-solving, decision-making and other forms of productive thinking, especially when that use is planned, monitored and evaluated.

There is an inevitable amount of overlap between the frameworks for thinking that we have classified as 'all-embracing' and those assigned to other family groups. However, the 'all-embracing' frameworks can be distinguished from most members of the critical thinking' family in that they are not simply concerned with 'higher-order' thinking, but also deal with acquiring and building knowledge and understanding through action, sensation, perception and memory. Although instructional design is an acknowledged aim of most of the 'all-embracing' frameworks, they also have a wider field of application, because they incorporate psychological theories. They differ from frameworks which are primarily explanatory models of cognitive structure and/or cognitive development in that they all have an applied educational purpose.

It is understandable that theorists should try to achieve a synthesis by taking into account previous models and frameworks and it is noticeable that two of the frameworks included here appeared in the present century. Two of the exceptions (Hauenstein and Romiszowski) have ancestries which can be traced back to Bloom's original intention to provide ways of classifying educational aims in the cognitive, affective and psychomotor domains (Bloom, 1956).

Time sequence of the all-embracing frameworks

Romiszowski's analysis of knowledge and skills (1981)
Romiszowski distinguishes between reproductive and productive learning in four skill domains: cognitive, psychomotor, reactive and interactive. He identifies 12 abilities which may be used in perception, recall, planning and performance.

Wallace and Adams' 'Thinking Actively in a Social Context' model (1990)
The 'TASC' problem-solving cycle has the following components: gather/organise; identify; generate; decide; implement; evaluate; communicate; learn from experience. An extended version of the model groups thinking skills under the headings: knowledge; attitudes and motivation; metacognition; and skills and processes.

Jonassen and Tessmer's taxonomy of learning outcomes (1996/7)
The major categories in this taxonomy are: declarative knowledge; structural knowledge; cognitive component skills; situated problem-solving; knowledge complexes; ampliative skills; self-knowledge; reflective self-knowledge; executive control; motivation (disposition); and attitude.

Hauenstein's conceptual framework for educational objectives (1998)

Acquisition, assimilation, adaptation, performance and aspiration are successive levels of learning in the cognitive, affective and psychomotor domains. At each level, and within each domain, Hauenstein identifies processes which help to build understanding, skills and dispositions.

Vermunt and Verloop's categorisation of learning activities (1999)

The cognitive categories are: relating/structuring; analysing; concretising/applying; memorising/rehearsing; critical processing; and selecting. The affective categories cover motivation and the management of feelings. The regulative categories are an elaboration of 'plan-do-review'.

Marzano's new taxonomy of educational objectives (2001a; 2001b)

The *self system* examines the importance of new knowledge, efficacy (ability to learn) and emotions associated with knowledge and motivation. The *metacognitive system* specifies learning goals and monitors execution, clarity and accuracy. The *cognitive system* deals with retrieval, comprehension, analysis and knowledge utilisation.

Sternberg's model of abilities as developing expertise (2001)

This model includes the analytical, creative and practical aspects of successful intelligence, metacognition, learning skills, knowledge, motivation and the influence of context.

Description and evaluation of seven all-embracing frameworks

Romiszowski's analysis of knowledge and skills

Description and intended use

Romiszowski's (1981) analysis of knowledge and skills forms part of his treatment of instructional design, which he places in the still wider context of human resources development. He aims to achieve a balanced approach to instructional design by taking into account information content, cognitive processing and behavioural responses.

He claims to provide a comprehensive means of classifying knowledge and skills (while recognising that knowledge of a particular topic is seldom of one type and that his categories are non-exclusive). Table 6.1 lists the types of knowledge which are described by Romiszowski in pp. 243–249 of his 1981 book.

Romiszowski then outlines a four-stage skill cycle, applicable in the cognitive, psychomotor, 'reactive' (self-management) and 'interactive' (social interaction) skill domains. What he calls 'reactive skills' are reactions expressing appropriate feelings, attitudes and values. Similarly, 'interactive skills' express, in interpersonal contexts, appropriate

Table 6.1. Romiszowski's knowledge categories

1.1 *concrete facts*

    1.1.1 concrete associations (things observed and remembered)

    1.1.2 verbal (symbolic) information (including all knowledge of a factual nature that has been gained by means of a symbolic language)

    1.1.3 fact systems (structures or schemata)

1.2 *procedures*

    1.2.1 linear procedures (chains)

    1.2.2 multiple discriminations (distinguishing similar information)

    1.2.3 algorithms (procedures which may be complex but which guarantee successful performance if followed correctly)

2.1 *concepts*

    2.1.1 concrete concepts (classes of real objects or situations)

    2.1.2 defined concepts (concepts which are classes of other concepts and cannot be learned without the use of a suitable language)

    2.1.3 concept systems (structures or schemata)

2.2 *principles*

    2.2.1 rules of nature (principles we can observe to be in operation in the world either by direct observation of by inference from their effects)

    2.2.2 rules of action (general heuristics regarding the appropriate actions or reactions to specific situations)

    2.2.3 rule systems (theories or strategies suitable for a given class of problems).

---

feelings, attitudes and value systems: 'voluntary reactions and actions, planned to lead to certain goals and involving the skills of self-control' (p. 226). The four stages of the cycle (*perceive, recall, plan,* and *perform*) are said to be usually but not always involved in skilled performance.

The 'expanded' skill cycle is presented in figure 6.1. Romiszowski (1981, p. 257) presents the skill cycle as 'a language for analysing skills', helpful in identifying gaps between performance requirements and trainee abilities. It is 'a taxonomy if you like', but 'no hierarchical dependencies are implied'.

The complete model of skill development therefore involves the operation of a skill cycle in which knowledge is selected for a particular purpose and used according to a plan. This produces results which act as new information to be evaluated in relation to purpose and plan.

Skills which require little planning and show little variation in execution from one instance to another are described as 'reproductive' while those which require strategic planning and show substantial variations in execution are termed 'productive'. Reproductive skills generally map onto Bloom's categories of *knowledge, comprehension* and *application,* while productive skills involve *analysis, synthesis* and

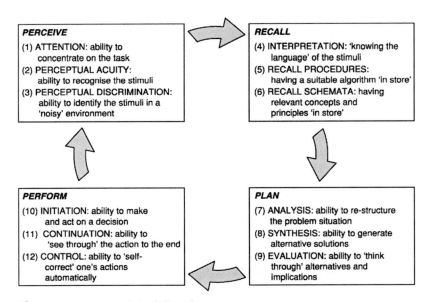

Fig. 6.1. Romiszowski's skill cycle.

evaluation. In table 6.2 the reproductive – productive skill continuum is shown to apply to skilled performance in all four domains. This skills schema is intended as a means of analysing instructional objectives so as to determine sources of difficulty, before one looks for effective ways to overcome them.

Table 6.2. Romiszowski's schema of skill categories

	Type of 'knowledge content'	
	Reproductive skills Applying procedures (algorithms)	**Productive skills** Applying principles and strategies
Cognitive skills Decision-making, problem-solving, logical thinking, etc.	Applying a known procedure to a known category of 'problem', e.g. dividing numbers, writing a grammatically correct sentence.	Solving 'new' problems; 'inventing' a new procedure, e.g. proving a theorem, writing creatively.
Psychomotor skills Physical action, perceptual acuity, etc.	Sensori-motor skills; repetitive or automated action, e.g. typewriting, changing gear, running fast.	'Strategy' skills or 'planning' skills; arts and crafts, e.g. page layout design, 'road sense', playing football.
Reactive skills Dealing with oneself; attitudes, feelings, habits, self-control.	Conditioned habits and attitudes, e.g. attending, responding and valuing, and approach/avoid behaviours.	'Personal control' skills, developing a 'mental set' or a value system; self-actualisation.
Interactive skills Dealing with others.	Social habits; conditioned responses, e.g. good manners, pleasant tone, verbal habits.	'Interpersonal control' skills, e.g. leadership, supervision, persuasion, discussion, salesmanship.

Evaluation

Although Romiszowski provides clear definitions for most of the key concepts, he does not try to pretend that real-life learning is easy to analyse. He recognises that a lot of mental activity is subconscious or unconscious and that teachers have little influence on many aspects of learning (especially abilities and attitudes).

Romiszowski uses four knowledge categories where Bloom used three, since he identifies conceptual knowledge as a separate category, distinct from knowledge of principles. Apart from this and his treatment of metacognition as a process rather than a distinct type of knowledge, Romiszowski's categories closely resemble those used twenty years later by Anderson and Krathwohl (2001) in their revision of Bloom's taxonomy.

The expanded skill cycle provides a coherent conceptual framework for understanding thinking and learning. It is comprehensive in scope since it deals with knowledge content (under *recall*), with experiential learning processes, and with mental and physical activity in all skill domains. Cognitive, affective and conative aspects of thinking and learning are covered, and the emphasis on a cycle of planning, acting, monitoring and evaluating shows that metacognitive processes are seen as very important (although Romiszowski uses different terminology). It is worth noting that what Romiszowski terms *reactive* and *interactive* skills correspond closely to what Gardner (1983; 1993) called 'intrapersonal' and 'interpersonal' intelligence; and to what Marzano calls the 'self system'.

The skill cycle *perceive, recall, plan, perform* is not unlike Kolb's (1984) experiential learning cycle *concrete experience, reflective observation, abstract conceptualisation, active experimentation*. It has the advantage of using simpler terms and expanding each category into three subcategories. However the distinction between *perceive* and *recall* is one that is often not easy to make, since the terms have overlapping meanings and individual differences and learning histories come into play.

It is interesting that Romiszowski places Bloom's *analyse, synthesise, evaluate* under the single heading of planning skills and in fact subsumes the whole of Bloom's taxonomy under only half of the skill cycle: *recall* and *plan*. This makes good sense in that planning is for a purpose and results in action (mental or physical performance), while the inclusion of a *perceive* quadrant usefully allows for instructional objectives which depend on learning to see, hear or feel things differently, in academic as well as in practical and social activities.

While there is no unifying principle underlying Romiszowski's categorisation of knowledge, he does see skilled performance as depending on the availability of prerequisite knowledge. His skill cycle schema is consistent with conceptions of problem-solving, learning and instruction as goal-directed exploratory processes which arrive at solutions through successive approximations as well as by using linear algorithmic procedures.

So far as values are concerned, no list of appropriate or desirable competencies, attitudes or dispositions is provided. However Romiszowski makes it clear that he believes that instructional technology can help more people reach high levels of skilled performance, although this is limited by whatever constraints are imposed by time and money.

Like many other instructional designers, Romiszowski adopts a rationalist technological approach derived from systems engineering. However he is eclectic in seeing value in psychological and pedagogical theories from behaviourist, humanistic and cognitive traditions. He settles for a mix of algorithmic and heuristic approaches and for 'guided discovery' in preference to solely expository or discovery pedagogical approaches. The mix and balance will depend on the type of task, on situational factors and on learner characteristics. When he applies his conceptual framework in the design of group as well as individualised learning experiences, Romiszowski (1984) takes a learner-centred stance.

By linking planning with the productive quality of a skill, Romiszowski is giving pride of place to constructive and creative mental processes inside the 'black box'. He thereby acknowledges the limitations of the behavioural 'performance type' approach of Mager and Beach (1967).

The great strength of Romiszowski's analysis is its simplicity and avoidance of idiosyncratic terminology. It should certainly be meaningful and useful to teachers and other educational professionals and it is also readily accessible to learners. Of all the classification systems we have examined, this one ranks highly in its potential relevance for lifelong learning, since Romiszowski draws on literature and extensive consultancy experience in post-compulsory contexts. There are many examples provided in the 1981 book to show how the analysis can be applied to 'diagnose' inadequate performance in real-life situations, in the workplace and in educational and training settings.

The concept of a skill cycle is an attractive one, as it sustains the idea of meaningful goal-directed activities rather than of isolated components, even though in practice thinking and learning may consist of a large number of cycles (some of them incomplete) arranged in many different ways.

One possible weakness of an all-embracing analysis is that it may not be sufficiently detailed for specific areas of application, but Romiszowski readily acknowledges this. He does, however give considerable importance to knowledge and skills in the psychomotor and affective domains.

Romiszowski has provided a flexible classificatory framework which is highly compatible with variations on a 'plan-do-review' instructional model. It would be a fruitful exercise to examine its goodness of fit with key skills as identified in the UK and many other countries.

Summary: Romiszowski

Purpose and structure	Some key features	Relevance for teachers and learning
Main purpose(s): • to improve instructional design • to identify gaps between objectives and performance	**Terminology:** • clear, simple and understandable by learners as well as teachers	**Intended audience:** • designers of instruction • teachers and trainers • researchers
Domains addressed: • cognitive • conative • affective • psychomotor • social	**Presentation:** • small print size: not an easy read	**Contexts:** • education • work • citizenship • recreation

Broad categories covered:	Theory base:	Pedagogical stance:
• self-regulation • reflective thinking • productive thinking • building understanding • information-gathering	• eclectic and integrative, drawing on Ausubel, Skinner, Gagné, and Piaget (among others)	• guided discovery • use of a learning or skill cycle
Classification by:	Values:	Practical illustrations for teachers:
• phase in skill cycle • productive–reproductive skill dimension • skill domain	• rationalist • technological	• Illustration provided for planning, teaching and assessment

Wallace and Adams' 'Thinking Actively in a Social Context' (TASC)

Description and intended use

This framework was developed by Adams and Wallace (1990) to support curriculum developers, teachers and parents in enhancing the 'thinking capacity' of pupils in primary and secondary schools. It is described as a problem-solving framework and was first used in the context of disadvantaged communities in South Africa. It was intended to have wide applicability, irrespective of age and culture.

By identifying and formulating problems which are relevant to themselves, children should be explicitly taught that problems occur when there are obstacles to achieving goals. They should then be introduced to the TASC problem-solving model, but not to the exclusion of all others.

The TASC model is presented as a cyclical process, represented by a wheel with eight sectors (figure 6.2).

Each of these eight areas of thinking is then broken down into 5–10 subskills or 'tools', which are supported with a rationale and examples of questions for parents or teachers to ask to support that kind of thinking. An abbreviated version is given in table 6.3.

TASC is supported by a thoroughly worked out set of pedagogical principles, extensive K–12 resource materials (Wallace et al., 1993) and

Fig. 6.2. The TASC problem-solving model.

suggestions for teacher development. It also incorporates an extended analysis of 'basic thinking skill categories' which are said to be especially relevant for work with less successful learners in all areas of the curriculum. These are grouped under the broad headings:

- knowledge
- attitudes and motivation
- metacognition
- skills and processes.

As there is a considerable amount of overlap between the extended analysis and the original, we present here only the more elaborated components. The elements included in table 6.4 are not intended to provide a comprehensive coverage, nor to be entirely original.

Table 6.3. Selected tools for effective thinking, using the TASC framework

Gather / organise	• systematic exploration, using senses and memory • question available data • problem recognition
Identify	• search for additional information • explore goals • question – what is needed? • represent information clearly
Generate	• produce ideas • consult with others • compare options
Decide	• look at possible consequences • other people's views for and against • establish priorities • select a course of action • make a case for the chosen course of action • plan steps and ways of monitoring
Implement	• monitor progress and check efficiency • consider alternatives and revise plan if necessary
Evaluate	• how far goals have been achieved • efficiency of personal and group processes and strategies
Communicate	• justify decisions • evaluate the evidence that informed decisions • exchange ideas on interaction and group organisation • recall, recount and explain succinctly
Learn from experience	• analyse and reflect on the problem-solving process • compare present with past performances • revise the whole problem-solving procedure • seek to generalise and transfer what has been learned

Evaluation

TASC offers a practical framework to support problem-solving through the structure of its organising 'wheel' or stages of the process.

The broad categories of thinking constitute a framework rather than a taxonomy, as a number of the skills in the different sections overlap. The TASC model includes all the cognitive and metacognitive categories one might expect, including strategic thinking and reflection on what has been learned. The TASC 'Tools for Effective Thinking' comprise a mixture of strategies that accommodate logical, creative and practical thinking. Dispositions are included under *attitudinal and motivational factors*, as well as under the *communication* heading. The framework is offered as a guide to structure and develop thinking, especially through collaborative problem-solving and by enabling parents, teachers and learners to break each of the stages down into manageable skill areas where this is needed.

Table 6.4. Elaborated descriptions of selected TASC skill areas

Attitudinal and motivational factors	• being purposeful and optimistic • interacting actively with the environment • avoiding impulsive responses • recognising the need for systematic exploration, accuracy and precision, making comparisons, summarising experiences, planning, being flexible in approaching problems, being persistent • being willing to work co-operatively or independently as the occasion demands
Metacognition	• being aware of incongruity, incompletion, the existence of a problem • selecting appropriate modes of problem representation • selecting cognitive strategies • allocating attentional resources • solution monitoring • sensitivity to feedback • awareness of one's strengths and weaknesses, and *acting* accordingly • balance between critical, analytical and creative thinking • planning

Using gathered information to identify and solve problems	• relating new data to previous experiences • being aware of disequilibrium, incompletion, incongruity • distinguishing between relevant and irrelevant information • selecting of representation: e.g. codes, conventions, symbols, diagrams, pictures, drawings, tables, charts, summaries, keywords, spider diagrams • seeking relationships between objects, events, experiences • keeping in mind various pieces of information • comparing objects, events, experiences • finding the class or set to which objects, events, experiences belong • understanding and using spatial and temporal references and patterns, including various viewpoints • analysing information, problems into parts • synthesising ideas from various sources • thinking about different possibilities and consequences • using logical evidence to prove things and defend opinions
Communicating with co-learners and communicating the outcome	• avoiding egocentric communication – thinking things through before beginning to communicate • being clear and precise – avoiding blocking • selecting an appropriate mode for communication • giving instructions clearly – using logical evidence to defend opinions • being an active listener
Learning from experience	• comparing new experiences with previous ones • classifying objects, events, experiences, problems, solutions • considering other circumstances in which the information, experience, outcome, insight might apply • deriving rules and principles from experiences • hypothesising and predicting about related problems/issues

The importance of motivation is appropriately stressed by Wallace and Adams, and in the books which support TASC there are many examples of problem-solving which learners will find emotionally engaging.

As with Halpern's approach to teaching critical thinking (Halpern, 2002), the TASC framework is intended to help with the development of lifeskills (Wallace, 2003). To this end it encourages discussion and dialogue, as well as the public sharing of thinking after the event. The emphasis on addressing real-life problems is part of the authors' attempt to facilitate the transfer and future use of problem-solving skills.

The TASC approach draws on a rationale based on the work of Vygotsky (1978) and the importance of social interaction in developing higher psychological processes. Other information-processing theories of intelligence and cognitive development are also cited, in particular Sternberg's (1985) 'Triarchic Theory of Intelligence', and Borkowski's model of the executive system (Borkowski, 1985). Metacognition is treated so as to bring out its *knowledge* and *working* aspects, and the descriptors used convey the importance of cognitive self-regulation through what cognitive psychologists call *executive function*. A simpler way of describing TASC is that it is not only about problem-solving, it is about learning how to learn.

As to the detail included within each sector or area of the model, the authors make no claim for comprehensive coverage. The extended analysis was developed after early classroom trials had indicated that a more specific focus was needed in certain areas. The language used is not intended to be prescriptive, but it is meant to be *shared*, with alternative simpler phrasing negotiated with learners where needed. This pragmatic approach to framework development is a highly distinctive feature of TASC.

Teachers will find the TASC cycle easy to understand and will welcome the fact that they can adapt it to the needs of pupils in different areas of the curriculum. It does, however, present significant challenges in that teachers are expected to model the processes they wish to develop, to provide frequent opportunities for learners to practise problem-solving and to move learners towards much greater autonomy.

Some evaluation of the impact of the TASC approach has been undertaken: on problem-solving (Maltby, 1995), on gifted pupils in South Africa (van der Horst, 2000) and as a means of staff development (Adams and Wallace, 1991).

Summary: Wallace and Adams

Purpose and structure	Some key features	Relevance for teachers and learning
Main purpose(s): • to support the development of problem-solving and thereby improve achievement and attitudes • to prepare students for active roles in society	**Terminology:** • very clear terminology in everyday language, to be used by learners in discussion and reflection	**Intended audience:** • curriculum developers • educational psychologists • teachers and parents • learners, including those for whom English is a second language
Domains addressed: • cognitive • affective • conative • social	**Presentation:** • as a series of practical guides for teachers with the theoretical rationale developed in articles	**Contexts:** • education • work • citizenship • recreation
Broad categories covered: • self engagement and self-regulation • reflective thinking • productive thinking • building understanding • information-gathering	**Theory base:** • Vygotsky's development of higher psychological processes • Sternberg's 'Triarchic Theory of Intelligence' • Bandura's social learning theory	**Pedagogical stance:** • start with real-life problems • collaborative problem-solving as a practical context in which to develop transferable skills • move from modelling to guided activity to autonomy • provide ample practice in strategy use • emphasise motivation and self-regulation

Classification by:	Values:	Practical illustrations for teachers:
• broad stages in the problem-solving process with identified sub-skills or 'tools'	• to develop self-confident and motivated learners.	• plenty of practical examples are included in a series of books for pupils, teachers and parents

Jonassen and Tessmer's taxonomy of learning outcomes

Description and intended use

This taxonomy was created by Jonassen and Tessmer (1996/7) primarily 'for the development and evaluation of computer-based learning systems for higher order thinking skills' (Jonassen, Tessmer and Hannum, 1999, p. 30). They argue that current taxonomies should be adapted to take account of developments in instructional technology and educational research, particularly the development of multimedia and Internet-based instruction (Jonassen, Prevish, Christy, Stavurlaki, 1999). They specifically seek to take account of higher-order dimensions of thinking such as ampliative (knowledge extension) skills, self-awareness and self-control.

The taxonomy, as shown below, has 11 broad categories of learning outcome, with a total of 35 sub-categories:

- **declarative knowledge**
  - cued propositional information
  - propositional information
  - acquiring bodies of information
- **structural knowledge**
  - information networking
  - semantic mapping / conceptual networking
  - structural mental models
- **cognitive component skills**
  - forming concepts
  - reasoning from concepts
  - using procedures
  - applying rules

- applying principles
- complex procedures found in well-structured problems
- **situated problem-solving**
  - identifying/defining problem space
  - decomposing problems
  - hypothesising solutions
  - evaluating solutions
- **knowledge complexes**
  - mental modeling
- **ampliative skills**
  - generating new interpretations
  - constructing/applying arguments
  - analogising
  - inferencing
- **self-knowledge**
  - articulating content (prior knowledge)
  - articulating sociocultural knowledge
  - articulating personal strategies
- **reflective self-knowledge**
  - articulating cognitive prejudices or weaknesses
- **executive control strategies**
  - assessing task difficulty
  - goal setting
  - allocating cognitive resources
  - assessing prior knowledge
  - assessing progress/error checking
- **motivation (disposition)**
  - exerting effort
  - persisting on task (tenacity)
  - engaging intentionally (willingness)
- **attitude**
  - making choices.

Jonassen and Tessmer believe that their categories are suitable for widespread general use in education and training and regard their taxonomy as a suitable instructional design tool in tasks such as mapping a curriculum and developing materials and assessments.

They seek to combine the steps of task analysis and outcome classification to make them 'a concurrent design process' (Jonassen, Tessmer
and Hannum, 1999, p. 31). They suggest that knowledge of a taxonomy can facilitate task analysis in instructional design (Jonassen
et al., 1989). In 1999 they make the stronger claim that 'if you are
unable to articulate the kind of thinking (by classifying the kind of
learning outcome required) that you expect learners to accomplish,
you have no business trying to design instruction to support that
learning' (Jonassen et al., 1999, p. 31).

Evaluation

This is a broad-brush framework rather than a coherently-structured
taxonomy. The authors do not specify a single organising principle used to distinguish different kinds or features of thinking, although they do see task analysis in terms of creating learning
hierarchies in which a higher-order outcome (such as problem-solving-
or constructing a mental model) depends upon lower-order outcomes
(such as concept formation or information processing) which need to
be mastered by the learner first. As it stands, however, the scheme is
not strictly hierarchical and is therefore best seen as a framework.

All kinds of learning outcome, whether cognitive, motor or psycho-
social, can be categorised by using the framework. It brings together
cognitive, metacognitive, affective and conative (motivational) dimensions. While it can be argued that the main categories are comprehensive, some areas are treated in more detail than others, the
section on motivation (dispositions) being far from complete. In a later
paper Jonassen provides more detail about problem-solving, setting
out 11 types of problem-solving outcome along the well-structured to
ill-structured dimension (Jonassen, 2000).

Gagné's taxonomy (Gagné, 1985) and Merrill's Component Display
theory (Merrill, 1983) are acknowledged by the authors as influencing
their own thinking (Jonassen et al., 1999). Cognitive and constructivist
ideas predominate and the analytic assumption is made that 'knowledge and human activity can be characterised as discrete cognitive
states' (Jonassen et al., 1999, p. 30). All of the learning outcomes are
expressed in mentalistic rather than behavioural terms and some (such

as 'allocating cognitive resources' and 'defining problem space') would be very difficult to operationalise.

The theoretical constructs for the framework come from contemporary educational research in psychology and sociology, as well as drawing on philosophical concepts. For example the importance given to metacognitive and motivational aspects of learning implies an active model of knowledge construction. The authors also acknowledge the importance of context for learning, by including a category of situated problem-solving (see Jonassen, 1997; 2000).

We concur with the authors' claim to have improved on the taxonomies of Bloom, Gagné and Merrill by including learning outcomes which:

a. *reflect learned behaviours* (by which they seem to mean abilities rather than skills) including inferencing, analogising, assessing task difficulty and decomposing problems;
b. *reflect cognitive structures acquired in learning* such as structural knowledge, self-knowledge and mental models; and
c. *are traditional*, such as attitudes, procedures, rules, concepts and problem-solving.

In each of the main categories there are some headings and terms which are somewhat different from those used in other taxonomies, such as 'ampliative skill' and 'structural knowledge' (Jonassen, Beissner and Yacci, 1993). However, it is possible to relate these to other conceptualisations. For example, a 'conceptual network' is what other theorists have called a 'schema' and 'ampliative skills' refer to aspects of critical and creative thinking.

By having an 'ampliative skills' category (by which they mean how a learner reasons beyond given information through analogy and inference), Jonassen and Tessmer imply that the issue of transfer in learning is not included or well covered in other accounts. Here they draw on Moore's work in critical and creative thinking (Moore, 1968) and claim that these 'knowledge enhancement skills' aim to make learning more efficient and personally relevant, as learners generate new knowledge and make meaningful connections within what they already know.

As the framework explicitly draws on a number of fields, the terminology includes some unfamiliar terms, which may make it challenging for teachers. On the other hand, the inclusion of 'traditional' learning outcomes such as attitudes and concepts makes it more accessible, as does the idea of 'ill-structured' problem-solving situated in the real world. The authors also have a possible communicative advantage in that they talk about self-knowledge and executive control strategies instead of metacognition and self-regulation.

As the authors point out, the usability, comprehensiveness and productivity of a taxonomy can only be properly assessed by applying it in many contexts. One example of the successful application of the taxonomy is a task analysis of what is involved in understanding the structure, functions and powers of the US Department of Defense.[1]

We believe that their framework offers considerable promise, especially in the field of computer-assisted learning, for which it was designed. Although it has more categories than Marzano (2001a) uses, it is a serious contender for widespread use in school-age as well as post-16 contexts. It is broad in scope, focuses on a range of learning outcomes and can cope with the application of knowledge and skills in complex situations such as problem-solving and work-based learning.

Summary: Jonassen and Tessmer

Purpose and structure	Some key features	Relevance for teachers and learning
Main purpose(s): • instructional design, especially of computer-based learning systems to help develop higher-order thinking skills	**Terminology:** • far from simple	**Intended audience:** • designers of instruction and assessment • researchers

[1] See: http://www.kihd.gmu.edu/immersion/dod/deliverables/task_analysis.htm

Domains addressed:	Presentation:	Contexts:
• cognitive	• academic	• education
• conative		• work
• affective		• citizenship
• psychomotor		• recreation
• social		

Broad categories covered:	Theory base:	Pedagogical stance:
• self-regulation	• eclectic, including educational psychology (e.g. Gagné)	• constructivist
• reflective thinking		• the sociocultural and situated nature of thought and knowledge are recognised
• productive thinking	• cognitive psychology and instructional design (e.g. Merrill)	
• building understanding		
• information-gathering		

Classification by:	Values:	Practical illustrations for teachers:
• types of knowledge	• learner autonomy	• not worked out
• features of thinking	• higher-order thinking	
• types of disposition		

Hauenstein's conceptual framework for educational objectives

Description and intended use

It was in 1972 that Hauenstein first published an integrated taxonomical framework in which he accommodated the cognitive, affective and psychomotor domains (Hauenstein, 1972). His 1998 book sets out a revised version of the original, based on the idea that teachers should not lose sight of the whole person as a learner, since 'We are what we believe, what we think, and most of all, what we do' (Hauenstein, 1998, p. 125). He identifies the long-term aims of education as being to produce *knowledgable, acculturated* and *competent* individuals. Arguing that the development of feelings, values and beliefs is just as important as gaining knowledge, and critical of the devaluing of practical skills in favour of the academic, Hauenstein points out that all learning involves feeling and doing as well as thinking. He advocates experiential learning and hopes that the use of his framework by teachers will enable students 'to develop their critical, reflective and problem-solving abilities and skills' in all three domains (1998, p. 29). More specifically, his objectives are that 'teachers and curriculum planners will have a better understanding of the learning process, be able to classify their objectives accurately, be more cognizant of student learning levels, and be better equipped to provide appropriate interconnected subject matter, objectives and lessons for their students.' (1998, p. xii).

Hauenstein offers three hierarchical taxonomies as well as one in which all three are integrated. The main organising principle is that of a learning hierarchy in which lower-order processes are prerequisites for higher-order processes. He claims that his taxonomies are comprehensive, with mutually-exclusive categories and he seeks to use terms which 'communicate the intent of the objectives to teachers in the field'. All categories include sub-categories, ordered according to the same principle which applies between levels in the hierarchy.

The composite *Behavioural Domain* taxonomy has five levels, defined (in brief) in the following way:

1. **Acquisition** – Ability to receive, perceive and conceptualise a concept, idea, or phenomenon in a specific context.
2. **Assimilation** – Ability to comprehend and make appropriate responses in a situation. Ability to transfer and transform concepts, ideas and perceptions to a similar situation.
3. **Adaptation** – Ability to modify knowledge, skills and dispositions which conform to ascribed qualities, criteria and standards. Ability to demonstrate intellectual and physical abilities and skills with desired qualities and characteristics to do a task or solve a problem in practical or simulated contexts and exhibit a preference for certain values.
4. **Performance** – Ability to evaluate situations and be productive. Includes the act of analysing, qualifying, evaluating and integrating knowledge, values and beliefs to act in accord with the situation.
5. **Aspiration** – Ability to synthesise knowledge and seek to master skills and demonstrate these in behaviour. Students can synthesise, hypothesise and resolve complex problems, and seek to originate and perfect their abilities and skills.

(based on Hauenstein, 1998, pp. 116–119)

In table 6.5 the complete framework is set out in abbreviated form, with a distinction being made in all cases between short-term (achievable within a single lesson) and longer-term objectives. It is important

Table 6.5. Hauenstein's abbreviated taxonomy of educational objectives

Behavioural Domain	Cognitive Domain	Affective Domain	Psychomotor Domain
Short-Term Objectives			
1 *Acquisition*	Conceptualisation	Receiving	Perception
• *Receiving*	• Identification	• Awareness	• Sensation
• *Perception*	• Definition	• Willingness	• Recognition
• *Conceptuali-sation*	• Generalisation	• Attentiveness	• Observation
			• Predisposition
2 *Assimilation*	Comprehension	Responding	Simulation
• *Responding*	• Translation	• Acquiescing	• Activation
• *Compre-hension*	• Interpretation	• Complying	• Imitation
• *Simulation*	• Extrapolation	• Assessing	• Coordination
3 *Adaptation*	Application	Valuing	Conformation
• *Valuing*	• Clarification	• Accepting	• Integration
• *Application*	• Solution	• Preferring	• Standardisation
• *Conformation*		• Confirming	
Long-Term Objectives			
4 *Performance*	Evaluation	Believing	Production
• *Believing*	• Analysis	• Trusting	• Maintenance
• *Evaluation*	• Qualification	• Committing	• Accommodation
• *Production*			
5 *Aspiration*	Synthesis	Behaving	Mastery
• *Behaving*	• Hypothesis	• Demonstrating	• Origination
• *Synthesis*	• Resolution	• Modifying	• Perfection
• *Mastery*			

(based on Hauenstein, 1998, p. 124)

to note that the Behavioural Domain is not an additional domain, but a composite in which there are only 15 sub-categories, in place of a total of 63 in the cognitive, affective and psychomotor domains.

Hauenstein's treatment of both the affective domain and the behavioural composite closely resembles Krathwohl, Bloom and Masia's (1964) classification of educational goals in the affective domain.

There is also a family resemblance between Hauenstein's cognitive domain taxonomy and the pioneering work of Bloom and his team (1956). We shall now compare and contrast these two cognitive domain taxonomies.

At Level 1 Bloom and Hauenstein both include the process of remembering (recall and recognition). Hauenstein calls Level 1 *Conceptualisation*, which has the sub-categories of 'Identification', 'Definition' and 'Generalisation' (by which he means the ability to explain a term or outline a process). At Level 2 (*Comprehension*) the sub-categories in the two taxonomies are identical and at Level 3 (*Application*) the only difference is that Hauenstein has two sub-categories, *Clarification* and *Solution* of problems. Despite the fact that *Conceptualisation* includes some processes (such as explaining) which Bloom may have seen as demonstrating comprehension, the two taxonomies are very similar at this level of 'short-term objectives'.

Hauenstein claims that his treatment of 'long-term objectives' provides a better account of critical thinking, reflective thinking, problem-solving and decision-making than Bloom's 'higher-order' categories *analysis, synthesis* and *evaluation*. Hauenstein uses only two categories, *Evaluation* and *Synthesis*, each with two sub-categories. He sees 'Analysis' as a necessary part of *Evaluation*, preceding measurement against a criterion or standard (which he calls 'Qualification'). *Synthesis* follows *Evaluation* and is defined as 'ability to hypothesise and resolve complex problems which yield new arrangements and answers' (Hauenstein, 1998, p. 49). *Synthesis* is seen as the highest level of thought, as it can include creative, innovative thinking. Hauenstein differs from Bloom in placing *Evaluation* below *Synthesis* and in treating 'Analysis' as only a sub-category.

Evaluation

Hauenstein's conceptual framework is a worthy attempt to fulfil Bloom's original vision of an all-encompassing system for classifying educational goals (Bloom, 1956). The Behavioural Domain framework provides a simple and useful general tool for understanding learning, while the Cognitive Domain framework is similarly useful for understanding thinking. In both Hauenstein places as much if not more emphasis on psychological processes as on educational goals.

As with Bloom's taxonomy, Hauenstein's work provides a heuristic framework rather than a theory. However, it is compatible with Piagetian theory (Piaget, 1952) and focuses attention on the learning process and on the long-term acquisition of valued dispositions. It covers all domains of human experience and performs a useful function in drawing attention to the importance of practical abilities through its treatment of the psychomotor domain and of the cognitive domain category Application.

Within the cognitive domain the terminology and definitions used are clear and accessible, with four of the categories being the same as those used by Bloom. Within the composite Behavioural Domain, the meanings of the terms 'simulation' and 'conformation' are unclear unless reference is made to the definitions and examples provided.

Hauenstein's claim for comprehensiveness seems a reasonable one, especially as he includes affective and psychomotor processes and makes frequent references to will, self-discipline and effort. However, his claim for mutually-exclusive categories can be challenged, as overlaps can be found. For example, within the cognitive domain, conceptualisation and comprehension may at times be hard to distinguish, as may be the problem-solving involved in Application and Synthesis, while varying degrees of analysis may be involved in lower-order processes than Evaluation. Overlaps within the affective and composite behavioural domains are even more likely to occur, as public access to feelings, beliefs and dispositions is more problematical than in the case of knowledge and understanding.

There appear to be two principles for organising all domains in Hauenstein's framework: a hierarchy based on skill and performance prerequisites and the progressive internalisation that takes place through learning. However, he does not provide many examples to illustrate how consistently those principles operate and it is where he combines categories from three domains to create the Behavioural Domain that their applicability is hardest to test. The first principle can be questioned as it does not always seem necessary for knowledge to be applied before evaluation takes place (e.g. the evaluation of a truth claim). The separation of Analysis and Synthesis is also problematical, since these processes are always complementary, both requiring awareness of part–whole relationships. So far as internalisation is concerned, this principle is perhaps more applicable in the affective and psycho-motor domains than in the cognitive domain. Complex concepts may require as much if not more internalisation than the procedures used in evaluation, and creative synthesis may become less, not more, likely if knowledge is internalised to the extent that its use becomes too rigid or predictable. It is certainly true that critical thinking and reflective thinking are facilitated by internalised dispositions, but the same can be said of Level 1 processes such as definition (where a disposition for cognitive clarity is very helpful).

Hauenstein believes that: 'individuals construct their own know-ledge from their experience; individuals learn as whole persons; sub-ject matter from various disciplines is interconnected, and that curriculum and instruction should be student-centered' (Hauenstein, 1998, p. ix). The holistic experiential-learning approach is clear, al-though the emphasis is on individual much more than social and societal development. Throughout the book there is frequent allusion to the value of accepting and conforming to the ideas and values of more experienced adults, with the model of an ideal student being encapsulated in the following descriptors: 'hard-working, clean, well groomed, athletic, healthy, moral, ethical, patriotic, law-abiding, a lady, a gentleman' (1998, p. 79).

It is not clear that Hauenstein has provided a better account of higher-order thinking (including critical and creative thinking) than Bloom. Both approaches are open to the criticism that evaluation (judgment of worth based on the application of standards or criteria) can be holistic and intuitive and does not necessarily depend on analysis. Indeed, evaluation can be seen as a metacognitive monitoring component operating at all phases and levels of thought. Bloom's argument that, although evaluation is not necessarily the last step in thinking or problem-solving, it requires to some extent all the other categories of behaviour, has some force (since the processes and products of synthesis and creative thinking are also evaluated). Both Bloom and Hauenstein link evaluation closely with the affective processes of valuing, liking and enjoying.

Although this framework has a welcome conceptual neatness and simplicity and makes a useful distinction between short- and long-term objectives, it is not fully worked out for classroom use, as it does not relate processes to curriculum content through a range of examples and vignettes. Hauenstein has four knowledge categories (symbolic, prescriptive, descriptive and technological), so a 5×4 matrix with four types of knowledge for each cognitive process could be easily constructed, as Anderson and Krathwohl (2001) have done.

Hauenstein does not explicitly take account of metacognition in his book, but his framework is broad enough to accommodate this. It is a strong contender for use in schools and in further and higher education, especially if taken as a flexible starting point for planning courses and systems of assessment where the development of personal qualities and practical skills are just as important as cognitive performance.

Summary: Hauenstein

Purpose and structure	Some key features	Relevance for teachers and learning
Main purpose(s): • to improve instructional design • to help teachers be more aware of learning levels	**Terminology:** • not always transparent	**Intended audience:** • curriculum planners teachers
Domains addressed: • cognitive • conative • affective • psychomotor • social	**Presentation:** • logical and well structured • rather abstract, with few concrete examples	**Contexts:** • education
Broad categories covered: • self-regulation • reflective thinking • productive thinking • building understanding • information-gathering	**Theory base:** • draws heavily on taxonomies by Bloom and others • uses Piagetian ideas of assimilation and adaptation • knowledge is constructed	**Pedagogical stance:** • objectives-driven • emphasises cross-curricular links • student-centred and holistic • experiential learning

Classification by:	Values:	Practical illustrations for teachers:
• short-term v. long-term objectives • domain of experience • level in hierarchy of prerequisites for learning • internalisation of knowledge, skills and dispositions	• tension between habitual conformity and open-mindedness • emphasis placed on individual rather than on social development	• few

Vermunt and Verloop's categorisation of learning activities

Description and intended use

In his doctoral research project, Vermunt developed a theoretical framework for categorising approaches to learning, especially in higher education (Vermunt, 1992). He built the framework around cognitive, affective and metacognitive (regulative) dimensions. He drew on several lines of research dating back to the 1970s, including Flavell's ideas about metacognition (e.g. Flavell, 1979). In 1999 Vermunt and Verloop use the same dimensions to present what they call a taxonomy or categorisation of learning activities. Their treatment of the affective and regulative dimensions is rather more developed than in Vermunt's earlier work (1996, 1998), while cognition is treated in very much the same way. Vermunt and Verloop hope that their formulation will be used to guide theory and research into learning and instruction and will not prove too simple or too complex for that purpose. The 'taxonomy' is not presented as an 'ultimate solution' and its authors do not claim that the categories are either exhaustive or mutually exclusive. The various categories of learning activities are summarised in table 6.6.

It should be noted that Vermunt and Verloop use the terms 'metacognitive' and 'regulative' interchangeably when referring to a type of learning activity (the other types being cognitive and affective). They define the metacognitive regulation of learning processes as 'exerting control over one's own cognitive and affective processing of subject matter' (1999, p. 262).

Table 6.6. A categorisation of learning activities

Cognitive processing	Affective/ motivational	Metacognitive regulation
Relating/structuring	Motivating/expecting	Orienting/planning
Analysing	Concentrating/exerting effort	Monitoring/testing/ diagnosing
Concretising/applying	Attributing/judging oneself	Adjusting
Memorising/ rehearsing	Appraising	Evaluating/ reflecting
Critical processing	Dealing with emotions	
Selecting		

(Vermunt and Verloop, 1999, p. 259)

Vermunt and Verloop expand on the meaning of each category, but mostly at an abstract or general level. Some paraphrased examples are given below:

Relating/structuring means looking for connections, including part-whole relationships and those between new information and prior knowledge.

Analysing means breaking down a whole into its parts and studying those parts or aspects in a step-by-step fashion.

Concretising/applying includes thinking of examples and using subject matter to interpret experiences and solve problems.

Critical processing means forming a personal judgment of the correctness of information presented.

Selecting means finding and studying the most important parts.

Attributing means ascribing learning outcomes to causal factors.

Appraising means deciding whether a learning task is worth the time and effort.

Dealing with emotions means being positive and coping with negative feelings.

Monitoring/testing/diagnosing means observing, during task performance, whether the learning process proceeds according to plan, and if not, finding a reason.

Evaluating means judging how far the learning proceeded as planned and was successful.

Reflecting means thinking over what has happened as well as about learning experiences in general.

Although they clearly favour a high degree of student self-regulation, the authors develop further pedagogical implications of their framework by taking each learning function and giving examples of things teachers can do to activate learning where there is either *shared regulation of learning* or *strong teacher regulation*. Thus, for example, with *shared regulation,* a teacher might promote critical processing by 'having students present arguments, presenting conflicting views, organising a group discussion' (1999, p. 268), whereas with *strong teacher regulation* a teacher might proceed by 'telling arguments in favour of and against a point of view, pointing out different possible conclusions' (p. 267).

It is the hope of the authors that their framework will provide a common language for teachers and researchers to communicate about student learning processes, especially in upper-secondary and post-secondary education. They argue that using the framework to analyse learning tasks, questions, assignments and examination questions will help achieve a better balance of activities and will help avoid what they term as 'destructive frictions' (1999, p. 270) between teachers and learners.

Evaluation

This categorisation is better described as a framework than as a taxonomy, since it does not have a consistent classificatory principle within each domain.

The proposed set of categories is neither complete nor without overlap, and several of them are combinations of processes which for some purposes it would be helpful to distinguish. Vermunt and Verloop's framework is similar in many ways to Pintrich's more elaborate framework for self-regulated learning which appeared a year later (Pintrich, 2000). When compared with Pintrich's framework, it becomes clear that it deals only with mental activities, not explicitly with behaviour.

The authors succeed only partially in their purpose of identifying core learning activities (most of which can equally be described as thinking activities), since they do not fully embrace the idea that students can extend as well as reconstruct knowledge, for example through dialogic or experimental enquiry.

Vermunt and Verloop designed their framework with older adolescents and adults in mind, but there is no reason to suppose that it is not applicable at the primary stage. It does, however, have the limitation that it was designed to apply primarily to academic rather than practical learning.

In its present form, this categorisation of learning activities is more appropriate for outlining a research agenda rather than for practical use in the classroom. It has the advantage of being closely related to two other dimensions of Vermunt's research: conceptions of learning and orientation to learning. It may have more appeal in higher education than elsewhere, in view of its potential for informing research on congruence and friction between individual differences in the self-regulation of learning and teacher control.

Summary: Vermunt and Verloop

Purpose and structure	Some key features	Relevance for teachers and learning
Main purpose(s): • to provide a theoretical framework for guiding research and practice in learning and instruction	**Terminology:** • clear definitions for all categories • uses some specialist vocabulary • some overlap between categories	**Intended audience:** • researchers • teachers
Domains addressed: • cognitive • conative • affective	**Presentation:** • academic journal article	**Contexts:** • education

Broad categories covered:	Theory base:	Pedagogical stance:
• self-engagement • reflective thinking • productive thinking • building understanding • information-gathering	• cognitive and educational psychology, with an emphasis on active learning	• process-oriented teaching as the facilitation of self-regulated knowledge construction by learners
Classification by: • domain of experience • time sequence in regulation	**Values:** • learning should be meaningful and have practical applications • independence in thought and action	**Practical illustrations for teachers:** • examples provided are at a general level

Marzano's new taxonomy of educational objectives

Description and intended use

Marzano's initial purpose (1998) was to produce a theory-driven meta-analysis of educational instruction using categories specific and functional enough to provide guidance for classroom practice. In his later book (2001a), the theory is presented as a taxonomy to help teachers and others design educational objectives, spiral curricula and assessments.

As illustrated in figure 6.3, the theoretical model is a hierarchical system in which the *self system* controls the *metacognitive system* which in turn controls the *cognitive system*. Each of these operates on the retrieved content of an individual's knowledge domain, which comprises stored information and knowledge of mental and psychomotor procedures. This knowledge can be represented linguistically, non-linguistically or in an affective (emotional) form.

The three systems in figure 6.3 are said to form a hierarchy in terms of the downward flow of information, once the self system has decided to engage in a task (Marzano, 2001b). Marzano (2001a) makes the additional claim that each level requires more conscious thought than the one below it.

At the top of the hierarchy of consciousness and control is the self system, in which attention and motivation are controlled in

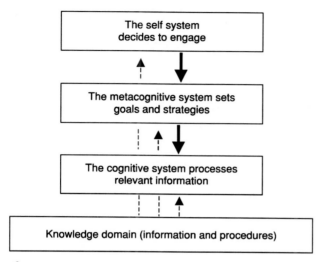

Fig. 6.3. The basic structure of Marzano's theory-based taxonomy.

accordance with beliefs and calculations of discrepancies between perceived and desired states. 'Because the mechanisms in the self-domain are the working elements that define motivation and volition in human behaviour, they have historically been referred to as conative structures' (2001a, p. 10). The self system is said to exert control over the metacognitive system, which is concerned with goal specification, process specification, process monitoring and disposition monitoring. The metacognitive system in turn 'exerts control over the cognitive system that operates in the knowledge domains' (2001a, p. 65). Marzano also (2001b) sees the cognitive system as hierarchical, in that knowledge retrieval is a prerequisite for comprehension, which is a prerequisite for analysis, without which knowledge cannot be used.

The functions of Marzano's three systems are shown in table 6.7, grouped into six levels, each of which corresponds to a class of educational objectives. It is clear that all levels of thinking from information-gathering to strategic and reflective thinking are included in this taxonomy.

For each of the functions at the six levels, Marzano (2001b) provides for teachers illustrative instructional objectives, cues or questions, the question for *generalising* being: 'What generalisations can be inferred from this knowledge?' (2001b, p. 187).

Table 6.7. Marzano's six levels of educational objectives

System	Level	Function	
Self	6	Examining the importance of the knowledge Examining efficacy (ability to learn) Examining emotions associated with knowledge and motivation	
Metacognitive	5	Specifying learning goals Monitoring the execution of knowledge Monitoring clarity Monitoring accuracy	
Cognitive	4	Knowledge utilisation	decision-making problem-solving experimental enquiry investigation
	3	Analysis	matching classifying error analysis generalising specifying
	2	Comprehension	synthesis representation
	1	Retrieval	recall execution

(based on Marzano, 1998, pp. 129-130 and Marzano, 2001b, p. 183)

The knowledge domain is comprised of declarative and procedural knowledge. Declarative knowledge is subdivided into *organising ideas* (principles and generalisations) and *details* (episodes, cause–effect sequences, time sequences, facts and vocabulary terms). Procedural knowledge is said to consist of more or less complex mental and psychomotor processes and skills. Mental skills are broken down into *tactics, algorithms* and *single rules*.

Marzano's new taxonomy is both a system for classifying educational objectives and a theoretical model of mental processes. At least two classificatory principles are employed between the *self, metacognitive* and *cognitive* systems: level of conscious control and direction of information flow. However, within the *cognitive* system the hierarchical principle is expressed not in terms of conscious control but in terms of logical or psychological necessity.

The taxonomy is presented as explanatory as well as descriptive, since Marzano began by constructing a theory to support his taxonomic framework. He does not discuss the values implicit or explicit in his theory, but it is certainly not value-neutral, as it is highly individualistic, using the metaphor of a control system with a powerful authority in charge.

Insofar as it yields predictions about 'what works' educationally, Marzano intends his taxonomy to be used prescriptively. He suggests that his levels should be built into a spiral curriculum which emphasises process more than content, but seems more in sympathy with teachers who set objectives and try to enthuse learners into adopting them rather than with those who seek to develop participatory, enquiry-based approaches to learning.

In Marzano's writing, there is an all-pervasive emphasis on rationality, to such a degree that emotions seem to be there not to be experienced, but to be analysed to see if they are reasonable. At the same time, he adopts a pragmatic approach, arguing that teachers should base their practice on the evidence of 'what works', as established through meta-analysis.

Evaluation

The scope of Marzano's taxonomy is certainly very broad, based as it is on a theory of thinking and learning which aims to be comprehensive. It covers objectives which relate to mental activity, values, beliefs and dispositions as well as observed behaviour. It builds on earlier work (e.g. Marzano et al., 1988; Marzano, 1992), but differs in that it has relatively little to say about creative thinking. It takes account of conative and affective aspects of thinking, but does not attempt to account for individual and situational differences in those domains.

The knowledge categories proposed by Marzano appear to be comprehensive, not least because they are said to contain all 'facts' and 'vocabulary terms'. However, he does not include 'pattern' or 'system' in his list, nor terms which refer to probabilistic knowledge of social situations. His treatment of sub-categories is generally in need of greater justification: for example, it is not self-evident that the sub-categories of knowledge utilisation are mutually exclusive nor that they offer comprehensive coverage.

Although Marzano's theory is clearly expressed, with clear definitions and examples, there are some instances in which he defines terms in unfamiliar ways. For example, he defines synthesis as 'the process of distilling knowledge down to its key characteristics' (2001a, p. 34), which contrasts with the more familiar idea of putting together parts so as to form a (sometimes complex) whole. For Marzano, matching involves the detection of differences as well as similarities and in this case the term 'compare' or 'compare and contrast' would be more appropriate.

Marzano's taxonomy has not been tested to see whether its structure is sufficiently robust to ensure consistent classification of instructional objectives and/or thinking skills. One possible area of confusion is the inclusion of error analysis in the cognitive rather than the metacognitive system. Marzano uses this heading to cover the evaluation of the logic and reasonableness of knowledge claims and provides a list of informal fallacies which can be detected through critical thinking. However, while the evaluation of another person's thinking is a cognitive activity, monitoring and detecting errors in one's own thinking involves metacognition.

Marzano (2001a, 2001b) makes many comparisons between his new taxonomy and Bloom's taxonomy of educational objectives (cognitive domain) (1956). The main differences are his addition of the metacognitive and self systems and his replacement of complexity with flow of information as an organising principle. Other differences lie largely in the detail, but especially in Marzano's treatment of analysis which incorporates elements from Bloom's higher-order categories of analysis, synthesis and evaluation.

We have here a largely coherent theory which draws on a wide research in cognitive and educational psychology more than on theory development in the fields of critical and creative thinking. Its basic three-tier structure is similar to that developed independently by Demetriou and Kazi (2001). Both Marzano and Demetriou distinguish between cognitive, metacognitive (termed hypercognitive by Demetriou) and self systems (self-representation for Demetriou). Demetriou and Kazi have accumulated an impressive amount of empirical support for their model, which is even broader in scope than Marzano's. Marzano pays rather less attention than Demetriou and Kazi to non-cognitive aspects of personality and says little about sensitivities to the situational and interpersonal factors which affect learning. His tendency to ignore sociocultural aspects of knowledge construction is an undoubted weakness. Nonetheless, his theory is compatible with a large number of the frameworks considered in this book, including those of Anderson and Krathwohl, Bloom, Halpern, Hauenstein, Jonassen and Tessmer, Pintrich, Presseisen, Romiszowski, and Stahl and Murphy.

It remains to be seen how far Marzano's theory will yield verifiable predictions and findings with practical implications for teachers and learners. One of its key features, the 'downward' direction of the flow of information, is highly speculative and probably over-simplified. His ideas about the amount of conscious thought needed at each level and the dependence of each level on those below also await critical analysis and experimental enquiry.

The three-tier structure of Marzano's taxonomy has only a modest level of empirical support from his own large-scale meta-analysis of research on instruction (1998). The mean differences in achievement gain produced by educational interventions making use of the three systems are not great (27 percentile points for the self system, 26 for the metacognitive system and 21 for the cognitive system). The standard deviations are so large that it is simply not possible to argue that it is better to aim for change via the self system rather than through the cognitive system.

Marzano seems to think of the metacognitive system as a sort of computer, unlike the self system which deals with motivation, beliefs and feelings. This does not accord with subjective experience, in which motivation, beliefs and feelings are not disassociated from planning, monitoring and evaluating, either when engaging in an activity or when seeing it through. Conative, affective and cognitive aspects of thought are not easily separable and all three are involved in planning, monitoring and evaluating. Although Marzano does acknowledge this when writing about the self system, we believe that the distinction he makes between the self and metacognitive systems is too rigid.

We also believe that the flow of information which constitutes 'control' is more complex and interactive than Marzano suggests. It cannot all be downwards, as he claims. For example, there are many examples in the literature of self-concept and self-efficacy being enhanced as a result of cognitive skill acquisition. The brain does not function like a strictly hierarchical military organisation. When Marzano states that without a clear goal, task execution will break down (2001b), he is evidently not thinking about many stages of creative thinking. Representations of the self are formed through experiences at all levels of consciousness and control. In Demetriou's empirically-supported model of the mind, there is more dynamic interaction between levels and modules (Demetriou and Kazi, 2001) than Marzano allows for.

Marzano's theory has considerable potential for use in instructional design, teaching, assessment, research and evaluation. He summarises both general and specific instructional implications for practitioners, many of which are applicable irrespective of the age range of learners. He has already demonstrated its value as a research tool and plans to extend what he claims to be the largest meta-analysis ever undertaken (Marzano, 1998).

The fact that Marzano has already provided many illustrations of how his new taxonomy may be used in primary and secondary education makes it useful to teachers and other educational professionals. It is not too complex for everyday use by teachers and learners and by encouraging the clear statement of educational goals, it may help teachers systematise and improve their practice. However, there are a few cases where boundaries between categories may not be entirely clear, because of the way in which the descriptors are defined.

The inclusion of a knowledge utilisation level, dealing with the orchestration of thinking, makes Marzano's taxonomy meaningful in real-life problem-solving contexts in the workplace and elsewhere. This feature, together with the importance given to the metacognitive and self systems may help bring about improvements in formative and summative assessment in relation to higher-level key skills and similar learning objectives.

While this taxonomy is likely to stimulate various forms of enquiry, it could have the effect of de-emphasising creativity as well as collaborative thinking and learning. Its most significant limitation is the strength of its emphasis on individual cognitive performance, compared with its treatment of interpersonal, cultural and systemic aspects.

Summary: Marzano

Purpose and structure	Some key features	Relevance for teachers and learning
Main purpose(s): • to provide a theory-grounded taxonomy for designing educational objectives and assessments • to provide a research tool for classifying educational interventions	**Terminology:** • generally clear but sometimes idiosyncratic	**Intended audience:** • designers of instruction and assessment • teachers • researchers
Domains addressed: • cognitive • conative • affective • psychomotor	**Presentation:** • Marzano has published his ideas in accessible forms for a variety of audiences	**Contexts:** • education • work • citizenship • recreation
Broad categories covered: • self-regulation • reflective thinking • productive thinking • building understanding • information-gathering	**Theory base:** • eclectic, drawing on the fields of cognitive psychology, neuropsychology, linguistics, critical thinking and informal logic	**Pedagogical stance:** • the effective teacher has clear objectives at all levels of the taxonomy and makes decisions based on theory-based understanding and research evidence • prerequisites should be mastered before moving to higher levels • skills should be orchestrated and applied in meaningful ways

Classification by:	Values:	Practical illustrations
• levels in a hierarchy of control	• individualism	**for teachers:**
• level of consciousness	• empiricism	• many and varied
• direction of flow of information	• high importance given to self-regulation and other productive habits of mind	

Sternberg's model of abilities as developing expertise

Description and intended use

Well known for his 'triarchic' theory of critical, creative and practical intelligence and to a lesser extent for his model of thinking styles (1997), Sternberg has also written about abilities as forms of developing expertise (Sternberg, 2001; Sternberg and Grigorenko, 2002). He claims that the development of expertise involves the interaction of at least the following elements:

1. *Metacognitive skills:* these refer to people's understanding and control of their thought processes. For example, such skills would encompass what an individual knows about writing an essay or solving arithmetic problems, both with regard to the steps involved and with how these steps can be executed effectively. Seven particularly important metacognitive skills are: problem recognition; problem definition; problem representation; strategy formulation; resource allocation; monitoring of problem-solving; and evaluation of problem-solving. All of these skills are deemed to be modifiable, yet Sternberg (2001) notes that students are often resistant to metacognitive training.

2. *Learning skills:* these are seen as sometimes explicit, when we make an effort to learn, or implicit when we pick up information incidentally, without any systematic effort. Examples of learning skills are: selective encoding, which involves distinguishing relevant from irrelevant information; selective combination, which involves putting together the relevant information; and selective comparison, which involves relating new information to information already stored in memory.

3. *Thinking skills:* there are three main kinds of thinking skill that individuals need to master –
   - *critical (analytical)* thinking skills, including: analysing, critiquing, judging, evaluating, comparing and contrasting, and assessing;
   - *creative* thinking skills, including: creating, discovering, inventing, imagining, supposing, and hypothesising;
   - *practical* thinking skills, which are 'involved when intelligence is applied to real world contexts' (Sternberg at al, 2000, p. 31) and depend heavily on 'tacit knowledge, namely the procedural knowledge one learns in everyday life that usually is not taught and often is not even verbalized' (Sternberg et al., 2000, p. xi).

   These three aspects are viewed as comprising 'successful intelligence', which Sternberg et al. (2000, p. 93) define as 'the ability to achieve success in life, given one's personal standards, within one's sociocultural context. Ability to achieve success depends on capitalizing on one's strengths and correcting or compensating for one's weaknesses through a balance of analytical, creative, and practical abilities in order to adapt to, shape, and select environments.'

4. *Knowledge: declarative* knowledge is knowledge of facts, concepts, principles, laws etc. – 'knowing that'. *Procedural* knowledge is knowledge of procedures and strategies – 'knowing how'. Sternberg does not devalue teaching for knowledge outcomes, as without this foundation students cannot think critically about what they know.

5. *Motivation:* while noting that it is indispensable for school success, Sternberg has tended not to consider motivation to the same extent as the cognitive elements. In setting out his model, he briefly refers to McClelland's (1961) theory of achievement motivation and Bandura's self-efficacy (1997), but makes no reference to more contemporary work. He gives the following examples of desirable attitudes:
   a. combating the tendency to procrastinate,
   b. organising oneself to get work done,
   c. figuring out how one learns best,
   d. avoiding the tendency to use self-pity as an excuse for working hard, and
   e. avoiding blaming others for one's own failings (Sternberg, 2002, p. 389).

6. *Context:* all the elements above are seen as characteristics of the learner, but Sternberg notes that all these processes are affected by, and can in turn affect, the context in which they operate. In a recent review (Sternberg, 2002a) provides illustrations from a variety of cultures to support his argument that while processes underpinning intelligence are universal, the ways in which these are manifested are not. Criticising the common tendency of psychologists to apply Western measures to other cultures, he argues that while it is currently impossible to create culture-free or culture-fair tests, 'we can create culture-relevant tests, and that should be our goal' (p. 336).

Sternberg emphasises the interactive nature of the above six elements:

At the centre, driving the elements, is motivation. Without it, the elements remain inert . . . Motivation drives metacognitive skills, which in turn activate learning and thinking skills, which then provide feedback to the metacognitive skills, enabling one's level of expertise to increase. The declarative and procedural knowledge acquired through the extension of the thinking and learning skills also results in these skills being used more effectively in the future (Sternberg and Grigorenko, 2002, pp. 8–9).

For more than twenty years Sternberg has sought to demonstrate the validity and practical utility of his triarchic theory. He argues that:

a. Western educational systems have placed undue emphasis upon analytical reasoning (which is highly valued in academic contexts) and have neglected creative and practical reasoning;
b. Triarchic teaching approaches (that utilise all three aspects) will result in superior learning outcomes to those using traditional methods;
c. Focusing teaching and learning approaches to the particular strengths of students will maximise learning.

Evaluation

Unlike some of the authors studied by our group, Sternberg does not seek, at least in his more recent publications, to list exhaustively all the various components of, for example, metacognition. Rather, he provides broad-brush strokes that yield key factors which contribute to expertise, and for each of these he offers examples. He incorporates his triarchic theory of intelligence within this broader theory and divides thinking skills into three main areas.

Sternberg and his colleagues have sought to apply their triarchic model to the practice of education at both school and university level. Sternberg et al. (1999) and Grigorenko et al. (2002) found that teaching triarchically tends to result in superior performance, even when traditional memory-based measures were employed as tests of achievement. Williams et al. (2002) report on the Practical Intelligence for School (PIFS) intervention in which emphasis was given to analytical, creative and practical ways of using and developing intelligence (according to Sternberg's triarchic theory), within each of Gardner's seven multiple intelligence domains. Large effect sizes on outcome measures of practical intelligence (but much less impressive academic gains) were found in one area where class sizes were small and where 90% of the PIFS lessons were delivered. However, in another area, despite receiving weekly support, teachers became more selective in their use of the programme in the second year, with the result that the differences in outcome between experimental and control groups were negligible.

Sternberg's triarchic theory has been challenged, especially by those who defend the concept of general intelligence (g). Quite recently, his conception of 'practical intelligence' and the research programme to validate it were meticulously and comprehensively critiqued (Brody, 2003a; 2003b, Gottfredson, 2003a; 2003b). While Sternberg has countered their arguments (Sternberg, 2003b; 2003c), pointing out, for example, that Brody's critique was of an outdated test, he does accept that, as yet, there is no published test of triarchic abilities and existing research-based measures require further development (Sternberg, 2004b).

As noted above, Sternberg sees motivation as being central to learning, yet he provides little systematic examination of related theoretical or conceptual issues. In a similar way, he creates his model of abilities as developing expertise by aggregating elements, rather than by providing a detailed theoretical rationale or empirical evidence base.

Nonetheless, the greater part of Sternberg's model of developing expertise is uncontroversial and is easily communicated to others so as to inform practice. As noted above, Sternberg's team have produced, and are continuing to produce, curricular interventions based upon the triarchic model with encouraging results. As a result of their particular emphasis upon the creative and the practical, their focus may be seen as different to, and potentially more powerful than, many thinking skills programmes which seek to draw upon cognitive approaches to analytical reasoning.

Summary: Sternberg

Purpose and structure	Some key features	Relevance for teachers and learning
Main purpose(s): • to improve teaching and learning • to provide more sensitive tests of intelligence and expertise	**Terminology:** • clear	**Intended audience:** • designers of instruction and assessment • teachers • researchers
Domains addressed: • cognitive • conative • affective	**Presentation:** • accessible, broad-brush outline, but more illustrative than exhaustive	**Contexts:** • education
Broad categories covered: • self-engagement • reflective thinking • productive thinking • building understanding • information-gathering	**Theory base:** • largely Sternberg himself (e.g. triarchic theory of intelligence)	**Pedagogical stance:** • provide an optimal degree of challenge • teach 'triarchically' for analytic, creative and practical learning
Classification by: • steps in problem-solving and in information processing • type of knowledge	**Values:** • emphasis tends to be placed upon individual development • emphasises the importance of cultural context	**Practical illustrations for teachers:** • some examples are provided • a number of educational interventions, based upon the theory, are currently being undertaken and evaluated

Some issues for further investigation

- What are the similarities and differences between the different treatments of *knowledge*?
- What evidence is there that perceiving and remembering are seen as processes in which meaning is constructed?
- Do any of the authors present the interplay of cognition and emotion as a holistic, dynamic process?
- Which, if any, of the new technical terms used by these authors are illuminative?
- Does any framework include important features which are not found elsewhere?
- Which framework presents the most helpful account of problem-solving?
- Which frameworks best accommodate creative thinking and which are themselves creative?
- How do the frameworks differ in dealing with the development and power of attitudes and dispositions?
- Are there any substantive differences between these authors in their understanding of self-regulation?
- Are any of these frameworks incompatible with the others or with parts of others?
- Which of these authors have also developed models of cognitive or learning style and how do such models relate to those considered here?
- Which frameworks are influenced by developmental stage models of human cognition and how are these influences apparent?
- What kinds of moral judgment are implicit and explicit in the various frameworks?
- Which of these frameworks is the most mechanistic and which the most humanistic – and why?

7

Moving from understanding to productive thinking: implications for practice

Overview

This chapter reviews the potential contribution of the various frameworks, models and taxonomies presented in the book and summarises a number of issues which have arisen. It examines how various taxonomies can inform and support differing aspects and areas of education. It will summarise some problems inherent in classification and theoretical models of thinking. We highlight evidence from meta-analysis to show that thinking skills approaches can be very effective, especially those targeted at the skills of metacognition and self-regulation. Turning to matters of theory, we note a degree of rapprochement between cognitive, constructivist and some recent behaviourist formulations. However, we do not believe that it has been established that meaningful learning can take place only when there is a low level of teacher direction (Hattie, 2002). We point out that a great deal of educational practice is based on sets of widely accepted but usually untested beliefs, values and assumptions. Finally, we outline the value of a practical four-category framework (information gathering; building understanding; productive thinking; strategic management/reflective thinking) that has arisen from our work in this field.

Thinking, learning and teaching

Everyone who is involved in learning needs to have some understanding of its nature and purpose. A framework for understanding thinking and learning can be used at different levels; for example, as a general guide to the formulation of a mission statement or in formulating specific learning objectives and precise assessment items. When a theoretical framework is used consistently and explicitly, it is likely that communication within an educational or training context will be enhanced, as well as communication with the outside world. This should therefore be of direct benefit to teachers and learners as well as others involved such as parents, employers, policy-makers and the educational research community.

There are a number of subject disciplines which have as their focus the study of human beings. These include philosophy, psychology, sociology and anthropology, where almost every aspect of human behaviour is of potential interest. Geographers and historians are clearly interested in a broad spectrum of human behaviour and we could add other disciplines to the list. The point is that in the humanities, just as much as in the sciences, there are benefits to be obtained through collaboration and this too requires a shared language about how people think and learn. It is certainly possible for a thinking skills framework to be drawn up for each subject area, but if this were done, the differences would probably lie only in the detail. In our view, many benefits would flow from the interdisciplinary development of a common framework, especially if care were taken to avoid the use of the kind of esoteric or abstruse language which tends to maintain artificial boundaries between traditional academic subjects.

Understanding thinking and learning is important not only in academic study, but also in professional and vocational courses and in working effectively with younger learners. Some kinds of teaching have traditionally included the philosophical study of theories of knowledge, but most have not included any study of theories of learning. However, it would make good sense for thinking and learning to form the core of such studies, associated with another subject of choice in which human behaviour is the focus. An understanding of thinking and learning frameworks should inform the planning of appropriate curricula for all kinds of learning, in order to ensure that they are realistic and achievable.

How are thinking skills classified?

Altogether, we identified a total of 16 different kinds of principle that were used in the frameworks we have evaluated to classify thinking and/or its outcomes. As can be seen from the evaluative summaries, most frameworks are structured by only two or three principles and none by a comprehensive set. We list the principles used in all 42 frameworks in the present handbook under four main headings as follows:

Domain

- area of experience
- subject area

Content

- types of objective
- types of product (including knowledge products)

Process

- steps/phases in a sequence or cycle
- complexity
- level in a hierarchy
- type of thinking or learning
- quality of thought/action

Psychological aspects

- stage of development
- structural features of cognition
- nature and strength of dispositions
- internalisation of learning
- orchestration and control of thinking
- degree of learner autonomy
- level of consciousness.

It was no surprise to find that the most comprehensive frameworks (according to the number and range of principles they embody) are members of the all-embracing and instructional design families. We found ten frameworks which are based on a selection of principles from each of the generic categories: domain, content, process and psychological aspects. Five of these are the all-embracing frameworks of Romiszowski (1981), Wallace and Adams (1990), Jonassen and Tessmer (1996/7), Hauenstein (1998) and Marzano (2001a; 2001b).

Four more are the instructional design frameworks of Gagné (1965; 1985), Williams (1970), Hannah and Michaelis (1977) and Gouge and Yates (2002). Demetriou's (1993) integrated developmental model of the mind also belongs in this category. It is worth noting that Bloom's overall taxonomic achievements would qualify him for membership of this group, if we were to take into account his work in the cognitive, affective and psychomotor domains.

The all-embracing frameworks are more likely than others to include some coverage of the affective and conative domains as well as cognitive skills. The more recent frameworks also include an explicit treatment of metacognition.

Several instructional design frameworks also extend beyond the cognitive domain, but members of this family are distinctive because their purpose is to categorise different kinds of learning objective and subject content or how far knowledge and skills are internalised.

Our examination of the classificatory principles used in the critical and productive thinking frameworks showed that the presence or absence of reflective and metacognitive processes and of dispositions with conative and affective features are often highlighted (as in the frameworks of Ennis, Paul and Lipman; see Chapter 4). However, there are some frameworks which are limited to the cognitive and metacognitive domain; such as Allen, Feezel and Kauffie (1967). Another feature of critical thinking frameworks is that (apart from valuing progress toward better critical thinking) their authors do not specify different kinds of objective (e.g. global or specific, short-term or long-term).

Among the frameworks dealing with cognitive structure and development there are some in which classificatory principles from only one category are used (such as Belenky et al., 1986, Koplowitz, 1987 and King and Kitchener, 1994). Again, within this type of framework, with the exception of Guilford's (1956) *products* dimension, different types of objective or outcome are not identified.

As at least 16 different kinds of principle have been used to classify thinking skills, it is most unlikely that a comprehensive and manageable framework can be constructed which uses all of them: a hypertaxonomy or 'meta-taxonomy' perhaps. It is perhaps for this reason that Romiszowski (1981) presents three separate models: a categorisation of knowledge; a skill cycle; and a schema of skill categories. Romiszowski, Gagné (1965; 1985), Hannah and Michaelis (1977),

Hauenstein (1998) and Marzano (2001a; 2001b) all come close to providing comprehensive coverage of thinking and learning in all areas of experience, but each have their own weaknesses and cannot be regarded as complete solutions for general use as they stand.

We did not therefore find one framework which can be recommended for widespread application as a way of giving purpose and structure to the experience of teaching and learning. At one stage we thought that we might be able to recommend Marzano's new taxonomy of educational objectives above all others (Marzano, 2001a and 2001b). His framework has two main advantages. It is built on psychological theory, and has been used to classify the outcomes of educational interventions in a very extensive meta-analysis (Marzano, 1998). However, there are certain problems with Marzano's approach. Firstly, we do not believe it is helpful to distinguish as strongly as Marzano does between the self system and the metacognitive system, since we see these as being in dynamic interaction. Secondly, Marzano's set of knowledge utilisation categories omits reasoning and creative thinking. Thirdly, in his first three cognitive categories, he defines some terms in ways which diverge from common usage and from the well-known meanings in other taxonomies.

We can identify three complementary frameworks which together provide comprehensive coverage. Pintrich's framework of self-regulated learning (see page 235) best conveys the meaning of strategic and reflective thinking, using a variation of the familiar plan-do-review cycle. Halpern (1997) provides a popular productive thinking framework (see page 140), accompanied by resource materials designed for school and college use (Halpern 2002). Anderson and Krathwohl's (2001) updated and extended revision of Bloom's taxonomy (see page 49), which can be used with any age and ability group, provides a vocabulary for describing specific knowledge and skill objectives. It covers basic thinking skills as well as single processes which, especially when combined, constitute productive thinking.

Using thinking skills frameworks

There are many ways in which the use of thinking skills frameworks can support teachers in their practice and be built into both teacher training and further professional development. Teachers need regular opportunities to reflect on their own learning and style of teaching. Without such opportunities, they will not be prepared to engage learners in similar discussions. Thinking skills frameworks can help to provide the necessary lexicon of thinking and learning, to develop a common language applicable across subject areas.

Elsewhere in this book we have referred to the use of thinking skills frameworks in the planning of instruction, in teaching, in assessment, and in the alignment of all three. This is clearly one of the most valuable functions of these frameworks. Planning can be done at several different levels, but it is the teacher who has, on the basis of formative and summative assessments, to make constant adjustments while teaching in order to facilitate learning. The skills required cannot be learned from textbooks alone, but are undoubtedly capable of development and fine-tuning using models and frameworks which make some aspects of thinking more explicit. The teacher's job is to ensure that learning takes place, and as teachers develop expertise, their constructs about teaching and learning become more sophisticated. Being able to discuss those constructs within a community of practice and in relation to theory-based frameworks makes a teacher not only a learner, but a practitioner–researcher. Indeed there is evidence that this kind of professional enquiry is in itself an effective way to support more effective teaching (Fennema et al., 1996; Franke et al., 1998).

It is not just teachers, but learners who need to develop a mature understanding of thinking and learning, especially in contexts where learners have to take a large share of the responsibility for their own progress. They need to consider not only their immediate needs, but the possible value of 'transferable skills' (the thinking that underlies key skills initiatives, for instance). Good communication, effective working with others and a commitment to improving one's own learning and performance are clearly valuable qualities. They can be developed in many ways, not just through formal education and training. As Lipman (1991) argues, it is far from clear that the best way to develop an intrinsic interest in thinking and learning is through prescribed activities. Lipman advocates the community of enquiry approach to thinking and learning, through philosophical discussion of issues of concern to a group. Yet even here, participants need to understand the theoretical framework within which the community operates.

Another use of a framework for understanding thinking and learning is as a research and evaluation tool. For example, Vermunt and Verloop (1999) write persuasively about congruence and friction between learning and teaching. They suggest that 'congruence' exists both when either teacher direction is high and student self-regulation low, and when student self-regulation is high and teacher direction low. A theory-based framework of approaches to learning like the one produced by Vermunt (1996) can lead to new ways of assessing psychological and pedagogical aspects of learning environments. It then becomes possible to relate what are presumed to be indicators of quality to outcome measures. There is a serious lack of evidence-based information of this kind, without which any inspection or quality assurance regime lacks credibility.

Which frameworks are best suited to specific applications?

Two of the complementary frameworks identified above (Halpern, 1997 and Anderson and Krathwohl, 2001) are written in a particularly accessible style. There is continuity between Bloom (1956) and Anderson and Krathwohl (2001) in that David Krathwohl was a member of Bloom's original team. In fact, teachers can still learn a lot from Bloom's famous book, which was written with college students in mind and shows few signs of its age. It has the advantage of being very concise and well written. Pintrich's framework of self-regulated learning can be understood in tabular form, but does need a more accessible exposition.

These three frameworks are, however, not the only ones that can help teachers acquire what we have called a 'lexicon of thinking and learning'. An outstanding professional resource is Costa's *Developing Minds* (2001), which contains chapters by Baron, Ennis, Marzano, McTighe, Paul, Perkins, Presseisen and Tishman, among others. This enables practitioners to select and develop ideas from these perspectives and grapple with the vocabulary and language that each perspective promotes. Those wanting an off-the-shelf practical framework, expressed in simple language and designed to be understood by learners as well as teachers, will find that the TASC model (Adams and Wallace, 1990) goes a long way towards meeting their needs.

We believe also that the following frameworks can help the reader better understand thinking and learning (which is not to say that all the original sources are accessible): Baron, Carroll, Gardner, Guilford, Hannah and Michaelis, Jewell, Koplowitz, Lipman, Quellmalz, Presseisen, Romiszowski, Sternberg, Vermunt and Verloop, Wallace and Adams, and Williams. The work of Gardner, Presseisen, Sternberg, Wallace and Adams and Vermunt is readily available and particularly relevant for teacher educators.

If the subject of thinking skills, especially critical thinking, is approached from a philosophical perspective, the frameworks of Ennis, Lipman and Paul can be usefully compared and contrasted. An indepth but also very practical psychological perspective on critical thinking is provided by Halpern (1997). As Sternberg's earlier work on critical thinking is available only on microfiche (1986), we recommend the latest edition of his general textbook on cognitive psychology (2003a). For understanding developmental perspectives on critical thinking, King and Kitchener's (1994) book is the best source, with Perry (1970) and Belenky (1986) providing both historical and theoretical context.

For instructional design purposes, we have highlighted Anderson and Krathwohl's revision (2001) of Bloom's taxonomy (1956). Readers who want a comprehensive treatment of instructional design should consult Jonassen, Tessmer and Hannum (1999). In addition, we suggest that consideration be given to the frameworks developed by Romiszowski (1981), Hannah and Michaelis (1977) and Hauenstein (1998). These all deal with psychomotor and affective learning objectives (as well as cognitive ones) and are concerned with stages in the development of understanding as well as with the end result. If the focus of instructional design is creative thinking, the most useful frameworks are those of Gouge and Yates (2002) and Williams (1970), while the work of Halpern and Lipman is also relevant.

Of all the authors we have reviewed, Marzano is noteworthy for translating research findings into teaching recommendations, framing these within the structure of his new taxonomy (Marzano, 1998, 2001a). His is a pragmatic approach to pedagogy. In contrast with Lipman and Paul, neither Marzano nor Anderson and Krathwohl seem to call for radical transformation of educational practice.

Developing appropriate pedagogies

A wide spectrum of views about what constitutes effective pedagogy is represented in the work we have evaluated. Theorists usually have preferences about ways of encouraging good thinking, meaningful learning and deep or strategic approaches to study. For example, ten Dam and Volman (2004) argue that, as one of the main purposes of critical thinking is to learn how to resist social injustice, more attention should be paid in schools to the political nature of issues which 'relate to the world, to students' own position and that of others and to students' opportunities to influence this position' (2004, p. 373). They argue for a social constructivist critical pedagogy but see value in a wide range of methods (e.g. fishbowling and creative controversy) thought to enhance critical thinking.

All theorists agree that learning and thinking are active processes in which new connections are made and the value of applying thinking in meaningful real-life situations is widely supported. If strategic and reflective thinking are to be developed, learners need to be in situations where they have opportunities to use that kind of thinking. However, it would be unwise to assume that thinking skills can only be developed in particular kinds of learning environment that are advocated by certain theorists or are fashionable at the time. Again the flexibility of the TASC approach is a positive feature, since it was designed to be used in very diverse cultural and educational environments.

Vermunt and Verloop (1999) place approaches to learning and instruction on a continuum between teacher-regulated and student-regulated, and point out that there may be differences between pedagogical practice and beliefs, and student conceptions of learning and their ability to regulate it. The continuum of theoretical positions in the work we have reviewed ranges from Gagné (1965; 1985) and Ausubel at the teacher-regulated end to those like Feuerstein (1980),

Hannah and Michaelis (1977) and Romiszowski (1981), who favour forms of 'guided discovery', to those like Lipman and Paul who advocate learner-centred approaches. Learner empowerment through the social construction of knowledge is strongly valued by Belenky et al. (1986), King and Kitchener (1994), and Jonassen and Tessmer (1996/7). Gardner and Vermunt believe in the importance of tailoring instruction to meet group and individual needs. Vermunt, in common with very many other theorists, emphasises process over content in much of his writing, arguing that self-regulation rather than the accumulation of knowledge, is the key to lifelong learning. The only theorists to deal adequately with what teachers and learners can do to improve the acquisition and retention of knowledge and skills are Halpern and Wallace and Adams. We believe this to be a neglected but still very important area.

In the actual practice of teaching, it is possible for a teacher to keep a simple framework in mind, as a means of monitoring the kind of thinking expected of students. This is especially important in the process of questioning and when discussing a topic with a class, group or individual. The simple four-category system developed in this project (see below) is very suitable for this purpose. Anderson and Krathwohl's (2001) six process categories (remember, understand, apply, analyse, evaluate, create) can also be used in this way. Many teachers find they can readily internalise Gardner's seven (or more) kinds of intelligence (see p. 206) in order to monitor learning activities in those terms. The '3Cs' of critical, creative, caring thinking, which are derived from Lipman and used by Jewell (1996) are also easily memorised and applied, as are the eight phases of problem solving in the TASC 'wheel'.

However, we do not wish to give the impression that any of the 3Cs are easy. As Petty argues for creative thinking, there is a lot of 'perspiration' involved. One example of a highly complex framework which we believe to be of great value is Altshuller's TRIZ. Our brief description and evaluative summary of this theory of inventive prob-lem solving (TRIZ) (1996; 1999; 2000) does not do it justice. It is now taught in a number of universities in the UK and has been widely taken up in many countries where technological innovation is valued. It has the unique quality of organising creative thinking. Although coming up with inventive solutions to practical problems still depends on analogical thinking and looking for patterns, the task is much simplified by applying Altshuller's 'algorithmic' procedures. These are the result of many years of systematic data gathering and his analysis of existing patented solutions.

Other applications of the frameworks and models

Consultancy (whether in educational or business contexts) is another area in which frameworks of thinking and learning are widely used. We have not attempted to identify all the frameworks that inform practice in this field, many of which are models of learning styles rather than thinking skills. Others (e.g. Senge, 1990) are simply sets of problem-solving heuristics. We mention here three particular frameworks. One of the early rational problem-solving approaches was the Kepner–Tregoe (Kepner and Tregoe, 1965) tenets of effective decision making – rational thinking. Koplowitz (1987) has applied his theory of stages in adult cognitive development in business settings and argues that better decisions are made when people move beyond logical analysis to more systemic and holistic ways of thinking. Although it was not devised with consultancy applications in mind, Vermunt and Verloop's categorisation of learning activities (1999) appears to us to be highly applicable as a way of understanding how learning develops (or not) in any organisation.

Assessment is another major area in which thinking skills frameworks, especially those dealing with educational objectives, are extremely relevant. As Ennis recognises, the assessment of critical thinking is a problematic area, despite being one in which he is personally involved (Ennis and Millman, 1985; Ennis and Weir, 1985). We believe, however, that the most useful framework for developing the quality of assessment is the SOLO taxonomy of Biggs and Collis (1982). This has the merit of being easily communicable to students. Examples of relevant work in the appropriate subject area can be presented to students to illustrate each of the five SOLO levels. Students can also assess such pieces of work (including their own).

When it comes to the assessment of personal qualities and dispositions, especially as displayed in group situations, further problems arise. However, these are not necessarily insuperable. The lists of dispositions produced by the following authors may be helpful in this context: Baron (1985), Ennis, Halpern, Jewell (1996) and Paul. Costa and Kallick's (2000a, 2000b) 16 'habits of mind' and the seven dispositions put forward by Perkins, Jay and Tishman (1993) as the basis of their dispositional theory of thinking are also worth considering. Costa, Kallick and Perkins (2000) address the topic of assessing and reporting on 'habits of mind' (a phrase originally coined by John Dewey, 1938).

Thinking skills frameworks are also valuable in research and evaluation. Pintrich is a good example of a researcher who developed ways of assessing learning, aided by his theoretical framework of self-regulated learning. Sternberg is another, with his triarchic theory of successful intelligence and his claim that 'triarchic teaching' is more effective than traditional approaches (2002a). Vermunt and Verloop's (1999) categorisation of learning activities and Vermunt's broader framework for understanding approaches to learning (1996) have led them and other researchers to find ways of assessing psychological and pedagogical aspects of learning environments. Feuerstein's Instrumental Enrichment (IE) intervention programme (1980) is typically evaluated using closely related cognitive measures from the Learning Potential Assessment Device (Hattie, Biggs and Purdie, 1996; Romney and Samuels, 2001). Demetriou's (1993) developmental model of the mind could usefully be tested out in more countries. In fact, all thinking skills frameworks can be used to generate research questions.

Finally, meta-analysis can be structured by using categories from thinking skills frameworks. This makes it possible to compare the effect sizes produced by different types of educational intervention. It was in this way that Hattie, Biggs and Purdie (1996) were able to evaluate the effects of learning skills interventions on student learning. They did so by using the SOLO taxonomy (Biggs and Collis, 1982) to categorise interventions as being unistructural, multistructural, relational or extended abstract. They also compared 'near transfer' with 'far transfer' effects. We believe that future meta-analyses should build on this kind of approach.

Marzano's (1998) meta-analysis was broader in scope and larger in scale than any other we have found. Marzano categorised all studies, including 147 studies at college level, using the categories and sub-categories from his new taxonomy of educational objectives. Marzano's overall conclusion (1998, p. 135) was as follows:

The effective teacher is one who has clear instructional goals. These goals are communicated both to students and to parents. Ideally, the instructional goals address elements of the knowledge domains as well as the cognitive, meta-cognitive, and self-system. Even if the instructional goals focus on the know-ledge domains only (as is frequently the case in public education), the teacher still uses instructional techniques that employ the cognitive system, the metacognitive system, and the self-system. Perhaps, above all, the teacher understands the interrelationships among the knowledge domains, the cog-nitive system, the metacognitive system, and the self-system, and uses that understanding to make the myriad of instructional decisions that occur in a single lesson.

In which areas is there extensive or widely accepted knowledge?

Theorists and taxonomists who categorise thinking skills do so on the assumption that the terms they use have meaning: in other words, that there are at least some skills, abilities or dispositions which are recognisable in different contexts. The question as to how far people are able to make use of those skills, abilities and dispositions in new situations, especially when learning is required in addition to prepared-ness and recall, is one requiring an answer based on experience, not theory. In our view, empirical research has amply confirmed that thinking and learning skills can be taught in such a way that the skills can successfully be applied in different (albeit usually closely related) areas.

We refer here to two relevant meta-analyses. In each of these, a thinking skills framework was used to categorise the results; and in both cases, it was found that interventions directed at metacognitive thinking skills were highly effective.

Hattie, Biggs and Purdie (1996) confined their interest to 271 effect sizes in 51 'learning skills interventions'. They found that 'unistruc-tural' approaches (interventions directed at single-skill outcomes) were the most effective, with a large mean effect size of 0.83. Among the most effective unistructural interventions were those addressing memory and reproductive performance. However, 'relational interventions' with 'near transfer' were also highly effective, the mean effect size being 0.77. The authors say (1996, p. 105) that relational interventions 'are integrated to suit the individual's self-assessment, are orchestrated to the demands of the particular task and context, and are self-regulated with discretion'. Relational interventions frequently have a metacognitive emphasis and include a small number of attributional retraining studies with a mean effect size of 1.05. Using 'structural aids' (with a strategy emphasis) was also moderately effective, the mean effect size being 0.58. Overall, in line with the weight of previous research, transfer effects were larger with 'near' than with 'far transfer'. Hattie, Biggs and Purdie also found that the mean effect size for self-directed interventions (0.70) was higher than for teacher-directed interventions (mean effect size 0.44).

Marzano (1998), found that college students responded just as well as school pupils when data from more than 4000 studies were aggregated. He confirmed Hattie, Biggs and Purdie's finding (1996) that techniques designed to be used by students led to significantly better results than those designed to be used by teachers. Although there was enormous diversity in the intervention studies selected by Marzano, ranging from a focus on specific skills (such as memorisation) to the use of disposition-monitoring strategies, he made the following claim (1998, p. 127) about the importance of metacognition:

instructional techniques that employed the metacognitive system had strong effects whether they were intended to enhance the knowledge domains, the mental process within the cognitive system, the beliefs and processes within the self-system, or the processes within the metacognitive system itself.

Overall, Marzano found that interventions which engage either the self system or the metacognitive system lead to better knowledge outcomes (by six and five percentile points respectively) than those which are directed only at the use of cognitive skills. Nevertheless, there are some types of very effective intervention at the cognitive skill level. These are interventions which address: experimental enquiry; using analogies; comparing and contrasting; idea representation; and the storage and retrieval of knowledge.

We can summarise these meta-analyses by saying that there is powerful empirical evidence that thinking skill interventions can be very effective at all levels, but especially if they are directed at meta-cognition, self-regulation and what may be termed 'value-grounded thinking'. Their effectiveness is likely to be greater if they are used for learner self-regulation rather than coming fully under teacher control. However, well-focused interventions at the cognitive level can also be very effective. These include interventions with a focus on experimental enquiry and idea representation, as well as approaches to study support such as using cues and questions to aid retrieval. Our own more modest work in this area reaches similar conclusions (Higgins et al., 2004).

In which areas is knowledge very limited or highly contested?

In our evaluations we have commented on the explicit and implicit value systems communicated by each theorist. There is considerable diversity among these and many philosophically and morally contested areas. Here we will not enter into debates which cannot be settled by research evidence, but will simply note the main areas of contention.

First, there are diverse views about the nature of knowledge and about how to access and use it. The power which people can exercise through thinking and communication also occupies many writers, who take positions ranging from various forms of elitism (intellectual, sociocultural or spiritual) to an egalitarian concern for human rights. There are also distinct moral and ethical belief systems – with some writers taking a pragmatic, technological view about the possible social and economic benefits of improved thinking; some espousing the values of a liberal–humanistic tradition; and others having a strong belief in rationalism.

We have also commented on a spectrum of views about nature and nurture and about individual freedoms and state control. Finally, opinions differ widely about which aspects of thinking should be taught and how they should be taught.

Of the contested issues listed above, those in the previous paragraph are, to varying degrees, open to systematic enquiry and research. The last of these (the nature and nurture debate) has been researched more than the others. For example, Pederson, Plomin and McClearn (1994) found substantial and broadly similar genetic influences on both general and specific cognitive abilities. Several studies have shown that genetic factors influence personality traits rather less than cognitive abilities (Loehlin, 1992). What is not known about thinking and learning is how far genetic influences impose limits on achievement when motivation is high and good-quality personal and environmental support are provided.

Most teachers accept that it is a core part of their role to take account of individual differences in learners, whether in terms of goals, preferences, ability, aptitude, or style of thinking and learning. There is no doubt that teachers are attracted by the idea that better results may be achievable if they capitalise on individual strengths, such as Gardner's multiple intelligences. However, in researching this area, there is a serious methodological difficulty in trying to control for the catalytic effects of enthusiasm on the part of those who take up novel approaches.

Just as the evidence base on the best ways to meet the individual needs of learners is weak, little is known about how to support teachers in being more effective in ways which respect their own individual differences and build on personal strengths. Apart from differences in the nature and extent of teacher direction and the facilitation of independent learning, teachers differ in other ways; for example, in creativity, in how they respond to a prescriptive curriculum, in their interest in abstract thinking, and in 'emotional intelligence'.

There is wide acceptance among psychologists and educators of the idea that thinking in individuals and groups is shaped through interpersonal interaction. Cognitive psychology is compatible with constructivist conceptions of learning and with the importance of person–situation interactions. As we have seen, theorists such as Pintrich and Vermunt see contextual factors as being highly important in relation to self-regulated learning. The sociocultural contexts in which learning takes place are also generally considered to exert powerful influences, even within the behavioural tradition. For example, Strand, Barnes-Holmes and Barnes-Holmes (2003, p. 105) suggest 'that advances in our understanding of choice behavior and verbal behavior put us within reach of a comprehensive framework for making sense of the interconnectedness of social, self, and academic development'.

The widely held view that constructivist beliefs about thinking and learning are incompatible with teacher-directed or behavioural approaches to instruction is an exaggerated position which has only a modest level of support from the meta-analytic findings which favour self-regulation over teacher direction. The fact is that teacher-directed approaches can also be effective in teaching thinking. Strand, Barnes-Holmes and Barnes-Holmes (2003) refer to several examples of this within the behaviourist paradigm. Hattie (2002) has compiled convincing evidence to show that 'direct instruction' can be highly effective and that pupils learn best when teachers provide high levels of appropriate feedback. As Ausubel argued, meaningful learning often requires a considerable amount of direction by teachers.

Constructing an integrated framework

As we have seen, there have been several attempts to produce an integrated framework for understanding thinking and learning. Those we called 'all-embracing' have variously taken into account cognitive, affective and conative aspects of thinking. Whether explicitly or implicitly, they also include metacognition as an important feature. However, while some authors associate metacognition only with thinking processes and skills at the 'higher' end of the cognitive domain, we believe that it makes more sense to consider all kinds of thinking, feeling and trying as potentially open to self-awareness and self-regulation. We decided to build our own integrated framework to reflect these ideas. We identified a set of core features and used them to develop a structurally simple framework suitable for a range of applications and formulated in clear and simple English.

All of the all-embracing frameworks in Chapter 6 have certain structural features in common and share all or some of these with every other framework, especially with those directed at instructional design. Bloom's taxonomy of educational objectives for the cognitive domain (1956) has clearly influenced many other formulations, and this gave us a starting point.

Bloom's taxonomy is basically a three-tier model, which we can describe in the following way. Thinking starts with and ends with knowledge, whether in the form of facts, concepts, rules or skills. An essential part of thinking is *information-gathering*, whether from memory or through perception. Basic thinking (which we call *building understanding*) consists of relatively simple ways of understanding, elaborating and using what is known. Higher-order thinking (or what we prefer to call *productive thinking*) is essentially a learning process which leads to a deeper understanding of the nature, justification, implications, and value of what is known.

All the frameworks we have evaluated include classifications of productive thinking. This may involve planning what to do and say, imagining situations, reasoning, solving problems, considering opinions, making decisions and judgments, generating new perspectives and designing and making valued products. Both critical and creative thinking are subsumed by the more general term 'productive thinking'. Productive thinking is very often supported by dispositions or habits of mind which take time to develop. Like other kinds of thinking, productive thinking may become so well practised as to be taken for granted, but when energised by feelings and determination, it can be, in Lipman's terms (1995), critical, creative and caring.

Although the Bloom-based model of *information-gathering, building understanding* and *productive thinking* is useful, we found it necessary to add another component. In seeking to identify what makes for good thinking and what facilitates meaningful learning, many theorists draw attention to conscious engagement and reflection as well as to relevant abilities and dispositions. We use the accessible and relatively uncontentious terms *strategic and reflective thinking* to capture these elements. In this way, we arrived at an integrated model and have found that it works well as a way of classifying the broad categories of thinking represented in the frameworks described and evaluated in this book.

Our model (see Figure 7.1) is made up of the three cognitive components which we identified in Bloom's taxonomy (1956) plus a self-regulatory/metacognitive system. This represents executive functioning as well as what Demetriou calls 'long-term hypercognition' (forms of knowledge about oneself as an agent and member of society, such as knowledge of personal qualities, values, roles and strategies).

STRATEGIC AND REFLECTIVE THINKING
Engagement with and management of thinking/learning, supported by value-grounded thinking (including critically reflective thinking)

⇕   ⇕   ⇕

COGNITIVE SKILLS		
Information-gathering	*Building understanding*	*Productive thinking*
Experiencing, recognising and recalling Comprehending messages and recorded information	Development of meaning (e.g. by elaborating, representing or sharing ideas) Working with patterns and rules Concept formation Organising ideas	Reasoning Understanding causal relationships Systematic enquiry Problem-solving Creative thinking

Fig. 7.1. An integrated model for understanding thinking and learning.

This model is not restricted to the cognitive domain and is intended to accommodate Lipman's critical, creative and caring thinking (1995). The terms 'engagement' and 'value-grounded' are meant to convey our interest in the conative and affective aspects of thinking. We see our model as applying to all kinds of thinking, including the 'emotional intelligence' areas which Gardner (1983; 1993) describes as interpersonal and intrapersonal intelligence. Although derived from models which are intended to represent an individual's thinking, our integrated model is just as applicable to the thinking of groups and organisations.

There is an essential difference between cognitive skills and strategic and reflective thinking in terms of the nature and quality of experience involved. Cognitive skills are procedures which can become automatised and are not necessarily associated with effort or emotion. However, strategic and reflective thinking are always highly conscious and are often experienced as involving will and/or emotion as well as cognition.

Strategic and reflective thinking are not easy, since they require sustained concentration, not only on the matter in hand, but also on how a task is conceived and whether or not there should be a change of strategy in the light of new and previous experience. Strategic and reflective thinking may involve considering the meaning of an activity in holistic as well as analytic ways. This kind of thinking is important when embarking on activities which make considerable demands on a person, such as an academic or vocational course or project. It can also be extremely valuable in dealing with much smaller issues, for example when there is a challenge to an assumption, belief or a communication problem. Most significantly, it is what changes what could be a routine process into a learning experience. The development of strategic and reflective thinking is acknowledged to be a major goal of higher education. We see it as equally important in lifelong learning at all ages and stages.

The two-way arrows between strategic and reflective thinking and cognitive skills in figure 7.1 do not fully represent the possible relationships between them. In many thinking and learning situations there certainly is two-way interaction. However, this does not always apply, since cognitive skills can be exercised effectively in unplanned and unreflective ways: for example, young children thinking creatively and developing productive problem-solving strategies, but being unable to give an account of the process (Alexander et al., 2004). On the other hand, it is impossible to operate at the level of strategic, value-grounded thinking without information-gathering and other cognitive skills coming into play. It is important to note that we are not making any claims about how thinking starts or about causality. The impetus for strategic or reflective thought may be situationally specific, as when a particular problem causes cognitive conflict, or it may flow from a well-established disposition or 'habit of mind'. What we do claim is that when thinking is strategic and reflective (involving the exercise of conscious purpose and a carefully executed plan), meaningful learning – to use Ausubel's phrase (1968) – is more likely to occur.

In the cognitive skill part of the framework, the three components (information-gathering, building understanding and productive thinking) are ordered from left to right, but this is not meant to imply that all thinking processes include the middle level of building understanding, as it is possible to go straight from information-gathering to productive thinking. Information-gathering is a prerequisite for either building understanding or productive thinking, but it is not necessarily a simpler or less conscious process. Although it very often happens that thinking develops through distinguishable (if overlapping) phases, from information-gathering to building understanding to a sound judgment or deeper understanding, this is not always the case, since these phases can take place in parallel or in complex systems with movement in both directions (as when it is found at a late stage of problem-solving that a vital piece of information is missing). The dotted lines in the diagram show that the boundaries between phases are far from rigid, since in the process of thinking, information can transmute into understanding and understanding into information.

The integrated framework proposed here is in some respects similar to the map of the thinking domain created by Swartz and Parks (1994). However, Swartz and Parks do not deal with information-gathering and use rather more categories to cover what we have called building understanding and productive thinking. Although they constantly stress the importance of metacognition, Swartz and Parks do not represent it on their map. Our integrated framework is not only simple in structure, but is compatible with the categories teachers are encouraged to use (such as in the National Curriculum for England or Scottish Curriculum Guidelines) as well as with leading theories about thinking and learning. The motivational and regulatory aspects of thinking (which cognitive psychologists think of as functions involving the 'central executive') are distinguished from cognitive skills; but, unlike Marzano, we do not see the need to distinguish between a self system and metacognitive system, since conscious planning, monitoring and evaluating functions are not neatly separable into two components, as presented in Marzano's model. This is recognised by Pintrich (2000), who includes Marzano's self-system and metacognitive-system functions within a unified framework of self-regulated learning.

We believe that the two-level structure of our model is a more accurate representation of how people think than a multilevel hierarchy. It also easily accommodates the various ways in which young and novice learners think strategically and reflectively as they develop information-gathering skills and build understanding. Without such a framework it is difficult for teachers to identify how comprehensive a particular curriculum is or, for example, to evaluate the claims of a thinking skills programme in covering aspects of critical thinking. We believe that our simple framework has potential as a tool for use in planning and evaluating courses and curricula, and constructing and grading of assessment tasks. In tables 7.1 and 7.2 we give two examples to illustrate how our broad categories are able to accommodate aspects of education for different age groups such as prompts and questions to support a range of thinking aimed at younger learners from 7–11 years old (table 7.1) and all of the key skills objectives appropriate for 14–19 year olds (table 7.2).

Summary

In this chapter we have reviewed the relative benefits of the different frameworks and models and their potential contribution to aspects of learning and teaching. We identified both the strengths and weaknesses of some of the general approaches which we have organised into family groups and the specific advantages and disadvantages of particular taxonomies and how they relate to what is currently known

Table 7.1. Problem-solving with young children

Area of thinking	Prompts and questions
Information-gathering	Think about what you know already.
	Have you done anything like this before?
	What information has been given to you?
Building understanding	Put the problem into your own words.
	What do you have to do?
	What will the final outcome look like?
Productive thinking	Think of ways to tackle the problem.
	What can you work out?
	What other approaches might work?
	Can you think of other possibilities?
Strategic management of thinking	Is this approach going to get you there?
	Have you overcome difficulties like this before?
	How good an answer will this be?
	What ideas of thinking might you be able to use in the future?
Reflective thinking	Keep track of what you are doing.
	How is it going?
	Did guessing the answers help at all?

Table 7.2. Meeting key skills objectives

Area of thinking	Tasks
Information-gathering	Identify the person you will see to review your progress and where and when this will take place.
Building understanding	Make changes suggested by your supervisor.
Productive thinking	Seek and actively use feedback and support from relevant sources to help you to meet targets.
Strategic management of thinking	Adapt your strategy to overcome difficulties and produce the quality of outcomes required.
Reflective thinking	Monitor and critically reflect on what you are learning and how you are learning, noting the choices you make and judging their effectiveness

about teaching and learning. Although our review did not identify one complete framework for general use, we recommended three complementary frameworks which provide comprehensive coverage. These are Pintrich's framework of self-regulated learning (see page 235) which covers the meaning of strategic and reflective thinking; Halpern (1997) who details a practical productive-thinking framework (see page 140); and Anderson and Krathwohl's (2001) revision of Bloom's taxonomy (see page 49), which can be used with any age and ability group and provides a valuable vocabulary for describing specific knowledge and skill objectives. The integrated model which we propose offers a practical tool to map these different models, frameworks and taxonomies in a way which should support those who wish to use the analysis and evaluation we offer in the earlier chapters of this handbook.

References

Adams, H. B. and Wallace, B. (1990). Developing the potential of children in disadvantaged communities: the TASC Project: Thinking Actively in a Social Context. In *The Challenge of Excellence: a vision splendid*, eds. S. Braggett, E. Bailey and M. Robinson. Sydney: The Australian Association for the Education of the Gifted and Talented, 250–266.

(1991). TASC: a model for curriculum development. *Gifted Education International*, 7(3), 104–113.

Adey, P. S. and Shayer, M. (1994). *Really Raising Standards: cognitive intervention and academic achievement*. London: Routledge.

Adey, P. S., Shayer, M. and Yates, C. (1989). *Thinking Science: the curriculum materials of the CASE project*. London: Thomas Nelson and Sons.

(1995). *Thinking Science: student and teachers' materials for the CASE intervention*, second edn. London: Nelson.

Adhami, M., Johnson, D. C. and Shayer, M. (1998). *Thinking Maths: the programme for accelerated learning in mathematics*. Oxford: Heinemann Educational Books.

Adorno, T. W., Frenkel-Brunswik, E., Levinson, D. J. and Sanford, R. N. (1950). *The Authoritarian Personality*. New York: Harper.

Ainscow, M. and Tweddle, D. (1988). *Encouraging Success*. London: David Fulton.

Alexander, J. M., Johnson, K. E., Leibham, M. E. and DeBauge, C. (2004). Constructing domain-specific knowledge in kindergarten: relations among knowledge, intelligence and strategic performance. *Learning and Individual Differences*, 15, 35–52.

Allen, R. R., Feezel, J. D. and Kauffie, F. J. (1967). *A taxonomy of concepts and critical abilities related to the evaluation of verbal arguments*. Wisconsin Research and Development Center for Cognitive Learning Occasional Paper No. 9. Madison, WI: University of Wisconsin.

Allinson, C. W., Chell, E. and Hayes, J. (2000). Intuition and entrepreneurial behaviour. *European Journal of Work and Organisational Psychology*, 9(1), 31–43.

Altshuller, G. (translated by L. Shulyak) (1996). *And Suddenly the Inventor Appeared: TRIZ, the theory of inventive problem solving.* Worcester, MA: Technical Innovation Center.

(1999). *40 Principles: TRIZ keys to technical innovation.* Worcester, MA: Technical Innovation Center.

(2000). *The Innovation Algorithm: TRIZ, systematic innovation and technical creativity.* Worcester, MA: Technical Innovation Center.

Altshuller, G. S. and Shapiro R. V. (in Russian) (1956). About a technology of creativity. *Questions of Psychology,* 6, 37–49.

Anderson, L. W. and Krathwohl, D. R. (eds.) (2001). *A Taxonomy for Learning, Teaching and Assessing: a revision of Bloom's taxonomy of educational objectives.* New York: Longman.

Anderson, R. D. (1983). A consolidation and appraisal of science meta-analyses. *Journal of Research in Science Teaching,* 20, 497–509.

Andrews, R., Costello, P. and Clarke, S. (1993). *Improving the Quality of Argument, 5–16.* Hull: The University of Hull.

Apter, M. J. (ed.) (2001). *Motivational Styles in Everyday Life: a guide to Reversal Theory.* Washington DC: American Psychological Association.

Arter, J. A. and Jenkins, J. R. (1979). Differential diagnosis–prescriptive teaching: a critical appraisal. *Review of Educational Research,* 49, 517–555.

Ashman, A. F. and Conway, R. N. F. (1997). *An Introduction to Cognitive Education: theory and applications.* London: Routledge.

Ausubel, D. P. (1967). *Learning Theory and Classroom Practice.* OISE Bulletin No. 1. Toronto: Ontario Institute for Studies in Education.

(1968). *Educational Psychology: a cognitive view.* New York: Holt, Rinehart and Winston.

(1978). *Educational Psychology.* New York: Holt, Rinehart and Winston.

Ausubel, D. P. and Robinson, F. G. (1969). *School Learning: an introduction to educational psychology.* New York: Holt, Rinehart and Winston.

Bachelor, P., Michael, W. B. and Kim, S. (1994). First-order and higher-order semantic and figural factors in structure-of-intellect divergent production measures. *Educational and Psychological Measurement,* 54, 608–619.

Baddeley, A. D. (1976). *The Psychology of Memory.* New York: Basic Books Inc.

(1996). Exploring the central executive. *Quarterly Journal of Experimental Psychology,* 49, 5–28.

Baddeley, A. D. and Hitch, G. J. (1974). Working memory. In *The Psychology of Learning and Motivation,* Vol. VIII: Recent advances in research and theory, ed. G. H. Bower. New York: Academic Press, 47–90.

Bailey, K. D. (1994). *Typologies and Taxonomies: an introduction to classification techniques.* London: Sage.

Bailin, S. (1998). Education, knowledge and critical thinking. In *Education, Knowledge and Truth*, ed. D. Carr. London: Routledge, 204–220.

Bailin, S., Case, R., Coombs, J. R. and Daniels, L. R. B. (1993). *A Conception of Critical Thinking for Curriculum, Instruction and Assessment*. Province of British Columbia: Ministry of Education.

(1999a). Common misconceptions of critical thinking. *Journal of Curriculum Studies*, 31(3), 269–283.

(1999b). Conceptualizing critical thinking. *Journal of Curriculum Studies*, 31 (3), 285–302.

Bandura, A. (1997). Self-efficacy: toward a unifying theory of behavior change. *Psychological Review*, 84, 191–215.

Barkley, R. A. (1996). Linkages between attention and executive functions. In *Attention, Memory and Executive Function*, eds. G. R. Lyon and N. Krasnegor. Baltimore, MD: Paul Brookes, 307–325.

Baron, J. (1985). *Rationality and Intelligence*. Cambridge: Cambridge University Press.

Baron-Cohen, S. (2003). *Essential Difference: men, women and the extreme male brain*. London: Allen Lane.

Bartlett, F. C. (1958). *Thinking*. New York: Basic Books.

Bateson, G. (1973). *Steps to an Ecology of Mind*. London: Paladin.

Baumfield, V. M. (2004). Thinking for yourself and thinking together: the community of inquiry as a pedagogy for self-regulated learning. In *Thinking about Thinking: what educators need to know*, eds. J. Ee, A. Chang and O. S. Tan. Singapore: McGraw Hill.

Baumfield, V., Higgins, S. and Lin, M. (2002). Thinking through teaching: professional development for innovation and autonomy. *Education Review*, London: National Union of Teachers, 61–67.

Baxter Magolda, M. B. (1987). The affective dimension of learning: faculty–student relationships that enhance intellectual development. *College Student Journal*, 21, 46–58.

(1992). *Knowing and Reasoning in College: gender-related patterns in students' intellectual development*. San Francisco: Jossey Bass.

Begab, M. J. (1980). Foreward. In *Instrumental Enrichment: an intervention for cognitive modifiability*, eds. R. Feuerstein, Y. Rand, M. Hoffman and R. Miller. Baltimore, MD: University Park Press, xv.

Belenky, M. F., Clinchy, B. M., Goldberger, N. R. and Tarule, J. M. (1986). *Women's Ways of Knowing: the development of self, voice, and mind*. New York: Basic Books.

Bidell, T. R. and Fischer K. W. (1992). Beyond the stage debate: action, structure and variability in Piagetian theory and research. In *Intellectual*

Development, eds. R. J. Sternberg and C. A. Berg. Cambridge: Cambridge University Press, 100–140.

Biggs, J. (1995). Assessing for learning: some dimensions underlying new approaches to educational assessment. *The Alberta Journal of Educational Research*, 41(1), 1–17.

(1999). *Teaching for Quality Learning at University.* Buckingham: SRHE and Open University Press.

Biggs, J. B. and Collis, K. F. (1982). *Evaluating the Quality of Learning – the SOLO taxonomy*, first edn. New York: Academic Press.

(1991). Multimodal learning and the quality of intelligent behaviour. In *Intelligence: reconceptualization and measurement*, ed. H. A. H. Rowe. Hillsdale, NJ: Erlbaum, 57–66.

Blagg, N., Ballinger, M. and Gardner, R. (1988). *Somerset Thinking Skills Course Handbook*. Oxford: Basil Blackwell.

Blagg, N. R., Lewis, R. E. and Ballinger, M. P. (1993). *Thinking and Learning at Work: A report on the development and evaluation of the thinking skills at work modules*. Sheffield: Department of Employment.

Blatz, C. V. (1992). Contextual limits on reasoning and testing for critical thinking. In *The Generalisability of Critical Thinking: multiple perspectives on an educational ideal*, ed. S. P. Norris. New York and London: Teachers College Press, 206–222.

Bloom, B. S. (ed.) (1956). *Taxonomy of Educational Objectives: the classification of educational goals. Handbook 1: cognitive domain*. New York: McKay.

Boekaerts, M. (1997). Self-regulated learning: a new concept embraced by researchers, policy makers, educators, teachers and students. *Learning and Instruction*, 7, 161–186.

Boekaerts, M. and Niemivirta, M. (2000). Self-regulated learning: finding a balance between learning goals and ego-protective goals. In *Handbook of Self-Regulation*, eds. M. Boekaerts, P. R. Pintrich and M. Zeidner. San Diego, CA: Academic Press, 417–450.

Boekaerts, M., Pintrich, P. R. and Zeidner, M. (eds.) (2000). *Handbook of Self-Regulation*. San Diego, CA: Academic Press.

Boekaerts, M. and Simons, P. R. J. (1993). *Leren en Instructie. Psychologie van de leerling en het leerproces*. Assen: Dekker van de Vegt.

Borkowski, J. E. (1985). Signs of intelligence: strategy generalization and metacognition. In *The Growth of Reflective Thought in Children*, ed. R. S. Yussen. New York: Academic Press, 105–144.

Borkowski, J. G. and Burke, J. E. (1996). Theories, models, and measurements of executive functioning: an information processing perspective. In *Attention, Memory and Executive Function*, eds. G. R. Lyon and N. Krasnegor. Baltimore, MD: Paul Brookes, 235–261.

Borkowski, J. G. and Nicholson, J. (2004). Executive functioning: towards a research agenda on higher-level cognitive skills. *Journal of Cognitive Education and Psychology*, 4(2), 188–198.

Borkowski, J. G., Weaver, C. M., Smith, L. E. and Akai, C. E. (2004). Metacognitive theory and classroom practices: links between motivation and executive functioning. In *Thinking about Thinking: what educators need to know*, eds. J. Ee, A. Chang and O. S. Tan. Singapore: National Institute of Education.

Boulton-Lewis, G. M. (1995). The SOLO taxonomy as a means of shaping and assessing learning in higher education. *Higher Education Research and Development*, 14(2), 143–154.

Bowler, P. J. (1992). *The Environmental Sciences*. London: Fontana.

Brainerd, C. J. (2003). Jean Piaget, learning research, and American education. In *Educational Psychology: A century of contributions*, eds. B. J. Zimmerman and D. H. Schunk. Hillsdale, NJ: Lawrence Erlbaum Associates, 251–287.

Brody, N. (2003a). Construct validation of the Sternberg triarchic abilities test: comment and reanalysis. *Intelligence*, 31, 319–329.

(2003b). What Sternberg should have concluded. *Intelligence*, 31, 339–342.

Bronowski, J. (1967). *Human and Animal Languages*. Vol. I. The Hague: Mouton and Co.

(1977). Human and animal languages. In *A Sense of the future*, ed. J. Bronowski. Cambridge, MD: MIT Press, 104–131.

Brown, K. (2002). *The Right to Learn: alternatives for a learning society*. London: Routledge Falmer.

Büchel, F. P., Schlatter, C. and Scharnhorst, U. (1997). Training and assessment of analogical reasoning in students with severe learning dificulties. In *Educational and Child Psychology*, 14, 109–120.

Burr, A. (1995). *An Introduction to Social Constructionism*. London: Routledge.

Butler, D. L. and Winne, P. H. (1995). Feedback and self-regulated learning: a theoretical synthesis. *Review of Educational Research*, 65, 245–281.

Callahan, C. M., Tomlinson, C. A. and Plucker, J. (1997). *Project START: using a multiple intelligences model in identifying and promoting talent in high risk students*. University of Connecticut Technical Report. Storrs, CT: National Research Centre on the Gifted and Talented.

Campbell, L. and Campbell, B. (1999). *Multiple Intelligences and Student Achievement: success stories from six schools*. Alexandria, VA: Association for Supervision and Curriculum Development.

Cardellini, L. and Pascual-Leone, J. (2004). On mentors. Cognitive development, education and constructivism: an interview with Juan Pascual-Leone. *Journal of Cognitive Education and Psychology*, 4(2), 199–219.

Carroll, J. B. (1993). *Human Cognitive Abilities. A survey of factor-analytic studies.* Cambridge: Cambridge University Press.

   (2003). The higher-stratum structure of cognitive abilities: current evidence supports *g* and about ten broad factors. In *The Scientific Study of General Intelligence*, ed. H. Nyborg. Amsterdam: Elsevier, 5–21.

Case, R. (1985). *Intellectual Development: birth to adulthood.* New York: Academic Press.

Case, R. and Daniels, L. R. B. (eds.) (2000). *Critical Challenges Across the Curriculum.* Burnaby, BC: Faculty of Education, Simon Fraser University.

Cohen, J. (1971). *Thinking.* Chicago: Rand McNally.

Cohen, R. I. and Nealon, J. (1979). An analysis of short-term memory differences between retardates and nonretardates. *Intelligence*, 3, 65–72.

Cole, M. and Scribner, S. (1974). *Culture and Thought: a psychological introduction.* New York: John Wiley.

Collis, K. F. and Biggs, J. B. (1982). Developmental determinants of qualitative aspects of school learning. In *Learning and Teaching Cognitive Skills*, ed. G. T. Evans. Melbourne, Victoria: Australian Council for Educational Research, 185–207.

Collis, K. and Romberg, T. A. (1991). Assessment of mathematical performance: an analysis of open-ended test items. In *Testing and Cognition*, eds. M. C. Wittrock and E. L. Baker. Englewood Cliffs, NJ: Prentice Hall, 82–130.

Colom, R., Rebolloa, I., Palaciosa, A., Juan-Espinosa, M. and Kyllonen, P. C. (2004). Working memory is (almost) perfectly predicted by g. *Intelligence*, 32, 277–296.

Comte, A. (1830–42). *Cours de philosophie positive* (6 vols.). Paris: Bachelier.

Corno, L. (1993). The best-laid plans: modern conceptions of volition and educational research. *Educational Researcher*, 22, 14–22.

Corno, L. and Randi, J. (1999). A design theory for classroom instruction in self-regulated learning? In *Instructional Design Theory and Models: a new paradigm of instructional theory.* Vol. II, ed. C. M. Reigeluth. Mahwah, NJ: Erlbaum, 293–318.

Costa, A. L. (ed.) (1991). *Developing minds: a resource book for teaching thinking* (Vol. I). Alexandria, VA: Association for Supervision and Curriculum Development.

(2001) *Developing Minds. Vol. I: a resource book for teaching thinking.* Alexandria, VA: ASCD Publications.

Costa, A. L. and Kallick, B. (2000a). *Discovering and exploring habits of mind (Habits of Mind, Bk. 1).* Alexandria, VA: Association for Supervision and Curriculum Development.

(2000b). *Activating and engaging habits of mind (Habits of Mind, Bk. 2).* Alexandria, VA: Association for Supervision and Curriculum Development.

Costa, A. L., Kallick, B. and Perkins, D. (2000). *Assessing and reporting on habits of mind (Habits of Mind, Bk. 3).* Alexandria, VA: Association for Supervision and Curriculum Development.

Costanzo, M. and Paxton, D. (1999). Multiple assessments for multiple intelligences. *Focus On Basics*, 3(1) http://gseweb.harvard.edu/~ncsall/fob/1999/paxton.htm

Covington, M. V. (1992). *Making the Grade: a self-worth perspective on motivation and school reform.* Cambridge, MA: Cambridge University Press.

Cowan, N. (1995). *Attention and Memory: an integrated framework.* Oxford: Oxford University Press.

Craft, A. (2000). *Creativity across the Primary Curriculum: framing and developing practice.* London: Routledge.

Craik, K. (1943). *The Nature of Explanation.* London: Cambridge University Press.

Creer, T. L. (2000). Self-management of chronic illness. In *Handbook of Self-Regulation*, eds. M. Boekaerts, P. R. Pintrich and M. Zeidner. London: Academic Press, 601–629.

Csikszentmihalyi, M. (1990). The domain of creativity. In *Theories of creativity*, eds. M. A. Runco and R. S. Albert. Newbury Park, CA: Sage, 190–212.

Damon, W. (1995). *Greater Expectations.* New York: Free Press.

Dare, D. E. (2001). *Learner-Centred Instructional Practices Supporting the New Vocationalism. New directions for community colleges, No.115.* John Wiley, and Sons Inc, 81–91.

de Bono, E. (1976). *Teaching Thinking.* London: Temple Smith.

(1983). The direct teaching of thinking as a skill. *Phi Delta Kappan*, 64, 703–708.

(1985). *Six Thinking Hats.* New York: Key Porter Books.

(1987). *Letters to Thinkers.* London: Harrap.

de Corte, E. (2000). Marrying theory building and the improvement of school practice: a permanent challenge for instructional psychology. *Learning and Instruction*, 10, 249–266.

de Corte, E., Verschaffel, L. and van de Ven, A. (2001). Improving text comprehension strategies in upper primary school children: a design experiment. *British Journal of Educational Psychology*, 71, 531–559.

de Landsheere, V. (1989). Taxonomies of objectives. In *The International Encyclopaedia of Educational Technology*, ed. M. Eraut. Oxford: Pergamon.

Demetriou, A. (1990). Structural and developmental relations between formal and post formal capacities: towards a comprehensive theory of adolescent and adult cognitive development. In *Adult Development: Vol. II. Models and methods in the study of adolescent and adult thought*, eds. M. L. Commons, C. Armon, L. Kohlberg, F. A. Richards, T. A. Grozer and J. D. Sinnott. New York: Praeger, 147–173.

(1993). On the quest of the functional architecture of developing mind. *Educational Psychology Review*, 5, 1–18.

(1998a). Cognitive development. In *Lifespan Developmental Psychology*, eds. A. Demetriou, W. Doise and K. F. M. van Lieshout. London: Wiley.

(1998b). A three-level theory of the developing mind: basic principles and implications for instruction and assessment. In *Intelligence, Instruction, and Assessment: theory into practice*, eds. R. J. Sternberg and W. M. Williams. Mahwah, NJ: Lawrence Erlbaum, pp. 149–199.

(2000). Organization and development of self-understanding and self-regulation: toward a general theory. In *Handbook of Self-Regulation*, eds. M. Boekaerts, P. R. Pintrich and M. Zeidner. London: Academic Press, 209–251.

Demetriou, A., Christou, C., Spanoudis, G. and Platsidou, M. (2002). *The Development of Mental Processing: Efficiency, working memory, and thinking*. Monographs of the Society for Research in Child Development, 67 (1, Serial No. 268).

Demetriou, A. and Efklides, A. (1985). Structure and sequence of formal and post-formal thought: general patterns and individual differences. *Child Development*, 56, 1062–1091.

Demetriou, A., Efklides, A. and Platsidou, M. (1993). *The Architecture and Dynamics of Developing Mind: experiential structuralism as a frame for unifying cognitive developmental theories*. Monographs of the Society for Research in Child Development, 58 (5–6, Serial No. 234).

Demetriou, A. and Kazi, S. (2001). *Unity and Modularity in the Mind and the Self*. London: Routledge.

Demetriou, A. and Raftopoulos, A. (1999). Modeling the developing mind: from structure to change. *Developmental Review* 19, 319–368.

Denckla, M. B. (1996). A theory and model of executive function. In *Attention, Memory and Executive Function*, eds. G. R. Lyon and N. Krasnegor. Baltimore, MD: Paul Brookes, 263–278.

Dewey, J. (1933). *How We Think: a restatement of the relation of reflective thinking to the reflective process*, revised edn. Lexington, MA: Heath.

(1938). *Logic: the theory of inquiry.* Troy, MO: Holt, Rinehart and Winston.

(1958). *Experience and Nature*, second edn. New York: Dover.

Dosher, B. A. (2003). Working memory. In *Encyclopedia of Cognitive Science*, ed. L. Nadel. London: Nature Publishing Group, 569–577.

Eisner, E. W. (2004). Multiple intelligences: its tensions and possibilities. *Teachers College Record*, 106(1), 31–39.

Elder, L. and Paul, R. (1998). Critical thinking: developing intellectual traits. *Journal of Developmental Education*, 21(3), 34–35.

Eliasmith, C. (1996). The third contender: a critical examination of the dynamicist theory of cognition. *Philosophical Psychology*, 9(4), 441–463.

Elliott, J. G. (2000). The psychological assessment of children with learning difficulties. *British Journal of Special Education*, 27(2), 59–66.

Endler, N. S. and Kocovski, N. L. (2000). Self-regulation and distress in clinical psychology. In *Handbook of Self-Regulation*, eds. M. Boekaerts, P. R. Pintrich and M. Zeidner. London: Academic Press, 569–599.

Ennis, R. H. (1962). A concept of critical thinking. *Harvard Educational Review*, 32, 81–111.

(1985). A logical basis for measuring critical thinking skills. *Educational Leadership*, 43(2), 44–48.

(1987). A taxonomy of critical thinking dispositions and abilities. In *Teaching Thinking Skills: theory and practice*, eds. J. B. Baron and R. J. Sternberg. New York: W. H. Freeman, 9–26.

(1989). Critical thinking and subject specificity: clarification and needed research. *Educational Researcher*, 18(3), 4–10.

(1991). Critical thinking: a streamlined conception. *Teaching Philosophy*, 14 (1), 5–25.

(1996). Critical thinking dispositions: their nature and assessability. *Informal Logic*, 18(2 and 3), 165–182.

(1998). Is critical thinking culturally biased? *Teaching Philosophy*, 21(1), 15–33.

Ennis, R. H. and Millman, J. (1985). *Cornell Critical Thinking Test, level Z.* Pacific Grove, CA: Midwest Publications.

Ennis, R. H. and Weir, E. (1985). *The Ennis-Weir Critical Thinking Essay Test.* Pacific Grove, CA: Midwest Publications.

Eslinger, P. J. (1996). Conceptualizing, describing, and measuring components of executive function: a summary. In *Attention, Memory and Executive Function*, eds. G. R. Lyon and N. Krasnegor. Baltimore, MD: Paul Brookes, 367–396.

Facione, P. A. (1990). *The Delphi Report*. Millbrae CA: California Academic Press.

Fashola, O. S., and Slavin, R. E. (1997). Effective and replicable programs for students placed at risk in elementary and middle schools (Grant No. R-117D-40005). Washington, DC: US Department of Education, Office of Educational Research and Improvement.

Fennema, E., Carpenter, T. P., Franke, M. L., Levi, L., Jacobs, V. R. and Empson, S. B. (1996). A longitudinal study of learning to use children's thinking in mathematics instruction. *Journal for Research in Mathematics Education*, 27, 403–434.

Feuerstein, R. (1980). *Instrumental Enrichment: intervention programme for cognitive modifiability*. Baltimore, MD: University Park Press.

Feuerstein, R, Falik, L. H., and Feuerstein, R. S. (1998). The learning propensity assessment device: an alternative approach to the assessment of learning potential. In *Advances in Cross-cultural Assessment*, eds. R. J. Samuda, R. Feuerstein, A. S. Kaufman, J. E. Lewis and R. J. Sternberg. Thousand Oaks, CA: Sage, 100–161.

Feuerstein, R. and Jensen, M. (1980). Instrumental enrichment: theoretical basis, goals and instruments. *The Educational Forum*, 44, 401–423.

Feuerstein, R., Rand, Y. and Hoffman, M. B. (1979). *The dynamic assessment of retarded performers: the learning potential assessment device, theory, instruments, and techniques*. Baltimore, MD: University Park Press.

Finster, D. (1989). Developmental instruction part 1: Perry's model of intellectual development. *Journal of Chemical Education*, 66, 659–661.

　(1991). Developmental instruction part 2: application of the Perry model to general chemistry. *Journal of Chemical Education*, 68, 752–756.

Fischer, K. W. (1980). A theory of cognitive development: the control and construction of hierarchies of skills. *Psychological Review*, 87(6), 477–531.

Fishback, S. J. and Polson, C. J. (1998). The cognitive development of adult undergraduate students. In *Proceedings of the 17th Annual Midwest Research-to-Practice Conference in Adult, Continuing, and Community Education*, eds. G. S. Wood, Jr. and M. M. Webber. Muncie, IN: Ball State University, 81–86.

Fisher, R. (1998). *Teaching Thinking*. London: Continuum.

Flavell, J. (1976). Metacognitive aspects of problem solving. In *The Nature of Intelligence*, ed. L. Resnick. Hillsdale, NJ: Lawrence Erlbaum Associates, 231–236.

Flavell, J. H. (1979). Metacognition and cognitive monitoring: a new area of cognitive-developmental inquiry. *American Psychologist*, 34, 906–911.

Franke, M. L., Carpenter, T., Fennema, E., Ansell, E. and Behrend, J. (1998). Understanding teachers' self-sustaining generative change in the context of professional development. *Teaching and Teacher Education* 14(1), 67–80.

Friedman, R. C. and Lee, S. W. (1996). Differentiating instructions for high-achieving/gifted children in regular classrooms: a field test of three gifted-education models. *Journal for the Education of the Gifted*, 19 (4), 405–436.

Fuchs, L. S., Fuchs, D., Prentice, K., Burch, M., Hamlett, C. L., Owen, R. and Schroeter, K. (2003). Enhancing third-grade students' mathematical problem solving with self-regulated learning strategies. *Journal of Educational Psychology*, 95, 306–315.

Fusco, E. T. (1983). *The relationship between children's cognitive level of development and their response to literature.* Unpublished Ph.D. dissertation, Hofstra University, New York.

Gagné, R. M. (1965). *Conditions of Learning*, first edn. New York: Holt, Rinehart and Winston.

(1985). *Conditions of Learning*, second edn. New York: Holt, Rinehart and Winston.

Gagné, R. M. and Briggs, L. J. (1974). *Principles of Instructional Design*. New York: Holt, Rinehart and Winston.

Gardner, H. (1983). *Frames of Mind: the theory of multiple intelligence*. New York: Basic Books.

(1993). *Frames of Mind: the theory of multiple intelligence*, second edn. New York: Basic Books.

(1999). *Intelligence Reframed*. New York: Basic Books.

(2004). Audiences for the theory of multiple intelligences. *Teachers College Record*, 106(1), 212–220.

Gardner, H., Kornhaber, M. L., and Wake, W. K. (1996). *Intelligence: multiple perspectives*. Orlando: Holt, Rinehart and Winston.

Gathercole, S. E. (1998). The development of memory. *Journal of Child Psychology and Psychiatry*, 39, 3–27.

Geiselman, R. E. and Fisher, R. P. (1985). Interviewing victims and witnesses of crime. *Research in Brief, National Institute of Justice*, December, 1–4.

Gerlach, V. and Sullivan, A. (1967). *Constructing Statements of Outcomes.* Inglewood, CA: Southwest Regional Laboratory for Educational Research and Development.

Glatthorn, A. A. and Baron, J. (1991). The good thinker. In *Developing Minds.* Vol. I: a resource book for teaching thinking, ed. A. L. Costa. Alexandria, VA: ASCD Publications, 49–53.

Goffman, E. (1959). *The Presentation of Self in Everyday Life.* Garden City, NY: Doubleday.

Gottfredson, L. S. (2003a). Dissecting practical intelligence theory: its claims and evidence. *Intelligence,* 31, 343–397.

(2003b). On Sternberg's 'Reply to Gottfredson'. *Intelligence,* 31, 415–424.

Gouge, K. and Yates, C. (2002) Creating a CA programme in the arts: the Wigan LEA arts project. In *Learning Intelligence: cognitive acceleration across the curriculum from 5 to 15 years,* eds. M. Shayer and P. Adey. Buckingham: Open University Press.

Govier, T. (1988). Ways of teaching reasoning directly. In *Critical Thinking: proceedings of the first British conference on informal logic and critical thinking,* ed. A. Fisher. Norwich: University of East Anglia, 30–38.

Graham, S. and Harris, K. R. (1996). Addressing problems in attention, memory, and executive functioning. In *Attention, Memory and Executive Function,* eds. G. R. Lyon and N. Krasnegor. Baltimore, MD: Paul Brookes, 349–365.

Gregory, R. L. (ed.) (1987). *The Oxford Companion to The Mind.* Oxford: Oxford University Press.

Gregson M. (2003). Learning to be reflective. Unpublished doctoral thesis, University of Newcastle upon Tyne.

Griffin, S. and Case, R. (1997). Re-thinking the primary school math curriculum: an approach based on cognitive science. *Issues in Education: Contributions from Educational Psychology,* 3(1), 1–49.

Grigorenko, E. L., Jarvin, L. and Sternberg, R. J. (2002). School-based tests of the triarchic theory of intelligence: three settings, three samples, three syllabi. *Contemporary Educational Psychology,* 27, 167–208.

Groth-Marnat, G. (1997). *Handbook of Psychological Assessment,* third edn. New York: John Wiley and Sons.

Gruber, H., Law, L. C., Mandl, H. and Renkl, A. (1999). Situated learning and transfer: implications for teaching. In *Learners, Learning and Assessment,* ed. P. Murphy. London: Paul Chapman Publishing, 214–30.

Guilford, J. P. (1950). Creativity. *American Psychologist,* 5, 444–454.

(1956). The structure of intellect. *Psychological Bulletin,* 53, 267–293.

(1967). *The Nature of Human Intelligence*. New York: McKay.

(1977). *Way Beyond the IQ: guide to improving intelligence and creativity.* Buffalo, NY: Creative Education Foundation.

(1980). Cognitive styles: what are they? *Educational and Psychological Measurement*, 40, 715–735.

(1982). Cognitive psychology's ambiguities: some suggested remedies. *Psychological Review*, 89, 48–59.

(1983). Transformation abilities of functions. *Journal of Creative Behavior*, 17, 75–83.

(1986). *Creative Talents: their nature, uses and development*. Buffalo, NY: Bearly Ltd.

Guilford, J. P. and Hoepfner, R. (1971). *The Analysis of Intelligence*. New York: McGraw-Hill.

Gustafsson, J.-E. and Undheim, J. O. (1996). Individual differences in cognitive functions. In *Handbook of Educational Psychology*, eds. D. C. Berliner and R. C. Calfer. New York: MacMillan, 186–242.

Hacker, D. J. (1998). Definitions and empirical foundations. In *Metacognition in Educational Theory and Practice*, eds. D. J. Hacker, J. Dunlosky and A. C. Mahwah, NJ: Lawrence Erlbaum Associates, 1–23.

Halpern, D. F. (1984). *Thought and Knowledge: an introduction to critical thinking*. Hillsdale, NJ: Larwence Erlbaum Associates.

(1994). A national assessment of critical thinking skills in adults: taking steps toward the goal. In *The National Assessment of College Student Learning: identification of the skills to be taught, learned and assessed*, ed. A. Greenwood. Washington, DC: National Center for Education Statistics, 24–64.

(1997). *Critical Thinking Across the Curriculum: a brief edition of thought and knowledge*. Mahwah, NJ: Lawrence Erlbaum Associates.

(2002). *Thinking Critically About Critical Thinking*, fourth edn (workbook). Mahwah, NJ: Lawrence Erlbaum Associates.

Hamers, J. H. M. and Overtoom, M. T. (1997). *Teaching Thinking in Europe*. Utrecht: Sardes.

Handley, S. J., Capon, A., Beveridge, M., Dennis, I. and Evans, J. St. B. T. (2004). Working memory, inhibitory control and the development of children's reasoning. *Thinking and Reasoning*, 10, 175–195.

Hannafin, M. J., and Hooper, S. (1989). An integrated framework for CBI screen design and layout. *Computers in Human Behavior*, 5(3), 155–165.

Hannah, L. S. and Michaelis, J. U. (1977). *A comprehensive framework for instructional objectives: a guide to systematic planning and evaluation*. Reading, MA: Addison-Wesley.

Hattie, J. (2002). What are the attributes of excellent teachers? Paper presented at the New Zealand Council for Educational Research Annual Conference, the University of Auckland. http://www.nzcer.org.nz/pdfs/hattie02.pdf

Hattie, J., Biggs, J., and Purdie, N. (1996). Effects of learning skills interventions on student learning: a meta-analysis. *Review of Educational Research*, 66, 99–136.

Hauenstein, A. D. (1972). *Curriculum planning for behavioral development.* Worthington, OH: Charles A, Jones Publishing Co.

   (1998). *A Conceptual Framework for Educational Objectives: a holistic approach to traditional taxonomies.* Lanham, MD: University Press of America.

Hawkins, W. and Hedberg, J. G. (1986). Evaluating LOGO: use of the SOLO taxonomy. *Australian Journal of Educational Technology,* 2(2), 103–109.

Hawley, W. E. (1967). Programmed Instruction. In *Training and development handbook*, eds. R. L. Craig and L. R. Bittel. New York: McGraw Hill, 225–250.

Haywood, H. C., Brooks, P. H. and Burns, M. S. (1992). *Bright Start: cognitive curriculum for young children.* Watertown, MA: Charlesbridge Publishing.

Herrmann, N. (1989). *The Creative Brain.* Lake Lure: NC: Brain Books, The Ned Herrmann Group.

   (1996). *The Whole Brain Business Book.* New York: McGraw-Hill.

Higgins, S. and Baumfield, V. (1998). A defence of teaching general thinking skills. *Journal of Philosophy of Education* 32(3), 391–398.

Higgins, S., Baumfield, V., Lin, M., Moseley, D., Butterworth, M., Downey, G., Gregson, M., Oberski, I., Rockett, M. and Thacker, D. (2004). *Thinking skills approaches to effective teaching and learning: what is the evidence for impact on learners.* In Research Evidence in Education Library. London: EPPI-Centre, Social Science Research Unit, Institute of Education.

Hoerr, T. R. (2000). *Becoming a multiple intelligences school.* Alexandria, VA: Association for Supervision and Curriculum Development.

Hofer, B. and Pintrich, P. (1997). The development of epistemological theories: beliefs about knowledge and knowing in relation to learning. *Review of Educational Research*, 67(1), 88–140.

Horn, J. and Knapp, J. (1973). On the subjective character of the empirical base of Guilford's structure of intellect model. *Psychological Bulletin*, 80, 33–43.

Howe, M. J. A., Davidson, J. W. and Sloboda, J. A. (1998). Innate talents: reality or myth? *Behavioural and Brain Sciences*, 21, 399–422.

Illeris, K. (2004). *The Three Dimensions of Learning*, second edn. Roskilde: Roskilde University Press/Niace Publications.

Jarvis, P. (1992). *Paradoxes of Learning: on becoming an individual in society.* San Francisco: Jossey-Bass.

Jewell, P. (1996). A reasoning taxonomy for gifted children. Paper presented in Adelaide at the national conference of the Australian Association for the Education of the Gifted and Talented. http://www.nexus.edu.au/teachstud/gat/jewell1.htm

Jonassen, D. H. (1997). Instructional design model for well-structured and ill-structured problem-solving learning outcomes. *Educational Technology: Research and Development,* 45(1), 65–95.

(1999). Designing constructivist learning environments. In *Instructional Design Theories and Models: a new paradigm of instructional theory (Vol. II)*, ed. C. M. Reigeluth. Mahwah, NJ: Lawrence Erlbaum Associates, 215–239.

(2000). Toward a meta-theory of problem solving. *Educational Technology: Research and Development,* 48(4), 63–85.

Jonassen, D. H., Beissner, K. and Yacci, M. (1993). *Structural Knowledge: techniques for representing, conveying and acquiring structural knowledge.* Hillsdale, NJ: Lawrence Erlbaum Associates.

Jonassen, D. H., Hannum, W. H. and Tessmer, M. (1989). *Handbook of Task Analysis Methods.* New York: Praeger.

Jonassen, D. H., Prevish, T., Christy, D. and Stavurlaki, E. (1999). Learning to solve problems on the web: aggregate planning in a business management course. *Distance Education: an International Journal,* 20(1), 49–63.

Jonassen, D. H. and Tessmer, M. (1996/97). An outcomes-based taxonomy for instructional systems design, evaluation and research. *Training Research Journal,* 2, 11–46.

Jonassen, D. H., Tessmer, M. and Hannum, W. H. (1999). *Task Analysis Methods for Instructional Design.* Mahwah, NJ: Lawrence Erlbaum Associates.

Just, M. A. and Carpenter, P. A. (1996). A capacity theory of comprehension, *Psychological Review,* 103, 773–780.

Kail, R. and Pellegrino, J. W. (1985). *Human Intelligence: perspectives and prospects.* New York: W. H. Freeman.

Kallio, E. (1995). Systematic reasoning: formal or post formal cognition? *Journal of Adult Development,* 2(3) 187–192.

Kavale, K. A. and Forness, S. R. (1987). Substance over style: assessing the efficacy of modality testing and teaching. *Exceptional Children,* 54(3), 228–239.

Kepner, C. and Tregoe, B. (1965). *The Rational Manager*. New York: McGraw Hill Book Company.

Kezar, A. (2001). Theory of Multiple Intelligences: implications for higher education. *Innovative Higher Education*, 26(2), 141–154.

King, P. M. and Kitchener, K. S. (1994). *Developing Reflective Judgment: understanding and promoting intellectual growth and critical thinking in adolescents and adults*. San Francisco, CA: Jossey-Bass.

Kitchener, K. S. and King, P. M. (1981). Reflective judgment: concepts of justifications and their relation to age and gender. *Journal of Applied Developmental Psychology*, 2(2), 89–116.

Klauer, K. J. and Phye, G. D. (1994). *Cognitive Training for Children*. Seattle: Hogrefe and Huber Publishers.

Klausmeier, H. J., Quilling, M. R., Sorenson, J. S., Way, R. S. and Glasrud, G. R. (1971). *Individually Guided Education and the Multiunit Elementary School: guidelines for implementation*. Madison WI: University of Wisconsin, Wisconsin Research and Development Center for Cognitive Learning.

Klein, P. D. (2003). Rethinking the multiplicity of cognitive resources and curricular representations: alternatives to 'learning styles' and 'multiple intelligences'. *Journal of Curriculum Studies*, 35(1), 45–81.

Kohlberg, L. (1990). Which postformal levels are stages? In *Adult Development Vol. II: models and methods in the study of adolescent and adult thought*, eds. M. L. Commons, C. Armon, L. Kohlberg, F. A. Richards, T. A. Grozer and J. D. Sinnott. New York: Praeger, 263–268.

Kolb, D. A. (1984). *Experiential Learning: experience as the source of learning and development*. Englewood Cliffs, NJ: Prentice Hall.

Koplowitz, H. (1984). A projection beyond Piaget's formal-operations stage: a general system stage and a unitary stage. In *Beyond Formal Operations: late adolescent and adult cognitive development*, eds. M. Commons, F. Richards and C. Armon. New York: Praeger, 272–295.

(1987). Post-logical thinking. In *Thinking: the second international conference*, eds. D. N. Perkins, J. Lochhead and J. Bishop. Hillsdale, NJ: Lawrence Erlbaum Associates, 213–232.

(1990). Unitary consciousness and the highest development of mind: The relation between spiritual development and cognitive development. In *Adult Development: Vol. II. Models and methods in the study of adolescent and adult thought*, eds. M. L. Commons, C. Armon, L. Kohlberg, F. A. Richards, T. A. Grozer and J. D. Sinnott. New York: Praeger, 105–111.

Kornhaber, M. L. (2004). Multiple intelligences: from the ivory tower to the dusty classroom – but why? *Teachers College Record*, 106(1), 67–76.

Kornhaber, M. L., Fierros, E. and Veenema, S. (2004). *Multiple Intelligences: Best ideas from theory and practice*. Needham Heights, MA: Allyn and Bacon.

Kornhaber, M. L. and Krechevsky, M. (1995). Expanding definitions of teaching and learning: Notes from the MI underground. In *Transforming Schools*, eds. P. Cookson and B. Schneider. New York: Garland Press, 181–208.

Kozulin, A. (1998). *Psychological Tools: a sociocultural approach to education*. Harvard: Harvard University Press.

(2002). Sociocultural theory and the Mediated Learning Experience. *School Psychology International*, 23(1), 7–35.

Krathwohl, D. B., Bloom, B. S. and Masia, B. B. (1964). *Taxonomy of Educational Objectives: the classification of educational goals*. Handbook II: Affective Domain. New York: David McKay.

Kreitzer, A. E. and Madaus, G. F. (1994). Empirical investigations of the hierarchical structure of the taxonomy. In *Bloom's Taxonomy: a forty-year retrospective. Ninety-third Yearbook of the National Society for the Study of Education Part II*, eds. L. W. Anderson and L. A. Sosniak. Chicago: National Society for the Study of Education, 64–81.

Kuhn, D., and Pearsall, S. (1998). Relations between metastrategic knowledge and strategic performance. *Cognitive Development*, 13, 227–247.

Lane, R. D. and Nadel, L. (2000). *Cognitive Neuroscience of Emotion*. New York: Oxford University Press.

Lave, J. and Wenger, E. (1991). *Situated Learning: legitimate peripheral participation*. Cambridge: Cambridge University Press.

Lawton, D. and Gordon, P. (2002). *A History of Western Educational Ideas*. London: Woburn Press.

Leat, D. (1998). *Thinking through Geography*. Cambridge: Chris Kington Publishing.

Leat, D. and Higgins S. (2002). The role of powerful pedagogical strategies in curriculum development. *The Curriculum Journal*, 13, 71–85.

Lipman, M. (1991). *Thinking in Education,* first edn. Cambridge: Cambridge University Press.

(1995). Caring as Thinking. *Inquiry: Critical thinking across the disciplines.* 15(1).

(2003). *Thinking in Education,* second edn. Cambridge: Cambridge University Press.

(2004). Interview on Philosophy for Children. http://www.buf.no/e_resources/e_resources_c_3.html

Loehlin, J. C. (1992) *Genes and Environment in Personality Development.* London: Sage.

Losee, J. (1993). *A Historical Introduction to the Philosophy of Science*, third edn. Oxford: Oxford University Press.

Luna, B., Garver, K. E., Urban, T. A., Lazar, N. A. and Sweeney, J. A. (2004). Maturation of cognitive processes from late childhood to adulthood. *Child Development*, 75(5), 1357–1372.

Lyon, G. R. and Krasnegor, N. (eds.) (1996). *Attention, Memory and Executive Function.* Baltimore, MD: Paul Brookes.

Madaus, G. F., Woods, E. N. and Nuttal, R. L. (1973). A causal model analysis of Bloom's taxonomy. *American Educational Research Journal*, 10, 253–262.

Mager, R. F. and Beach, K. H. (1967). *Developing Vocational Instruction.* Belmont, CA: Fearon Publishers.

Maltby, F. (1995). The use of TASC to develop a selection of tools for effective thinking. *Gifted Education International*, 11(1), 18–23.

Mann, D. (2001). TRIZ thinking hats. *TRIZ Journal.* http://www.triz-journal.com/archives/2001/03/b/index.htm

(2002). *Hands-on Systematic Innovation.* Ieper, Belgium: CREAX Press.

Marchand, H. (2001). Some reflections on post-formal thought. *The Genetic Epistemologist*, 29(3).

Margolis, H. (1987). *Patterns, Thinking and Cognition.* Chicago: University of Chicago Press.

Martin, J. R. (1992). Critical thinking for a humane world. In *The Generalisability of Critical Thinking: multiple perspectives on an educational ideal*, ed. S. P. Norris. New York and London: Teachers College Press, 163–180.

Marzano, R. J. (1992). *A Different Kind of Classroom: teaching with dimensions of learning.* Alexandria, VA: Association for Supervision and Curriculum Development.

(1998). A theory-based meta-analysis of research on instruction. Aurora, CO: Mid-Continent Regional Educational Laboratory. www.mcrel.org/topics/productDetail.asp?topicsID=6&productID=83, 24 December 2002.

(2001a). *Designing a New Taxonomy of Educational Objectives.* Thousand Oaks, CA: Corwin Press.

(2001b). A new taxonomy of educational objectives. In *Developing Minds: a resource book for teaching thinking*, third edn, ed. A. L. Costa. Alexandria,

VA: Association for Supervision and Curriculum Development, 181–188.

Marzano, R. J., Brandt, R. S., Hughes, C. S., Jones, B. F., Presseisen, B. Z., Rankin, S. C. and Suhor, C (1988). *Dimensions of Thinking: a framework for curriculum and instruction.* Alexandria, VA: Association for Supervision and Curriculum Development.

Mayer, R. E. (2002). A step toward redesigning Bloom's taxonomy. *Contemporary Psychology APA Review of Books,* 47(8), 551–553.

McClelland, D. C. (1961). *The Achieving Society.* Princeton: D. van Nostrand.

McCrae, R. R., Arenberg, D. and Costa, P. T. (1987) Declines in divergent thinking with age: Cross-sectional, longitudinal, and cross-sequential analyses. *Psychology and Aging.* 2, 130–137.

McGuinness, C., Curry, C., Greer, B., Daly, P. and Salters, M. (1997). *Final Report on the ACTS project: Phase two.* Belfast, Northern Ireland: Council for Curriculum, Examinations and Assessment.

McPeck, J. (1981). *Critical Thinking and Education.* New York: St. Martin's.

Meeker, M. N. (1969). *The Structure of Intellect: its uses and interpretation.* Columbus, OH: Merrill.

Mercer, N., Wegerif, R., Dawes, L., Sams, C. and Higgins, S. (2002). *Language, Thinking and ICT in the Primary Curriculum: final project report to the Nuffield Foundation.* Milton Keynes: Open University.

Merrill, M. D. (1983). Component display theory. In *Instructional Design Theories and Models: an overview of their current status,* ed. C. M. Reigeluth. Hillsdale, NJ: Lawrence Erlbaum Associates, 279–333.

(2002). First principles of instruction. *Educational Technology Research and Development,* 50(3), 43–59.

Merrill, M. D., Jones, M. K. and Zhongmin Li (1992). Instructional design theory: classes of transactions. *Educational Technology,* 32(6), 12–26.

Merrill, M. D., Zhongmin Li and Jones, M. K. (1990a). Limitations of first generation instructional design (ID1). *Educational Technology,* 30(1), 7–11.

(1990b). Second generation instructional design. *Educational Technology,* 30 (2), 7–14.

Messick, S. (1992). Multiple intelligences or multilevel intelligence? *Psychological Inquiry,* 3, 365–384.

Meyer, B. J. F., Young, C. J. and Bartlett, B. J. (1989). *Memory Improved: reading and memory enhancement across the life span through strategic text structures.* Hillsdale, NJ: Erlbaum.

Mezirow, J. (1978). Perspective transformation. *Adult Education,* 28, 100–110.

(1998). On critical reflection. *Adult Education Quarterly,* 48(3), 185–198.

Miyake, A., Friedman, N. P., Rettinger, D. A., Shah, P. and Hegarty, M. (2001). How are visuospatial working memory, executive functioning, and spatial abilities related? A latent-variable analysis. *Journal of Experimental Psychology. General,* 130(4), 621–640.

Moore, W. E. (1968). *Creative and Critical Thinking.* London: Houghton Mifflin.

Moore, W. S. (1988). *The Measure of Intellectual Development: an instrument manual.* Olympia, WA: Center for the Study of Intellectual Development.

(1989). The learning environment preferences: exploring the construct validity of an objective measure of the Perry scheme of intellectual development. *Journal of College Student Development,* 30, 504–514.

Morris, R. D. (1996). Relationships and distinctions among the concepts of attention, memory, and executive function. In *Attention, Memory and Executive Function,* eds. G. R. Lyon and N. Krasnegor. Baltimore: Paul Brookes, 11–16.

Moseley, D. V., Baumfield, V., Higgins, S., Lin, M., Miller, J., Newton, D., Robson, S., Elliott, J. and Gregson, M. (2004). *Thinking skill frameworks for post-16 learners: an evaluation.* London: Learning and Skills Research Centre. http://www.lsda.org.uk/pubs/dbaseout/download.asp?code=1541

Moseley, D., Elliott, J., Gregson, M. and Higgins, S. (2005). Thinking skills frameworks for use in education and training. *British Educational Research Journal,* 17(3), 367–390.

Murris, K. and Haynes, J. (2001). *Storywise: Thinking through stories.* Newport: Dialogue Works.

Nathan, P. E. (1987). What do behavioral scientists know – and what can they do – about alcoholism? In *Nebraska symposium on motivation, 1986* (pp. 1–25). Lincoln, Nebraska: University of Nebraska Press.

National Education Goals Panel (1991). *The National Education Goals Report.* Washington, DC: US Department of Education.

Neber, H. and Schommer-Aikins, M. (2002). Self regulated science learning with highly gifted students: the role of cognitive, motivational, epistemological and environmental variables. *High Ability Studies,* 13 (1), 59–74.

Newton, D. P. (2000) *Teaching for Understanding.* London: Routledge-Falmer.

Nisbet, R. A. (1966). *The Sociological Tradition.* Oxford: Heinemann.

Noble, T. (2004). Integrating the revised Bloom's taxonomy with multiple intelligences: a planning tool for curriculum differentiation. *Teachers College Record*, 106(1), 193–211.

Norris, S. P. and Ennis, R. H. (1989). *Evaluating Critical Thinking*. Pacific Grove, CA: Critical Thinking Press and Software.

Nosich, G. M. (2000). *Learning to think things through: a guide to critical thinking across the curriculum*. Upper Saddle River, NJ: Prentice Hall.

Ohbayashi, M., Konishi, S. and Miyashita, Y. (2003). Executive function, models of. In *Encyclopedia of Cognitive Science*, ed. L. Nadel. London: Nature Publishing Group.

Ormell, C. P. (1974). Bloom's taxonomy and the objectives of education. *Educational Research*, 17, 3–18.

Palincsar, A. S. and Brown, A. L. (1984). Reciprocal teaching of comprehension-fostering and comprehension-monitoring activities. *Cognition and Instruction*, 1, 117–175.

Pascual-Leone, J. (1970). A mathematical model for the transition rule in Piaget's developmental stages. *Acta Psychologica* 32, 301–345.

  (1988) Organismic processes for neo-Piagetian theories: a dialectical causal account of cognitive development. In *The Neo-Piagetian Theories of Cognitive Development: towards an integration*, ed. A. Demetriou. Amsterdam, North-Holland, 25–64.

Paul, R. (1982) Teaching critical thinking in the strong sense: a focus on self-deception, world views, and a dialectical mode of analysis. *Informal Logic Newsletter*, 4(2), 2–7.

Paul, R. W. (1985). Bloom's taxonomy and critical thinking instruction. *Educational Leadership*, 42(8), 36–39.

Paul, R. (1987). Dialogical thinking: critical thought essential to the acquisition of rational knowledge and passions. In *Teaching Thinking Skills: theory and practice*, eds. J. Baron and R. J. Sternberg. New York: W. H. Freeman, 127–148.

Paul, R. W. (1991). Teaching critical thinking in the strong sense. In *Developing Minds: a resource book for teaching thinking*, Vol. I, ed. A. L. Costa. Alexandria, VA: Association for Supervision and Curriculum Development.

Paul, R. (1993). *Critical Thinking – what every person needs to survive in a rapidly changing world*, third edn. Santa Rosa, CA: Foundation for Critical Thinking.

Paul, R. and Elder, L. (2001). *Critical Thinking: tools for taking charge of your learning and your life*. Upper Saddle River, NJ: Prentice Hall.

Pederson, N. L., Plomin, R. and McClearn, G. E. (1994). Is there a G beyond g? (Is there genetic influence on specific cognitive abilities independent of genetic influence on general cognitive ability?) *Intelligence*, 18, 133–143.

Peel, E. A. (1971). *The Nature of Adolescent Judgement*. London: Staples Press.

Perkins, D., Jay, E. and Tishman. S. (1993). Beyond abilities: a dispositional theory of thinking. *The Merrill-Palmer Quarterly*, 39(1), 1–21.

Perry, W. G., Jr. (1968). *Patterns of Development in Thought and Values of Students in a Liberal Arts College: a validation of a scheme*. Cambridge, MA: Harvard University, Bureau of Study Counsel.

   (1970). *Forms of Intellectual and Ethical Development in the College Years: a scheme*. New York: Holt, Rinehart, and Winston.

Petty, G. (1997). *How to be Better at Creativity*. London: Kogan Page.

   (1998). *Teaching Today*, second edn. Cheltenham: Stanley Thornes.

Piaget, J. (first published in French, 1947) (1950). *The Psychology of Intelligence*. London: Routledge and Kegan Paul.

   (1952). *The origin of intelligence in children*. New York: International Universities Press.

Pintrich, P. R. (2000). The role of goal orientation in self-regulated learning. In *Handbook of Self-Regulation*, eds. M. Boekaerts, P. R. Pintrich and M. Zeidner. San Diego, CA: Academic Press, 451–502.

Pintrich, P. R. and De Groot, E. V. (1990). Motivational and self-regulated learning components of classroom academic performance. *Journal of Educational Psychology*, 82, 33–40.

Pintrich, P. R., Wolters, C. and Baxter, G. (2000). Assessing metacognition and self-regulated learning. In *Metacognitive Assessment*, eds. G. Schraw and J. Impara. Lincoln, NE: Buros Institute/The University of Nebraska, 43–97.

Pithers, R. T. and Soden, R. (2000). Critical thinking in education: a review. *Educational Research*, 42(3), 237–249.

Polanyi, M. (1958). *Personal Knowledge: towards a postcritical philosophy*. Chicago: University of Chicago Press.

Polya, G. (1945). *How to Solve it: a new aspect of mathematical method*. New York: Doubleday.

Posner, M. I. and Raichle, M. E. (1994). *Images of Mind*. New York: Scientific American Library.

Presseisen, B. Z. (1988). *At-risk Students and Thinking: perspectives from research*. Washington, DC: National Education Association Publications and Research for Better Schools, Inc.

(1991). Thinking skills: meanings and models revisited. In *Developing Minds: a resource book for teaching thinking*, first edn, ed. A. L. Costa. Alexandria, VA: ASCD Publications, 47–53.

(2001).Thinking skills: meanings and models revisited. In *Developing minds: a resource book for teaching thinking*, third edn, ed. A. L. Costa. Alexandria, VA: ASCD Publications, 47–53.

Pressley, M. (1986). The relevance of the good strategy user model to the teaching of mathematics. *Educational Psychologist*, 21, 139–161.

Pressley, M. and Associates (1990). *Cognitive Strategy Instruction that Really Improves Children's Academic Performance*. Cambridge, MD: Brookline.

Prosser, M. and Trigwell, K. (1999). *Understanding Learning and Teaching*. Buckingham: SRHE/Open University Press.

Quellmalz, E. S. (1987). Developing reasoning skills. In *Teaching Thinking Skills: theory and practice*, eds. J. R. Baron and R. J. Sternberg. New York: W. H. Freeman, 86–105.

Quellmalz, E. S. and Hoskyn, J. A. (1988). Making a difference in Arkansas: the multicultural reading and thinking project. *Educational Leadership*, 45(7), 52–55.

Rabbit, P. (1997). *Methodology of frontal and executive function*. Hove: Psychology Press.

Ree, M. J. and Earles, J. A. (1991) Predicting training success: not much more than *g*. *Personnel Psychology*, 44, 321–332.

Reigeluth, C. M. (1996). A new paradigm of ISD? *Educational Technology*, 36(3), 13–20.

(1997). Instructional theory, practitioner needs, and new directions: some reflections. *Educational Technology*, 37(1), 42–47.

Reigeluth, C. M. (ed.) (1999). *Instructional Design Theory and Models, Vol. II: a new paradigm of instructional theory*. Mahwah, NJ: Erlbaum.

Reigeluth, C. and Stein, F. (1983). The elaboration theory of instruction. In *Instructional Design Theories and Models*, ed. C. Reigeluth. Hillsdale, NJ: Erlbaum Associates, 335–381.

Renzulli, J. S. (1975). What makes giftedness? Re-examining a definition. In *Psychology and Education of the Gifted*, eds. W. B. Barbe and J. S. Renzulli. New York: Irvington, 55–65.

(1986). The three ring conception of giftedness: a developmental model for creative productivity. In *Conceptions of Giftedness*, eds. R. J. Sternberg and B. J. E. Davidson. Cambridge: Cambridge University Press, 53–92.

Resnick, L. (ed.) (1989). *Knowing, Learning, and Instruction*. Hillsdale, NJ: Lawrence Erlbaum Associates.

Rhodes, M. (1961). An analysis of creativity. *Phi Delta Kappan*, 42, 305–310.

Richelle, M. and Feuerstein, R. (1957). *Enfants Juifs Nord-Africains*. Jerusalem: Youth Aliyah.

Ritchie, S. M. and Edwards, J. (1996). Creative thinking instruction for aboriginal children. *Learning and Instruction*, 6(1), 59–75.

Roberts, A. C., Robbins, T. W. and Weiskrantz, L. (1998). *The Prefrontal Cortex: executive and cognitive functions*. Oxford: Oxford University Press.

Rogoff, B. (1990). *Apprenticeship in Thinking: cognitive development in social context*. New York: Oxford University Press.

Romine, C. B. and Reynolds, C. R. (2004). Sequential memory: a developmental perspective on its relation to frontal lobe functioning. *Neuropsychological Review*, 14, 43–64.

Romiszowski, A. J. (1981). *Designing Instructional Systems: decision making in course planning and curriculum design*. London: Kogan Page.

(1984). *Producing Instructional Systems: lesson planning for individualized and group learning activities*. London: Kogan Page.

Romney, D. M. and Samuels, M. T. (2001). A meta-evaluation of Feuerstein's Instrumental Enrichment. *Educational and Child Psychology*, 18(4), 19–34.

Runco, M. A. (1992). Children's divergent thinking and creative ideation. *Developmental Review*, 12, 223–264.

Salamatov, Y. (1999). *TRIZ: The right solution at the right time*. Hattem, Netherlands: Insytec B.V.

Säljö, R. (1979a). *Learning in the learner's perspective I – some common-sense conceptions. Reports from the Institute of Education No 76*. Gothenburg: University of Gothenburg, Department of Education.

(1979b). *Learning in the learner's perspective II – differences in awareness. Reports from the Institute of Education No 77*. Gothenburg: University of Gothenburg, Department of Education.

Salovey, P. and Mayer, J. D. (1990). Emotional Intelligence. *Imagination, Cognition and Personality*, 9, 185–211.

Schoenfeld, A. (1992). Learning to think mathematically: problem solving, metacognition and making sense in mathematics. In *Handbook of Research on Mathematics Teaching and Learning*, ed. D. A. Grouws. New York: MacMillan, 334–370.

Schunk, D. H. (1994). Self-regulation of self-efficacy and attributions in academic settings. In *Self-Regulation of Learning and Performance: issues and educational applications*, eds. D. H. Schunk and B. J. Zimmerman. Hillsdale, NJ: Erlbaum, 75–99.

Schunk, D. H. and Zimmerman, B. J. (eds.) (1994). *Self-Regulation of Learning and Performance: issues and educational applications.* Hillsdale, NJ: Erlbaum.

Seels, B. (1997). Taxonomic issues and the development of theory in instructional technology. *Educational Technology,* 37, 12–21.

Senge, P. (1990). *The Fifth Discipline: the art and practice of the learning organisation.* London: Century.

Shayer, M. and Adey, P. (2002). *Learning Intelligence.* Buckingham: Open University Press.

Skuy, M., Dunn, M., Durbach, F., Mentis, M., Gibson, M., Muller, F. and Lazar, C. (1991). *Cognitive Functions and Dysfunctions Working Manual.* Johannesburg: Cognitive Research Programme, Division of Specialised Education, University of the Witwatersrand.

Smith, E. (1979). *Taxonomy in Britain.* Report of the Review Group on Taxonomy (Chairman E. Smith). London: HMSO.

Smith, G. (2002). Thinking skills: the question of generality. *Journal of Curriculum Studies,* 34(6), 659–678.

Smith, K. C. P. and Apter, M. J. (1975). *A Theory of Psychological Reversals.* Chippenham: Picton.

Smith, L. (1996). The social construction of rational understanding. In *Piaget-Vygotsky: the social genesis of thought,* eds. A. Tryphon and J. Vonèche. Hove: Psychology Press, 107–22.

Smith, M. K. (2002). 'Howard Gardner and multiple intelligence', the encyclopedia of informal education. http:www.infed.org/thinkers/gardner.htm

Splitter, L. and Sharp, A. M. (1995). *Teaching for Better Thinking: the classroom community of enquiry.* Melbourne: Australian Council for Educational Research.

Spodak, R. (1999). Executive functioning – what is it and how does it affect learning? Washington Parent. http://www.washingtonparent.co. articles/9906/executive-functioning.htm

Stahl, R. J., and Murphy, G. T. (1981). The domain of cognition: An alternative to Bloom's cognitive domain within the framework of an information processing model. ERIC Document Reproduction Service No. ED 208 511.

Sternberg, R. J. (1985). *Beyond IQ: a triarchic theory of human intelligence.* Cambridge: Cambridge University Press.

   (1986). Critical thinking: its nature, measurement and improvement. ERIC Document Reproduction Service ED272882.

(1997). *Thinking Styles*. Cambridge: Cambridge University Press.

(1998). Principles of teaching for successful intelligence. *Educational Psychologist*, 33, 65–72.

(2001). Giftedness as developing expertise: a theory of the interface between high abilities and achieved excellence. *High Ability Studies*, 12(2), 159–179.

(2002a). Raising the achievement of all students: teaching for successful intelligence. *Educational Psychology Review*, 14(4), 384–393.

(2002b). Review of 'The Psychology of Intelligence' by J. Piaget. *Intelligence*, 30, 482–483.

(2003a). *Cognitive Psychology*, third edn. Belmont, CA: Wadsworth.

(2003b). Issues in the theory and measurement of successful intelligence: a reply to Brody. *Intelligence*, 31, 331–337.

(2003c). Our research program validating the triarchic theory of successful intelligence: reply to Gottfredson. *Intelligence*, 31, 399–413.

(2003d). Teaching for successful intelligence: Principles, practices and outcomes. *Educational and Child Psychology*, 20(2), 6–18.

(2004a). Culture and intelligence. *American Psychologist*, 59, 325–338.

(2004b). North American approaches to intelligence. In *International Handbook of Intelligence*, ed. L. Resnick. New York: Cambridge University Press, 411–444.

(2004, submitted). The Rainbow project collaborators, and the University of Michigan Business School project collaborators. Theory-based university admissions testing for a new millennium. *Educational Psychologist*, 39, 185–198.

Sternberg, R. J. and Bhana, K. (1986). Synthesis of research on the effectiveness of intellectual skills programs. *Intelligence* 5, 209–230.

Sternberg, R. J., Grigorenko, E. L., Ferrari, M., and Clinkenbeard, P. (1999). A triarchic analysis of an aptitude-treatment interaction. *European Journal of Psychological Assessment*, 15, 1–11.

Sternberg, R. J. and Grigorenko, E. L. (2000/2001). Guilford's structure of intellect model and model of creativity: contributions and limitations. *Creativity Research Journal*, 13(3 and 4), 309–316.

(2002). *Dynamic Testing: the nature and measurement of learning potential*. Cambridge: Cambridge University Press.

Stiggins, R. J., Rubel, E., and Quellmalz, E. S. (1988). *Measuring Thinking Skills in the Classroom*, revised edn. Washington, DC: NEA Professional Library.

Stott, D. H., Marston, N. C. and Neill, S. J. (1975). *Taxonomy of Behaviour Disturbance*. London: University of London Press.

Strand, P. S., Barnes-Holmes, Y. and Barnes-Holmes, D. (2003). Educating the whole child: implications of behaviorism as a science of meaning. *Journal of Behavioral Education*, 12(2), 105–117.

Swanson, H. L. (1999). *Interventions for Students with Learning Disabilities*. New York: Guilford Press.

(2000). Searching for the best cognitive model for instructing students with learning disabilities: a component and composite analysis. *Educational and Child Psychology*, 17(3), 101–120.

Swanson, H. L. and Sáez, L. (2003). Memory difficulties in children and adults with learning disabilities. In *Handbook of Learning Disabilities*, eds. H. L. Swanson, K. R. Harris and S. Graham. New York: Guilford Press, 182–198.

Swartz, R. J. and Parks, S. (1994) *Infusing the Teaching of Critical and Creative Teaching into Content Instruction: a lesson design handbook for the elementary grades*. Pacific Grove, CA: Critical Thinking Books and Software.

ten Dam, G. and Volman, M. (2004). Critical thinking as a citizenship competence: teaching strategies. *Learning and Instruction*, 14, 359–379.

Thagard, P. (1996). *Mind: Introduction to cognitive science*. Cambridge, MA: MIT Press.

Thayer-Bacon, B. (1998). Transforming and redescribing critical thinking: constructive thinking. *Studies in Philosophy and Education*, 17, 123–148.

Thelen, E. and Smith, L. B. (1994). *A Dynamic Systems Approach to the Development of Cognition and Action*. Cambridge, MA: MIT Press.

Torgensen, J. K. (1996). A model of memory from an information processing perspective: the special case of phonological memory. In *Attention, Memory and Executive Function*, eds. G. R. Lyon and N. Krasnegor. Baltimore: Paul Brookes, 157–184.

Torrance, E. P. (1966). *Torrance Tests of Creative Thinking*. Bensenville, IL: Scholastic Testing Service.

Toulmin, S. (1958). *The Uses of Argument*. Cambridge: Cambridge University Press.

Toulmin, S., Rieke, R., Janik, A. (1984). *An Introduction to Reasoning*. MacMillan: New York.

Trickey, S. and Topping, K. J. (2004). 'Philosophy for children': a systematic review. *Research Papers in Education*, 19(3), 365–380.

van der Horst, H. (2000). A problem solving strategy for gifted learners in South Africa. *Gifted Education International*, 15(1), 103–110.

van Gelder, T. (1995). What might cognition be if not computation? *Journal of Philosophy*, 91, 345–381.

van Gelder, T. and Port, R. (1995). It's about time: an overview of the dynamical approach to cognition. In *Mind as Motion: explorations in the dynamics of cognition*, eds. R. F. Port and T. van Gelder. Cambridge, MA: MIT Press.

van Gelder, T. J. (2000). Learning to reason: a Reason!–Able approach. In *Cognitive Science in Australia, 2000*. Proceedings of the Fifth Australasian Cognitive Science Society Conference, eds. C. Davis, T. J. van Gelder and R. Wales. Adelaide: Causal.

(2001). Critical thinking: some lessons learned. Adult Learning Australia, Adult Learning Commentary Number 12.

van Merriënboer, J. J. G. (1997). *Training complex cognitive skills*. Englewood Cliffs, NJ: Educational Technology Publications.

Velmans, M. (2000). *Understanding consciousness*. London: Routledge/Psychology Press/Taylor and Francis.

Vermunt, J. D. (1992). *Learning styles and regulation of learning processes in higher education: towards a process-oriented instruction in independent thinking*. Doctoral dissertation. Lisse: Swets and Zeitlinger.

(1996). Metacognitive, cognitive and affective aspects of learning styles and strategies: a phenomenographic analysis. *Higher Education*, 31, 25–50.

(1998). The regulation of constructive learning processes. *British Journal of Educational Psychology*, 68, 149–171.

Vermunt, J. D. and Verloop, N. (1999). Congruence and friction between learning and teaching. *Learning and Instruction*, 9, 257–280.

von Bertalanffy, L. (1950). An outline of General Systems Theory. *British Journal for the Philosophy of Science*, 1, 139–164.

Vygotsky, L. S. (1962). *Thought and Language*. Cambridge, MA: MIT Press.

(1978). *The Mind in Society: the development of higher psychological processes*. Cambridge, MA: Harvard University Press.

Wallace, B. (2001). *Teaching Thinking Skills across the Primary Curriculum: a practical approach for all abilities*. London: David Fulton Publishers.

(2003). What are the learning experiences that gifted and talented children need in order to develop life skills? *Gifted and Talented*, 7(2), 49–53.

Wallace, B., Adams, H. B., Maltby, F., and Mathfield, J. (1993). *TASC: Thinking actively in a social context*. Bicester: AB Academic Publishers.

Weiner, B. (1986). *An Attribution Theory of Motivation and Emotion*. New York: Springer-Verlag.

Weinert, F. E. and Weinert, S. (1998). History and systems of developmental psychology. In *Life-span Developmental Psychology*, eds. A. Demetriou, W. Doise and C. van Lieshout. Chichester: John Wiley and Sons, 1–33.

Welsh, M. C. and Pennington, B. F. (1988). Assessing frontal lobe functioning in children. *Developmental Neuropsychology*, 4, 199–230.

Wenger, E. (1998). *Communities of Practice: learning, meaning, and identity*. Cambridge: Cambridge University Press.

Wertheimer, M. (1959). *Productive Thinking* (enlarged edn). New York: Harper and Row.

White, J. (1998). *Do Howard Gardner's multiple intelligences add up?* London: Institute of Education, University of London.

Whyte, J. (2003). *Bad Thoughts: a guide to clear thinking*. London: Corvo.

Williams, F. E. (1970). *Classroom Ideas for Encouraging Thinking and Feeling*. Buffalo, NY: DOK Publishers.

(1972). *A Total Creativity Program for Individualising and Humanising the Learning Process*. Englewood Cliffs, NJ: Educational Technology Publications.

(1980). *The Creativity Assessment Packet*. Nerang East QLD: Pro-Ed Australia.

(1986). The cognitive–affective intervention model for enriching gifted programs. In *Systems and Models for Developing Programs for the Gifted and Talented*, ed. J. S. Renzulli. Mansfield Center, CT: Creative Learning Press, 461–484.

Williams, W. M., Blythe, T., White, N., Li, J., Gardner, H., and Sternberg, R. J. (2002). Practical intelligence for school: developing metacognitive sources of achievement in adolescence. *Developmental Review*, 22, 162–210.

Winne, P. (1995). Inherent details in self-regulated learning. *Educational Psychologist*, 30, 173–187.

Wong, B. Y. L. and Jones, W. (1982). Increasing metacomprehension in learning disabled and normally achieving students through self-questioning training. *Learning Disability Quarterly*, 5, 409–414.

Wood, D. J., Bruner, J. S., and Ross, G. (1976). The role of tutoring in problem solving. *Journal of Child Psychology and Psychiatry*, 17, 89–100.

Wood, R. (1977). Multiple choice: a state of the art report. *Evaluation in Education*, 1, 191–280.

Zangwill, O. L. (1980). Kenneth Craik: the man and his work. *British Journal of Psychology*, 71, 1–6.

Zeidner, M., Boekaerts, M. and Pintrich, P. R. (2000). Self-regulation: directions and challenges for future research. In *Handbook of Self-Regulation*, eds. M. Boekaerts, P. R. Pintrich and M. Zeidner. London: Academic Press, 750–769.

Zhang, L. F. (1999) A comparison of U.S. and Chinese university students' cognitive development: the cross-cultural applicability of Perry's theory. *The Journal of Psychology*, 133(4), 425–439.

Zimmerman, B. J. (1995). Self-regulation involves more than metacognition: a social cognitive perspective. *Educational Psychologist*, 29, 217–221.

(1998). Developing self-fulfilling cycles of academic regulation: An analysis of exemplary instructional models. In *Self-Regulated Learning: from teaching to self-reflective practice*, eds. D. H. Schunk and B. J. Zimmerman. New York: Guilford, 1–19.

(2000). Attaining self-regulation: a social cognitive perspective. In *Handbook of Self-Regulation*, eds. M. Boekaerts, P. R. Pintrich and M. Zeidner. San Diego, CA: Academic Press, 13–39.

Index

Adams, H. 26, 251, 259, 265, 302–303
Adey, P. 25, 27–28, 112–113
affective domain and affect 2, 14, 51,
    73, 77, 83, 137, 198, 246, 271,
    272–273, 279, 299
Allen, R.
  brief outline of framework 120
  description and intended use
      128–130
  evaluation 130–132
  summary 132–133
Altshuller, G. 305–306
  brief outline of TRIZ framework 120
  description and intended use 122–126
  evaluation 126–127
  generic nature of TRIZ 127
  summary 128
  TRIZ and creativity 131
Anderson, L. 300, 302
  brief outline of framework 49
  comparison with Bloom's taxonomy
      103–105, 110
  description and intended use 102–105
  evaluation 109–111
  knowledge dimension 104, 106–108
  organising questions 104–105
  summary 112
  treatment of metacognition 110
Anderson, R. 34, 40
Andrews, R. 132, 163
argument analysis 128–130, 131, 143,
    145–146

ARIZ algorithm for inventive problem
    solving 122, 125
Ashman, A. 13, 24
assessment 23, 57–58, 73, 88, 104–105,
    140–141, 156, 212, 306–307
attribution for success or failure
    237–238, 239, 309
Ausubel, D. 31
  brief outline of framework 47
  comparison with Bloom's
      categories 68
  description and intended use 67–69
  evaluation 69–70
  summary 70–71

Baddeley, A. 229, 244–245
Bailey, K. 33, 37, 38, 39
Bailin, S. 120
  brief outline of framework 122
  description and intended use 177–181
  evaluation 181–182
  summary 182–183
Bandura, A. 238
Barnes-Holmes, D. see Strand, P.
Barnes-Holmes, Y. see Strand, P.
Baron, J.
  brief outline of framework 121
  description and intended use 148–150
  evaluation 150–151
  model of the good thinker (authored
      with Glatthorn) 149–150
  summary 151–152

Lightning Source UK Ltd.
Milton Keynes UK
UKOW051253070412

190321UK00001B/28/P